ELECTING THE FRENCH PRESIDEN

Georgios Varouxakis
London, 18 November 1997

Also by Robert Elgie

POLITICAL LEADERSHIP IN LIBERAL DEMOCRACIES

THE ROLE OF THE PRIME MINISTER IN FRANCE, 1981–91

Electing the French President

The 1995 Presidential Election

Edited by

Robert Elgie
Lecturer in Politics
University of Limerick
Ireland

First published in Great Britain 1996 by
MACMILLAN PRESS LTD
Houndmills, Basingstoke, Hampshire RG21 6XS
and London
Companies and representatives
throughout the world

A catalogue record for this book is available
from the British Library.

ISBN 0–333–63084–X hardcover
ISBN 0–333–63085–8 paperback

First published in the United States of America 1996 by
ST. MARTIN'S PRESS, INC.,
Scholarly and Reference Division,
175 Fifth Avenue,
New York, N.Y. 10010

ISBN 0–312–16340–1

Library of Congress Cataloging-in-Publication Data
Electing the French president : the 1995 presidential election /
edited by Robert Elgie.
p.   cm.
Includes bibliographical references and index.
ISBN 0–312–16340–1 (cloth : alk. paper)
1. Presidents—France—Election—1995.   2. France—Politics and
government—1981–   I. Elgie, Robert.
JN2959.E39   1996
324.944'0839—dc20
96–21860
CIP

10   9   8   7   6   5   4   3   2   1
05   04   03   02   01   00   99   98   97   96

Printed and bound in Great Britain by
Antony Rowe Ltd, Chippenham, Wiltshire

Contents

List of Tables and Exhibits

TABLES

EXHIBIT

Acknowledgement

The editor would like to thank the Nuffield Foundation for the award received under the auspices of the Social Science Small Grants Scheme which funded research work in Paris in preparation for this book.

Preface
Robert Elgie

On 7 May 1995 Jacques Chirac was elected as the fifth President of the French Fifth Republic, winning the support of over fifteen and three-quarter million people or a total of 52.64 per cent of the votes cast. As befits such an event, tens of thousands of people converged on the Place de la Concorde in Paris and an impromptu victory party was held. And yet, when compared with the celebrations that accompanied the successes of his illustrious presidential predecessors, Charles de Gaulle (1958–69), Georges Pompidou (1969–74), Valéry Giscard d'Estaing (1974–81) and François Mitterrand (1981–95), the scenes of rejoicing at Chirac's victory seemed somewhat sober. Chirac won because he galvanised an initially lacklustre campaign and because he was the most convincing advocate of change. He won because he beat off the challenge from both his right-wing rival and fellow Gaullist, Edouard Balladur, at the first ballot and his left-wing opponent and socialist candidate, Lionel Jospin, at the second. But for all that, his victory failed fully to dispel the pall of *morosité* that hung over the country. It merely papered over the cracks of the country's *fracture sociale*. In short, Chirac's victory was the culmination of a period of intense and extremely entertaining political theatre, but, even on the night of 7 May, few were willing to believe that it had brought about a fundamental realignment of the French political system which might have been an event truly worthy of mass celebration.

This is a study of the 1995 French presidential election. Its central characters are the candidates, parties and voters whose behaviour determined the outcome of the campaign. Its context is the economic, social and political environment in which the election took place. In this respect, its aim is to provide a snapshot of French political life in 1995. At the same time, though, this book is designed to provide more than just a yellowing portrait of some perhaps soon-forgotten political figures. Instead, it also aims to examine

some of the longer-standing issues and debates in contemporary French politics. Elections are not just one-off
happenings. They are neither ahistorical nor inconsequen-
tial occurrences. Rather, elections are the culmination of
past events and the precursor to future ones. They are both
an epilogue and a prologue. As such, they can serve as an
extremely useful explanatory device. They can be used both
to illuminate that which has gone before and to indicate
that which is to come. They can operate as a vehicle to
demonstrate the rules of a country's political game and the
exceptions to them. As a result, this book uses the 1995
French presidential election as an instrument by which to
analyse the.Fifth Republic's institutional structures, the behaviour of its political parties, the attitudes of its citizens
and the nature of its governance.

In the opening chapter, David Hanley examines the issue
of continuity and change during the Mitterrand presidency
and introduces many of the themes that crop up in later
chapters. In the second chapter, Howard Machin charts the
course of the campaign and provides reasons for Chirac's
victory. In the third chapter, Robert Elgie identifies the rules
of the presidential election game in France and analyses
their political consequences. In the following two chapters,
Peter Fysh and Steven Griggs consider the nature of French
party politics and explore the intra- and inter-party strategies
of both left- and right-wing candidates at the 1995 election.
In the sixth chapter, Sonia Mazey looks at the changing
issue agenda of French politics and shows how candidates
reacted to it. In the seventh chapter, Alain Guyomarch teases
out the implications of the 1995 election for the established
models of French voting behaviour. In the final chapter,
Vincent Wright and Robert Elgie investigate the changing
nature of the presidency and the French public policy-making environment. Overall, these chapters aim both to give a
flavour of the 1995 French presidential election and to present
some thoughts on the functioning of the French political
system as a whole.

Notes on the Contributors

Robert Elgie is Lecturer in Politics in the Department of Government and Society at the University of Limerick. He has published articles on French politics in *Governance, Modern and Contemporary France, Political Studies, Public Administration* and *West European Politics*. He is the author of *The Role of the Prime Minister in France, 1981–91* and *Political Leadership in Liberal Democracies*.

Peter Fysh is Senior Lecturer in French in the Department of Modern Languages, Nottingham Trent University. He has published articles on French politics in *Parliamentary Affairs, Modern and Contemporary France* and the *International Journal of Public Opinion Research*. He is currently working on a study of the extreme right in France.

Steven Griggs is Lecturer in Politics at Staffordshire University. He has written on the French Socialist party in *Modern and Contemporary France*. He has also contributed to *Espace social européen*. His research interests include French political parties, the French state and comparative public policy-making.

Alain Guyomarch is Lecturer in West European Politics and Assistant Director of the European Institute at the London School of Economics and Political Science. He has published articles on French politics in journals such as *Parliamentary Affairs, Revue Française de Science Politique* and *West European Politics*. He also contributed to *Developments in French Politics* edited by Jack Hayward, Peter Hall and Howard Machin.

David Hanley is Professor of European Studies at the University of Wales, College of Cardiff. His books include *Keeping Left, Contemporary France: Politics and Society since 1945* (co-author with A. P. Kerr and N. H. Waites) and *Christian Democracy in Europe* (editor). He is the author of many articles on French Christian Democracy, the French Socialist party and French foreign and defence policy.

Howard Machin is Director of the European Institute at the London School of Economics and Political Science. He has published many articles on French politics in journals such as *French Politics and Society, Government and Opposition, Parliamentary Affairs* and *West European Politics.* He is the co-editor of *Developments in French Politics* with Jack Hayward and Peter Hall.

Sonia Mazey is University Lecturer in the Faculty of Social and Political Sciences at Cambridge University. Her publications include *Mitterrand's France* (co-edited with Michael Newman), *Lobbying in the European Community* (co-edited with Jeremy Richardson) and *The European Community: Economic and Political Aspects* (co-authored with V. Lintner). She has published articles on French politics in journals such as *Politics, Electoral Studies* and *West European Politics.* She also contributed to *Developments in French Politics* edited by Jack Hayward, Peter Hall and Howard Machin.

Vincent Wright is Fellow of Nuffield College, Oxford University. He is the co-editor of *West European Politics.* His books include *The Government and Politics of France, Continuity and Change in France* (editor), *Centre–Periphery Relations in Europe* (co-editor with Yves Mény) and *The Politics of Privatization in Western Europe* (co-editor with John Vickers). He has published articles on French politics in many leading journals including *Comparative Politics* and *Political Studies.*

1 Change and Continuity in the Mitterrand Years

David Hanley

Mitterrand's electoral triumph of 10 May 1981 was widely seen, possibly even by the victor himself, as heralding a period of unprecedented change in French social and political structures. The euphoria of his socialist supporters, not fearing to call their programme *Changer la Vie*, was matched only by the fear of his right-wing opponents as to the havoc which the 'alliance socialo-communiste' would wreak. Fourteen years on, the apocalyptic atmosphere had long since faded away, to be replaced by doubts and fears as to what any politicians, including those on both the right and the left, could do in the face of seemingly intractable problems. France changed much during the two Mitterrand *septennats*. Little of this change, though, came about in a manner or a direction envisaged by those who were victorious in 1981. Instead, much of it was imposed upon them by factors outside their control. In short, the socialists were unable to carry through many or indeed most of the changes on which they had originally set their hearts.

This chapter will chart the changing face of France in recent times and will make clear the context in which French voters went to the polls in April and May 1995, distinctly underwhelmed at the prospect of electing the Fifth Republic's fifth president. It will look first at the changes in the economic and social structure of France. It will then turn to the political process, where evidence will be given to suggest that there have been distinct changes in political practice, which apply both to the nature of presidential government and to the behaviour of French voters and those parties which (increasingly unsuccessfully it may be said) articulate their interests. Finally, it will consider the changing situation of France within the European Union. Underlying all these different spheres of change will be the persistent

1

sentiment that France in 1995 was a more volatile, less certain and more difficult country to govern than was the case in 1981.

CHANGING ECONOMIC AND SOCIAL STRUCTURES

Under Mitterrand's stewardship the French economy underwent a brusque phase of modernisation and internationalisation in keeping with the movement of its European and other partners. After the disappointments of the early voluntaristic, statist phase of economic policy,[1] French governments adopted a broadly liberal approach with the emphasis falling increasingly on deregulation, privatisation and supply-side measures such as tax incentives for businesses. The stated aim was to make firms more competitive in a market which French governments recognised was becoming inevitably ever more global. Older sectors of production, such as mining, steel or textiles, were allowed to decline rapidly as governments tried to encourage areas of high value-added where France enjoyed some comparative advantage.

The results of these policies were mixed. For example, the economy enjoyed a slow, sometimes stuttering growth, peaking at a rare 4.4 per cent per annum in the mini-revival of the late 1980s, whereas the usual rate was nearer 2 per cent. Nevertheless, inflation was certainly tamed, falling from 13.4 per cent in 1981 to some 1.6 per cent in 1994. One part of the anti-inflation strategy was to keep the parity of the franc as close as possible to the strong German mark. The price paid for this *franc fort* policy was unemployment, which crept up relentlessly from 1.9 million in 1981 to 3.3 million by the end of 1994. Moreover, those in employment did not benefit commensurately from any economic growth. It has been estimated that some 5 million French people could be described as genuinely poor in 1995 with the majority of the workforce still earning less than 7500 francs per month.[2] Another way of realising the social price paid for macroeconomic success is to consider the share of GDP taken by the state. Despite the best intentions of the socialists, they saw it rise from 42 per cent in 1981 to an obstinate 44 per cent today. The social security deficit tells the same story in different figures, with its rise from less than 7 billion francs in 1981 to over 50 billion by 1994.

The Mitterrand years also brought other kinds of socio-economic changes as France modernised apace. The number of property owners increased from 50 million to nearly 54 million, with increases in the acquisition of the conventional attributes of a consumer society, such as telephones, freezers and video machines.[3] By the end of the era, the number of students in higher education had gone up from 1.2 million to 2 million, while the number of graduates rose by 60 per cent in the same period. Health expenditure had risen by a factor of almost three by the end of 1993, reviving the old jokes about the French being the world's champion pill-poppers. These figures showed perhaps both the presence of increased wealth, but also of increased stress. Guy Carcassonne has shown how economic change was accompanied by changes in the law, inspired, as he rightly says, by the same liberalism that drove so much of economic policy.[4]

Initiatives occurred in a number of other directions as well. For example, older authoritarian measures, such as de Gaulle's emergency courts and the death penalty, were cleared off the statute book. Phone tapping was somewhat belatedly made the object of judicial supervision. A number of regulatory bodies were set up to cover areas such as stock exchange trading, broadcasting matters (too long the exclusive province of government) and competition policy. Major fiscal laws such as the *revenu minimum d'insertion* (RMI) or the *contribution sociale généralisée* attempted to set the welfare state on a more modern footing. The decentralisation laws were a response to demands in the provinces. The Constitutional Council upgraded its standing to become a fully-fledged institution of the Republic and the Council of State's 1990 decision enshrined the primacy of European Union (EU) law over domestic law. This anxiety to bring law into line with the forward movement of French economy and society often led, as Carcassonne remarked, to legislation on matters perhaps best handled at personal or community levels. One such example was the famous Evin anti-smoking law, more honoured in the breach than in the observance.[5]

The reshaping of the French economy naturally had

powerful effects on the country's social structure, the most
dramatic expression of which was the mutation of the working class. As the socialists rose to power through the 1970s,
this group, by then the most numerous in society, seemed
destined to grow steadily, providing an ever-expanding natural
social base for the revamped Socialist Party (PS). However,
even as the party's early attempts at 'Keynesianism in one
country' were foundering, it became apparent that France
was no more able than any other country to stand aside
from radical changes in the mode of production taking place
across the developed world. Several forces were at work here.
On the one hand, new technology enabled rapid productiv-
ity gains, leading to a reduction in the labour force. On
the other, the growing internationalisation of trade brought
increased competition among firms, forcing them to cut costs
more and to diversify production. At the same time, governments came under pressure to reduce public expenditure, leading to further job losses in the state sector, large
parts of which were in any case by now being privatised.[6]
Thus, the working class on which the socialist appeal had
been based underwent rapid changes during Mitterrand's
rule. Prior to his arrival, the working class represented 38.5
per cent of the total workforce. By 1990, the figure was 29.2
per cent. During the same period, the proportion of the
workforce employed in the tertiary sector rose from 50.9
per cent to 64.6 per cent.[7]

As Emmanuel Todd suggests, certain analysts, including
himself, overreacted initially to these changes, which they
saw as implying the virtual disappearance of the traditional
working class, subsumed into some nebulous tertiary salariat.[8]
It is true that the working class shrank in numbers, became
more diversified, was subject to permanent, structural unemployment and saw its general salience as a political force
decline. The eclipse of the Communist Party (PCF) was but
one symbol of these changes. However, Todd's more recent
work stresses the closeness between the changing working
class *stricto sensu* and the large mass of lower white-collar
workers, with whom manual workers intermarry and share
similar levels of income and lifestyle.[9] For him, the real social
cleavage today lies between this vast group, or *peuple*, and
what he calls a middle class of professionals and middle

and upper management.[10] Recent elections and other tests
of opinion like the 1992 Maastricht referendum make this
cleavage, he argues, increasingly apparent.

One group within French society whose salience has increased since 1981 are immigrants. Since the 1970s, the
number of incomers has fallen sharply and the type of new
arrival has changed. Instead of the unskilled migrant from
a traditional Third World rural background aiming for a
job in a car factory or on a building site, newcomers tend
to be younger, more educated and often more westernised
in outlook.[11] A priori, this should facilitate their integration
within French society, as indeed the rising number of mixed
marriages between native-born French and immigrants would
suggest.[12] However, integration is a very elusive goal. The
problem arises of course less from the willingness or capacity of the incomer than from the perception which native French have of 'the other'. Whereas the total foreign
population resident in France is *stricto sensu* some 3.6 million in a total of 56.6 million, representing 6.4 per cent of
the population compared with 4.4 per cent in 1946, there
are also some 5 million children of previous immigrants and
probably as many grandchildren again. It is a moot point
how long people have to live in a country before being accepted as equals by indigenous people, especially when they
are often different in appearance, accent and to some extent
lifestyle. When one adds to this the fact that immigrants
are three times more likely to live in a disadvantaged *quartier
prioritaire* and that they are twice as likely (two and a half
times as likely in the case of North Africans) to be unemployed as native French people, one begins to have some
idea of why they have become something of a political football over the past 15 years. At one level, it may well be that
many *beurs* and other second generation immigrants are living unselfconsciously and serenely in France. At another,
however, a succession of governments has reacted uncom-
fortably to an anti-immigrant scapegoating operation executed
without remorse by the Front National (FN) and its allies.
Immigration is, thus, bound to be a major issue in any election today.

Blue- and white-collar workers, whether native-born or
recently arrived, have grown accustomed to two other features

during the Mitterrand years. These are the high degree of
structural unemployment and, linked to it, the growing pre-
cariousness of those in work.[13] Part-time working and short-
term contracts advance remorselessly at the expense of
traditional public and private sector job security. Workforces
have had to be flexible and learn not to price themselves
out of a job. Despite the best efforts of the socialists, they
were never able to peg the rise of unemployment, apart
from a brief success at the start and a brief respite due to
the growth spurt of the late 1980s. The creation of the RMI
(see above) during the Rocard government (1988–91) was
an admission of the permanent character of structural unemployment. In 1995, it had 1.8 million recipients and there
have been few real reinsertions into the world of employment.

Towards the end of the Mitterrand era, a new term began to gain currency, that of exclusion. It figured prominently in the 1995 election campaign. It was not coterminous
with unemployment, although the long-term unemployed were
among the most prominent *exclus*. Exclusion did not just
mean poverty either, as some of the *exclus* would not qualify
as poor in most people's understanding of the word. Nor
did the term simply refer to those with particular problems,
such as the homeless, the handicapped or the acutely isolated. In a sense it encompassed all these groups.[14] It seemed
that a growing proportion of the French eked out an existence at the margins of society.[15] Debarred from participation in the life of the workplace, they were so much more
likely to be isolated and demoralised, badly housed and have
poorer physical and mental heath also. Above all they felt
excluded and peripheral to the movement of mainstream
society. Such a phenomenon is as much cultural as socioeconomic. It has often been linked to other pressures which
continued to make themselves felt during this period. A
decline of family life is one, as is the decrease of local neigh-
bourhood solidarities. This became apparent during the
second Mitterrand *septennat* with the creation of a high-profile Ministry of Urban Affairs to try and alleviate the growing alienation of crime-ridden, ill-conceived tower blocks in
the suburbs. The growing decline of religious identity is often
adduced as evidence of the decline of another, different
type of solidarity as is the waning of the PCF, which per-

formed a function of social aggregation. All these tendencies need to be set against the growth of liberal individualism, the cultural pendant of the economic policies which all governments of this period assumed, most of them with great willingness. The *exclus* were the inevitable losers of a liberal society, with its emphasis on individual success and prowess. It is not the intention here to suggest that these groups were a majority or anything approaching one. The majority of French people remained in work and enjoyed slowly rising standards of comfort throughout this period. But the *exclus* were a reminder of the harsh, competitive and less secure nature of the French society of the 1990s. When Mitterrand won in 1981, most of his voters expected steady growth in living standards, job security and guaranteed social benefits. By the time he left office, people's expectations were less and their fears much greater.

VOTERS, ATTITUDES AND PARTIES

By the end of the 1980s there were a number of disturbing signs concerning the relationship between voters and politics. Abstentions in all kinds of election seemed to be rising steadily. Voters seemed to identify much less with parties than before. Some commentators took this to mean either that French citizens were becoming less interested in politics or that the parties were no longer fulfilling their role of aggregating social demands into viable political projects. Hence, there was agonising about the 'crisis of political representation'.[16] More worryingly, politicians as a category were held in ever lower esteem in opinion polls. The proportion of voters who thought that politics was a dishonourable activity went from 20 per cent in the late 1970s to over 40 per cent by 1990.[17] At the same time, general scepticism seemed to be on the increase as to what politicians could actually achieve when in office. A slightly different expression of this latter sentiment took the form of the oft-repeated claim that there was no real difference nowadays between politicians, whatever their label, and that the hallowed left–right dichotomy could finally be dispensed with as an explanatory tool, along with much other ideological baggage from the

1789 revolution.[18] Clearly these preoccupations are linked and need to be studied in turn.

While it is true that the last years have seen some increase in abstention, the figures need to be placed in a comparative perspective. The turnout at the 1995 French presidential election was 78.38 per cent at the first ballot and 76.66 per cent at the second. By contrast, in Britain the turnout at the 1987 and 1992 general elections was 73.2 per cent and 77.7 per cent respectively. In the US, a mere 55 per cent of voters turned out to elect Bill Clinton in 1992. Therefore, the most one can say is that there has been a modest fall-off of electoral participation in France of late, from what has long been a very high level of participation comparatively. More serious might be an increased readiness of French voters to support parties or candidates who have no realistic chance of winning office. In recent elections some 40 per cent of voters have been ready to do so. It should be remembered, though, that many French elections are held under a two ballot majority system. This enables a more vocal protest to be made at the first ballot before one votes for real, as it were, at the second ballot (see Chapter 3). As an experienced French voter once put it more bluntly to the author: 'de toute façon, le premier tour, ça compte pas!' In addition, it is true that the 1995 presidential poll did see an unusually high percentage of spoiled ballots in the second ballot, but this may well be as much a commentary on the quality of the candidates in this particular contest as a symbol of some generalised discontent, or ras-le-bol. In short, we should be wary of reading off too many danger signals about the nation's political appetite from turnout figures. Instead, it is probably wiser to agree with Boy and Mayer that there has been not so much a turning away from politics as a change in the way people relate to politics.[19]

One trend which does seem clear is that voters are identifying less with parties.[20] It is perhaps unfair to cite the very low ratio of members to voters as proof of this (about 2 per cent for the PS in 1988). Historically, French parties have never performed well in this respect, even in the heyday of the PCF. Nor should one adduce the lack of significant sectors of the population, such as women or workers, among the ranks of party activists as a criterion of non-representativity.[21] The plain fact is that it has always been so and perhaps analysts should have remarked on it earlier. Be this as it may, by 1990 only 23 per cent of French voters felt that they were adequately represented by a political party and, for what it is worth, only 14 per cent by a trade union, although given that only about 9 per cent of the workforce is unionised this is in some ways an encouraging figure. Yet, at the same time, the proportion of voters expressing interest in politics has remained static (54 per cent in 1974, 52 per cent still in 1990). What this suggests is that mainstream parties are somehow failing to satisfy a political demand that is still extensive. Commentators seek evidence for this failure of party in an increased respect shown for local politics (mayors and councillors achieve much higher poll ratings than deputies or other national figures) as well as for non-party organisations, which are seen as better able to take care of citizens' needs.[22] Thus 65 per cent believe that consumers' organisations can do this better than parties (a mere 6 per cent). Mayer and Perrineau postulate that more and more citizens will put their faith in *ad hoc* politics, i.e. pressure groups.[23] The uncertain flickerings of the various ecology parties in France and their chronic inability to produce a durable and plausible structure despite continuing to attract an encouraging vote also suggest the inability of established parties to take new issues adequately on board. So too does the growth of the FN from insignificance in the early 1980s to a steady 10–15 per cent of the vote today.

Thus far, it would seem that French voters are aware of new issues and are to some extent seeking new vehicles to further them. This does not mean, however, that old political cleavages are being totally ousted by new ones. There has been a temptation to think that with rapid socioeconomic change, cultural and value changes have followed apace. That is to say, just as the old working class has declined in salience and changed in nature, just as conflict about the form of regime has virtually disappeared and just as religious practice has declined dramatically, then so must the bases of the old left–right conflict have faded away. It is easy to find opinion polls where only 20 per cent of people agree that the left–right conflict is still relevant. Yet the same people, when asked to situate themselves on a ten-point scale, where the far left is zero and the far right is ten, are usually happy to do so to the tune of 85 or 90 per cent.

What all this tells us is that there still is a basic sense of conflict among French people.[24] The stakes of this conflict may have changed in that left and right are no longer fighting about issues like the nature of the Republic or the place of the Church within it, or *a fortiori* about expropriating the expropriators. But it is still fair to say that there are two sensibilities in conflict. Grunberg speaks of the 'central character' of the left–right polarity in structuring ideological differences.[25] Right-wingers still dislike the state's intervention in the economy and its function as a major welfare provider. They believe that individual merit should win its own rewards. They also tend to be illiberal on a range of cultural matters, ranging from immigration to the death penalty, homosexuality, abortion and defence spending. Left-wingers, among whom most ecologists can be numbered, are less confident in their rugged individualism and are more equalitarian at bottom. They look to a strong, enabling state and tend towards relaxed stances on the cultural and moral issues. Two sensibilities are still clearly present, even if they cannot any longer be labelled in tight little formulae such as Birnbaum's *petits contre les gros*. But it is inevitable that they will find electoral expression somehow. Hence, few should have been surprised at Jospin's 1995 second ballot showing where he effectively rallied all the left behind him.

Recent talk of 'new voters' needs to be seen in this light.[26] It is probably true that less voters than before are voting instinctively and in conformity with deep-lying left or right sensibilities, themselves the product of heavy socialisation through class, job and family. Evidence suggests that a growing number of voters have become dealigned and are becoming more akin to 'issue voters'. The 1988 polls showed a certain tendency to make up one's mind at the last minute or to change it during the campaign. In some cases change was not confined to within one camp, such as communists voting socialist. Instead, voters actually crossed the left–right line. There was also evidence of a sort of split-ticket voting. Some voters opting for Mitterrand as president in 1988 then chose to send a right-wing deputy to the National Assembly so as to curb the freedom of their new head of state. But the voters concerned are still a minority which even the boldest estimates put between 10–15 per cent of the total. It is true that they are mostly well-educated people from the salaried middle class and the supposition is that they bring their critical faculties to bear on parties and candidates in an unsentimental, analytical way, voting on a pure basis of rational and highly conditional self-interest. Poll evidence suggests, as we have shown, however, that old instincts and patterns of socialisation lie not far beneath the surface and that we should be extremely sceptical about the ubiquity of the rational voter (see Chapter 7).

Whatever the values and emotions that structure their votes, an increasing number of French people are doubtful about the worth of their choice. It seems often that politicians may present their ideology-driven programmes, but once elected they are not able to carry them out with much success.[27] The failure of Mitterrand's voluntarism of 1981–82 is highly symbolic. As noted above, ever since then governments have pursued neo-liberal economic policies, like their counterparts across the developed world. Differences have been of degree rather than of kind. The wave of Chirac privatisations of 1986–88 did after all continue a movement begun under Fabius.[28] The growing internationalisation of economies has made distinctive policies even harder for governments to follow, though in truth most of them have willingly accepted if not actively pursued such internationalisation. Left and right have alternated in power, but the demands of voters of all parties still remain the same: job security, income protection, law and order.[29] The widespread admission by the presidential candidates of a 'social fracture' in France was testimony to the failure of all previous governments to deliver. It is hardly surprising that voters have no great faith in the ability of parties and leaders to solve problems.

By 1995 then, claims that the French were becoming depoliticised were hard to sustain. Concern with politics remained high and conflicting world views were still in contention, even if their substance had mutated somewhat. To a degree the French voter was willing to experiment with new forms of political expression, but not to the extent of fundamentally remodelling the party system. Presidential candidates would be aware of this, but they would also know that politicians in general were losing esteem progressively and that there was less faith in their ability to deliver lasting solutions to abiding problems.

PARTISAN RESPONSE: HOW PARTIES COPE WITH A CHANGING ELECTORATE

Before addressing the ways in which the party system has tried to adapt to the above changes within the electorate, it is necessary to clarify the relationship of parties to the presidential contest. In one sense, there should be none. The Gaullian concept of the presidency postulated a contract between one man and the nation, in which intermediaries had at best a minor place. Fortunately parties have proved strong enough to overcome this Rousseauesque mistrust and are now essential actors in any presidential campaign and subsequent governance (see Chapter 3).

To begin with, the main presidential challengers are nowadays always party people. The annals of failure are replete with would-be saviours campaigning without a party base and whose lead in the opinion polls soon proved no match for rivals with a base in a real organisation. Raymond Barre was a good example in 1988 and Edouard Balladur would have been in 1995, except that even he owed his initial prominence to a long career in the Gaullist machine under Pompidou and then Chirac. Michel Rocard, who never managed to capture the PS machine when it was still capable of winning something, would doubtless agree.

Secondly, we are told that elections are nowadays decided by the media and that a good communications staff is worth more than several hundred thousand activists. Perhaps the 1995 campaign should question this wisdom. Undoubtedly a part of Chirac's remarkable reeling-in of Balladur in the opinion polls was due to his networks on the ground. This *'homme de terrain'* (his favourite self-description) was able to count on a wide spread of mayors, councillors and local activists to push his claims against the media front-runner and thereby slowly swing opinion towards him. It is no accident that while most of the Rassemblement pour la République (RPR) ministers went early for Balladur, the great majority of back-bench parliamentarians supported Chirac, reflecting the pressure of grassroots opinion.[30] There is also the obvious point that a president needs a majority in the National Assembly in order to pass his legislation. This means discipline, which means party. In addition, while ministers and advisers may be freely chosen from any party or area of civil society, the hard core of them are always likely to come from the upper reaches of the party. These are after all the men and women who have worked with the leader for years, forging mutual links of loyalty and dependence. If they are to be rewarded at the highest level it will be through the eventual triumph of their *présidentiable*. A party is, among its many other identities, a community of career hopes and fierce loyalties. Anyone who forgets that, like some of the RPR élite who unwisely plumped for the usurper Balladur, is likely to have his or her wrist slapped with some relish by the eventual winner. In short, party is a key element of any presidential campaign and it is vital to see how the main forces presented themselves in 1995.

Broadly speaking, the parties knew that the 1995 contest had serious implications for the whole party system. As has been noted already, in recent elections voters had been ready to vote for peripheral parties in growing proportions. This reflected partly short-term exasperation with the rash of scandals that has plagued France of late and partly a deeper scepticism about the failure of both mainstream left and right to cope satisfactorily with persistent problems such as employment or security. Increasingly then, the core parties of government, PS on the left and the RPR/UDF (Union pour la Démocratie Française) tandem on the right, found themselves hemmed in by a growing spectrum of peripheral dissidents. The FN's challenge on the right was replicated by the PCF's on the left, while the core party leaders could be thankful that the ecologists' perennial personal and ideological feuding stopped them from turning a considerable capital of sympathy into a bigger vote. The 1994 elections to the European Parliament, which were held under a system of proportional representation, had thrown up further trouble, with the 'flash' votes for the left-radical businessman, Bernard Tapie, and Philippe de Villiers, once of the UDF, both of whom promptly began to exhibit presidential symptoms.[31]

As a result, by late 1994 it was clear that there would be the usual spread of presidential aspirants, but this time the vote would be scattered wider with probably no one having a big lead at the first ballot. Nevertheless, trends in voter opinion put the right as the firm favourite, the only questions being which of its champions, Chirac or Balladur, would win and would both be in the second round. There is in fact little to suggest that the parties or their candidates took any particular measures to counteract the alleged 'crisis of representation' other than at the level of their programmes and moderately at that (see Chapter 6). This is because at bottom they saw the presidential campaign as a means of both rallying support that was fragile or drifting and reinforcing internal unity. Clearly the victorious candidate would accomplish both these aims even better than his rivals, but any party that made the second round would inevitably benefit from a consolidation of its support. Here is one of the keys to the relative serenity with which the big parties treat the crisis of representation. They believe that at the first ballot one protests but that at the second one votes for real. Party behaviour needs to be seen with this factor in mind and the main parties will each be considered briefly.

For the RPR clearly much depended on winning back the Elysée. Another defeat would kill off Chirac in a way that his younger challengers had never managed, but it would also put huge strains on a party machine that was still vigorous enough to win seats at all levels but needed the prestige and resources that come with the presidency. The RPR's and Chirac's tactic was to do as little as possible after 1993, counting on lasting detestation of the Mitterrand years to see them into office. The only factor which perturbed this scenario was an unexpected internal one in the shape of Edouard Balladur. It is a tribute to the resilience and skill of Chirac that when Balladur tried to usurp his position, he was able to use the party machine to weaken his rival and at the same time present a more combative, socially aware image that contrasted favourably with Balladur's complacency. The party's main problem was to resist the sirens of the polls and stick with its historic leader. This it did without too much difficulty and its faith was rewarded handsomely (see Chapter 4).

The UDF showed once again the weakness of semi-federal parties with no obvious leader, or perhaps too many potential ones. As in 1988, it opted for a candidate from outside its ranks, so affirming its readiness to play second fiddle. While a generous helping of posts in the new Chirac government can soothe the pain of loss for the time being, it has to be asked whether the UDF can really carry on if it does not present its own candidate in future.

The PS approached the election in a state of panic. Knowing that it would lose, with its credibility in tatters after a succession of scandals and riven by factionalism which led to the eviction of Rocard as party leader in 1994, it sought a saviour in the person of Jacques Delors. The President of the European Commission was too wise and too old to play *deus ex machina* and announced in December 1994 that he would not stand as the PS's candidate. After some ungainly wrangling Lionel Jospin was subsequently chosen 'to lose with dignity' as one observer put it. Making up his manifesto as he went along, Jospin was concerned above all to present an acceptable face for his party, appearing with increasing success as a sensible, reformist pro-European social democrat far removed from the ideological ambitions of the old PS. His campaign succeeded beyond the PS's wildest dreams, showing that such a party can still rally nearly half the French, provided it behaves sensibly. Through his campaign Jospin has given the party a lease of life that it hardly deserved and which it will, one hopes, not squander (see Chapter 5).

Communists, frontists and ecologists used the campaign as a propaganda exercise, voicing the protests of their disgruntled clientele. For them a presidential election is like any other. They are not expecting to win or even to make the second round, but it is a chance to count support. The same was true of Philippe de Villiers, but he is now at a loose end precisely because he has no party relay to carry on his protests after the election.

The election then confirmed the importance of party for the candidates and of the candidates for their parties,

particularly the big ones. The latter remained basically confident that their traditional appeal would, with but slight
modification, continue to attract the majority of voters. While
there is still no room for complacency about the challenge
of smaller forces, it would seem on the whole that their
judgement was basically correct.

THE PRIZE AT STAKE: A CHANGING PRESIDENCY

There can be few offices which have attracted the wealth of
study devoted to the French presidency.[32] The varying character of its incumbents and the changing circumstances in
which they have operated have combined to leave a rich
legacy of case law. While there is broad agreement among
experts as to the parameters of the office (the big decisions
to the president and the price of milk to the prime minister, as the consecrated formula has it), this rough and ready
delimitation of the extent of presidential power conceals a
multitude of in-between cases and variants which are the
stuff of the everyday governance of France.[33] Much of it takes
place in a low key way with little controversy. It is safe to
say only that the extent and depth of presidential decision-
making varies according to how the president perceives the
rapports de force at any particular moment. The interest of
the two Mitterrand terms lies precisely in the fact that it
seems possible to distinguish a number of distinct periods,
each of which bespeaks a different style of presidential decision-making. There have even been hints that Mitterrand's
successor would inherit a presidency that had gradually
evolved into something irreversibly different from the ever
more powerful machinery developed by his predecessors.
Such assertions need to be treated with caution, but it seems
that the Mitterrand presidency has assumed different faces
at different times. However, whether these are due to anything more than realistic short-term calculations is another
question.

Mitterrand's criticisms of the presidential institution before assuming office, made from a classical Republican stand-
point, are well known, but so too are his declarations, once
in power, about how well the presidency suited him after

all.[34] This was not to say that it might not turn out to be dangerous again in the hands of someone less suitable, as he complacently remarked. Certainly there were no symbolic moves by Mitterrand to convey the impression that he was trying to develop a new, less autocratic style of presidency. He never went further than talking about shortening the mandate, although Pompidou at least managed to produce a bill to this effect, and Article 16, which grants the president emergency powers during times of national crisis, still remains in force. His presidency, then, can only be judged on acts, not on rhetoric.

The initial period is probably the one that shows clearest signs of the more spectacular type of leadership associated with previous presidents. The so-called 'reserved area' of high policy showed examples of clear personal decisions, particularly the unflinching Atlanticism of Mitterrand's prompt support for the NATO twin-track policy of countering Soviet medium-range missiles with cruise and Pershing counterparts. This was at variance with official PS policy and more significantly was executed within days of taking office, which was a sure signal of who was in charge. Similar bravura was shown in the Third Worldist declaration at Cancún shortly after. In domestic affairs, while Mitterrand's first prime minister, Pierre Mauroy, and his team (1981–84) featured prominently in the prosecution of the alternative economic strategy of 1981–82, it would be a mistake to think that Mitterrand was at odds with it, although he certainly he took a clear lead in settling the debate between Jacques Delors and the faction which wanted France to withdraw from the European Monetary System in 1983. Other less remarked decisions, such as the restoration of rights for the Algerian plotters of 1961 in anticipation of *pied noir* votes in the municipal elections of 1983, show a president prepared to push through ruthlessly any matter he deemed necessary, however much it stuck in the craw of the faithful. The same could be said of Mitterrand's 1984 termination of the bill to nationalise Catholic schools, where his decisive intervention saved the government and the party from a pit into which they were determinedly digging themselves.

In all this early period, this was a presidency more like its predecessors in that the major lines of policy were Mitterrand's

and that he felt free to mark his primacy by visible intervention in matters big or small. Like his predecessors also,
Mitterrand's right to do this went virtually unchallenged from
his own side (excepting the PCF in later stages). If change
took place towards the end of this first period and afterwards, it was change imposed from the outside.[35] Mitterrand
recognised simply how constrained were his options on the
socioeconomic front after the failed reflation in 1981. From
then on his watchword was one of total pragmatism, not
just in economics but in every area of domestic policy. This
was the period when the president's grip on the tiller was
much less evident in the media and where by contrast
Mauroy's replacement as prime minister, Laurent Fabius,
and his team (1984–86) were more exposed to criticism.

This tactical presidential retreat should not be confused
with a diminishing of presidential prerogative. If governing
is likely to be difficult, with options narrowed and supporters
likely to be disappointed, then what is the point of the president being associated too closely with decisions that are bound
to be unpopular? Consequently, during the Fabius administration the prime minister's vocation as a lightning conduc-
tor or fuse came into its own. As for the president, when
he wishes to hide, then he has a choice of places in which
to do so. An avuncular, paternal and less visibly political
persona is one such place. From dynamic manager of France
Inc., he can become a moral magistrate or pedagogue of
the nation. Another refuge is the sphere of high policy, which
always affords greater room for manœuvre simply because
its impact on everyday life is necessarily oblique. Everyone
appreciates at once the effects of a raise in VAT on fuel,
but how long does it take for the effects of a deal on competition policy in Brussels or the creation of a Franco-German army corps to filter through? It is no accident then
that the 1984–86 period saw Mitterrand position himself above
the partisan battlefield concerned with loftier matters such
as 'building Europe'.

Following the left's defeat at the 1986 parliamentary elections, the first period of *cohabitation* between a left-wing
president and a right-wing prime minister increased the
external pressures for a less commanding style of presidency.
The narrowness of the right's National Assembly majority,

together with the horizon of a presidential election in 1988, where both president and the new prime minister, Jacques Chirac, were obvious front runners, reduced the amount of open conflict between the two protagonists. But while Mitterrand fought with skill to preserve his corner of high policy and while he struck a deal with Chirac about sharing out appointments within the state apparatus, there is no denying that the major burden of domestic policy-making was abandoned to the government. True, the president held a watching brief, used his constitutional powers to delay some legislation (with few real consequences) and seized upon any government gaffe to full effect in the media, but guerrilla warfare of this type is very different from the regalian presidency which had been the norm.

During the period of *cohabitation* Mitterrand also stressed the paternal, above-politics image and devoted more energy to foreign policy, particularly the German connection. Crucial here was the Single European Act which on another level signified a further weakening of presidential prerogative, implying as it did a further loss of national economic autonomy. Given this drift of events, it was logical for Mitterrand to campaign for the 1988 election in a more apolitical way than before. Without a very clear manifesto, he stressed themes of stability and continuity, making Chirac out to be the real risk of change and turbulence. With his talk of *ouverture*, he was clearly bidding for support from beyond the normal confines of the left, aspiring to pull in the hypothetical two-thirds of Frenchmen who, as Giscard's book had it, want to be governed in the centre, committed to the dynamism of a market economy but with enough of a protecting state to cover them from risk. In 1988, this strategy was successful. Mitterrand defeated Chirac at the presidential election and, although the PS only won a relative majority at the subsequent parliamentary elections, the first period of *cohabitation* ended.

The second Mitterrand *septennat* never showed the gestural leadership that characterised the start of the first, unless one is to count the president's insistence on equipping Paris with a number of architectural landmarks clearly intended as monuments to his personal glory and guarantees of his place in History (commentators used the capital letter without embarrassment). The first prime minister of this period, Michel Rocard, was left to govern as he could with no proper majority in the National Assembly and little sign of presidential interference, until his sudden removal from office and replacement by Edith Cresson in 1991. Probably Mitterrand's most active contribution to policy was his attempts to exclude Rocard as his presidential successor, particularly through his pushing of Fabius as leader of the PS from 1991–93. The exception to this passive presidential style remained the European issue, where Mitterrand strove to inject a social dimension into growing economic integration.

All the above demonstrates the further cutback of presidential power after 1988. Energy went into grand foreign designs and short-term partisan politics. The major fields of domestic policy were left to the prime minister and his team in the main. The PS's crushing defeat at the 1993 parliamentary elections simply reinforced this retreat. A much more severe *cohabitation* ensued, which saw the government led by the new prime minister, Edouard Balladur, erode parts even of the high policy domain as witnessed by the April 1994 White Paper on defence, for example. This time Balladur offered fewer opportunities than Chirac for presidential sniping, although one exception was the revision of the Falloux education bill which was rushed through the Senate in barely an hour and was subsequently thrown out by the Constitutional Council. Mitterrand could only watch helplessly as the right limbered up for the 1995 election, which at one time seemed likely to be fought between two RPR men, so badly damaged were the PS and the left generally by policy exhaustion, scandal, the traumas of the 1993 election defeat and the PS's mauling in the 1994 European elections. Only in one area did presidential willpower show through, and this was in the final undoing of Rocard who was forced out of the 1995 presidential contest after the European election débâcle. Mitterrand's constant encouragement of rivals such as Tapie, Fabius and then Delors eventually had its effect.

We should be wary of concluding from any of this that Mitterrand sought to bequeath to the French a new, somehow less monarchical style of presidency. It is true that with time his direct involvement in domestic decision-making might be said to have decreased, but he could still intervene decisively when his supporters had a parliamentary majority. If he chose to do so less, then this is mainly a reflection of the difficulty of governing an advanced country with a sophisticated and demanding electorate in a period of long-term economic stagnation. Had the situation improved, we can be sure that the president would have assumed a much more prominent role in steering policy and claiming the credit for it. In foreign affairs, particularly Europe (though Africa would merit a special study, so closely does it fall under the Elysée's control), the president remained the agenda setter and main protagonist. It is true that the majority of the political class shared his basic assumptions, which eased his task.

In short, the presidency remains as potent an office as ever, especially now that following the 1995 parliamentary elections the National Assembly majority is in line with the Elysée once again. If he so wishes, Jacques Chirac has ample tools at his disposal to set in motion the voluntarist anti-unemployment and anti-exclusion policies which figured so prominently and so unspecifically in his campaign. He also has the means to inflect France's European policies in a more Eurosceptic sense. If he chooses not to do so, this will not be because he lacks the means but simply because he has concluded, against the instincts of many of his supporters whom he desperately strove to keep on board during the campaign, that France has really no alternative but to stay close to Germany and pursue monetary union, whatever the associated costs. What is crucial in shaping presidential policy style is not so much the pious intentions or innate decency of the incumbent but the external parameters. These are becoming more constraining for governments of all types, but within them we may expect any French president of the future to seek maximum influence when he thinks it advisable and maximum invisibility when he does not.

FRANCE IN EUROPE

The Mitterrand years have seen an ever deepening involvement in European integration.[36] Delors' famous remark that

by the end of the century some 80 per cent of French legislation would emanate from Brussels neatly encapsulates this
process. Mitterrand's governments actively pushed inte-
grationist measures, such as the single market, more voting
by qualified majority, the remodelling of the structural funds,
the Schengen Agreement to abolish internal frontiers and
above all the Maastricht Treaty on European Union with its
commitment to a single currency, common foreign and security policies and the social chapter. The Maastricht referendum of 1992, where the 'yes' vote triumphed by a whisker,
revealed a 'social fracture' within France, as large sectors of
the population expressed their fears about losing out in the
new, open European marketplace.[37] Although it was widely
deplored by commentators that Europe was scarcely an issue in the 1995 presidential campaign, this verdict needs
some revision. It would be truer to say that it was not an
issue for candidates from the core parties. However, for those
from more peripheral, protesting formations, the European
dossier often subsumed many of the fears and hopes of their
supporters. The three main contenders at the 1995 presidential election, Chirac, Balladur and Jospin, all expressed
the strong consensus among the political class that French
policy towards Europe could only continue to go in the same
direction. There was no alternative.[38] Their line could be
described as intergovernmentalist, but with a clear understanding that the status quo was untenable. There was certainly no idea that France could somehow keep the benefits
of a single market without further political collaboration,
even if none of them was willing to give too much detail as
to how they would address some of the mid-term questions.[39]
They were aware that the best way for France to maintain
her competitiveness was to work closely with allies within a
strong block. The 1992–93 GATT negotiations on world trade
were an eloquent illustration of this policy. They all stressed,
then, albeit with nuances (particularly from Chirac who had
to keep on board an avowedly more Eurosceptical electorate), their commitment to the *acquis communautaire* and to
the essentials of the Maastricht Treaty, especially common
foreign and security policy and single currency. While they
had ideas for institutional change within the EU, all favoured
deepening before widening. Above all they were explicitly

committed to the Franco-German partnership at the heart of the integration process.

It is small wonder that the three main candidates were not very keen to argue on Europe as there was a remarkably high degree of élite consensus on the above. This can be seen *a contrario* through the positions of the smaller candidates.[40] Leaders as different as Philippe de Villiers, Jean-Marie Le Pen for the FN and the communist Robert Hue were united in their opposition to a single currency and further loss of sovereignty. Hue refused a 'European super army'. De Villiers demanded more use of the national veto and he wanted to abrogate Schengen and weaken the role of the European Parliament not strengthen it (as Balladur or Jospin wished).

It seemed clear then that whoever won the presidential election, French policy towards Europe would change little, so high was the agreement among the main protagonists. It has been suggested that the centrality of the European dossier to policy-making in general has increased the presidentialisation of decision-making.[41] Hopes have been expressed that greater parliamentary involvement might occur under the new president. This is probably unlikely, but in any case one would have to ask whether it would make much difference to the outcome, so solid is the mainstream consensus. Whatever his other difficulties, the new president should have quite an easy ride on Europe.

CONCLUSION: FRANCE AND HER PRESIDENT IN 1995

The Mitterrand period has been a time of significant, sometimes rapid change for France. Her economy has been modernised to compete better in an increasingly global market and much of her civil and social legislation has been revamped apace. This strenuous effort has not been without social costs, particularly in terms of the old working class, shaken up and reduced in importance by the changes, but significant social polarities still remain within France. Thus, while the majority saw no erosion in their standard of living, insecurity about the future, related to employment, began to spread. In the case of a visible minority, unemployment and other forms of marginalisation combined to produce increasing numbers of *exclus*. Yet, during this time France continued to integrate slowly large numbers of people from different backgrounds, even though the difficulties of this process provided ammunition for politicians ready to exploit any kind of social problem. The French did not become politically apathetic, even though they expected less from their leaders. They were more willing to express political anger by voting for peripheral parties, but on major occasions would usually rally to the core forces, reflecting perhaps the fact that the major left–right divide continues to structure French political culture, even though it sometimes finds oblique ways of expression. Certainly the major parties remained confident, refusing to panic about 'crises of representation' and continuing to produce the only eligible candidates with (relatively) plausible programmes. The office sought by these contestants remains potentially as powerful as ever, particularly in so far as the winner has a big majority in both houses of parliament. But, as the last occupant of the Elysée discovered, heroic decision-making in these times is likely to be the exception rather than the rule. Presidents today are hemmed in by an increasing number of parameters from above and below and are more ready than before to accept that fact. One parameter accepted without question is the importance of continuing and increasing European collaboration, particularly via the German connection. Such was the France that the victor of 1995 inherited. A new president invariably takes office with high hopes, but enough lucidity to realise the resistances to action which exist. As Jacques Chirac contemplates the legacy of the Mitterrand years, he may well wonder how much real change he can set in motion within his seven-year span and how far his policies will be simply a reaction to events.

NOTES

1. See, for example, Machin and Wright (1985) and Hall (1986).
2. In 'François Mitterrand: 14 ans de pouvoir', *Le Monde*, Paris, 1995, p. 176.
3. See the article entitled 'Le confort à tout prix' in *La Croix*, 14 April 1995.

4. 'François Mitterrand: 14 ans de pouvoir', *Le Monde*, Paris, 1995, p. 172.
5. Ibid.
6. Wright (1994).
7. Todd (1994).
8. Todd (1988).
9. Todd (1994).
10. Ibid.
11. For example, 70 per cent of young male Maghrebin immigrants and 60 per cent of females do not practise any religion (see *La Croix*, 8 April 1995).
12. In 1992, the figure was 11.4 per cent of the total compared with 6.2 per cent in 1980 (ibid.).
13. See *La Croix*, 30 April–1 May 1995.
14. See *La Croix*, 25–26 September 1994.
15. Few would put figures on it, but at least 10 per cent of the population were concerned.
16. See, for example, Grunberg in Duhamel and Jaffré (1992) and Mossuz-Lavau (1994).
17. Mayer and Perrineau (1992), p. 143.
18. See Duhamel (1989) and Furet et al. (1988).
19. Boy and Mayer (1990), p. 199.
20. Mayer and Perrineau (1992).
21. Ibid., p. 145.
22. Lawson and Merkl (1988).
23. Mayer and Perrineau (1992).
24. Imbert and Julliard (1995).
25. Grunberg in Duhamel and Jaffré (1992), p. 200.
26. Habert and Lancelot (1988).
27. Ross (1987).
28. Wright (1994), p. 85.
29. Grunberg in Duhamel and Jaffré (1992), p. 211.
30. *Le Monde*, 8 October 1994.
31. See Buffotot and Hanley (1995) and Perrineau and Ysmal (1995).
32. Hayward (1990).
33. Elgie (1993).
34. Hayward (1990), p. 35.
35. See 'François Mitterrand: deux septennats, un bilan', in *La Croix* 14–15 May 1995.
36. Dreyfus et al. (1993).
37. Buffotot (1993).
38. See *Le Monde*, 22 March 1995.
39. See in *La Croix*, 5 May 1995.
40. See the various presidential programmes in *L'Express*, No. 2284, 13–19 April 1995 and *Le Monde*, 22 April 1995.
41. See *Le Monde*, 28 March 1995.

2 The 1995 Presidential Election Campaigns

Howard Machin

This chapter focuses on how candidates attempted to win votes at the first ballot and election to the Elysée at the second ballot of the 1995 presidential election, the features which distinguished the 1995 campaign from earlier campaigns and the methods by which Jacques Chirac won. Its concerns are the strategies adopted by the candidates and the resources and methods employed. The data are mainly derived from published sources, notably newspapers and studies of earlier elections.[1] Opinion polls also provide information not only about how public attitudes changed during the campaign, but also about the significant minority of voters who remained undecided about how to vote until very near the polling days. Whether or not those voters finally chose in a 'rational' way, as Habert and Lancelot have suggested,[2] their changes of preferences during the campaign explain not only why the *maillot jaune* passed from Edouard Balladur to Jacques Delors to Chirac, but also why the poll predictions for the first ballot proved so inexact.

In recent decades, political scientists have focused great efforts into the analysis of speeches and broadcasts by candidates to panel analysis of how and why potential voters changed or maintained their choices. To establish a standard for comparison, the findings of studies by Cayrol in 1985 and Mayer and Perrineau[3] in 1992 are considered in the first section of the chapter. In the second section we focus on the stages and dynamics of the campaign and consider how the different campaigns of the various candidates interrelated. This leads on to a final section comparing the campaign resources deployed by the candidates.

The analysis of presidential election campaigning is made problematic by the fact that the first ballot has different objectives for different candidates, since some are seeking election while others are gathering support for other purposes (see Chapters 3 and 7). Similarly, for the two first-ballot leaders, the campaign for the second ballot is inevitably different from that which they have just waged. Furthermore, all candidates do not start as equals: some may be well known or respected, some are backed by parties or coalitions with great popularity in the country.

In 1995, the first ballot objective for the Socialist Party candidate, Lionel Jospin, was to win sufficient votes to stand at the second ballot. Given the results of opinion polls and the PS scores at the 1993 National Assembly election and the 1994 European Parliament election, this was not an easy task. The objectives for the two Gaullist party candidates, Chirac and Balladur, if ostensibly similar to that of Jospin, were nonetheless distinct since all expected the leading candidate of the centre-right to win. They treated the first round as a 'primary' election within their coalition: each sought to maximise support without antagonising the supporters of their rival whose votes at the second ballot would be necessary for victory. For all the other first-ballot candidates, however, the goals were to marshal support for and to show the strength of their movement – a useful preparation for the June 1995 municipal elections. At the second ballot, Chirac had only to reassemble the coalition which had won the 1993 National Assembly election, whereas Jospin had not only to establish his own presidential credentials but also to build a new electoral coalition. Jospin proved far more effective a campaigner than most observers had expected, but Chirac's head start and professional approach to the campaign ensured his victory.

TRADITIONAL PATTERNS OF PRESIDENTIAL ELECTION CAMPAIGNING

Since 1965, presidential elections have been organised in four phases. The first and longest phase, the 'pre-campaign', may start many months before the votes take place. It is characterised by both uncertainty about the precise nature of the competition, as none of the candidates admits a willingness, let alone a desire, to stand, and by attempts of the would-be candidates to win over groups and to secure favourable opinion poll results. Determined and financially secure candidates proceed to establish campaign teams with branches in all parts of the country. The second phase, the 'open' campaign, usually starts a few months before the election when candidates formally announce their intention of standing and organise campaign teams and their first public meetings. They seek the official endorsement of the parties and issue numerous statements intended to 'make news' (since paid political advertising is banned). This leads smoothly on to the third phase, the 'official first ballot campaign', which begins just two weeks before that ballot when the candidate lists are closed, the official campaign advertising boards are erected in every commune and the normal flow of television and radio programmes starts to be interrupted by the regulated broadcasts of the candidates. The final phase begins on the evening of the first ballot, as soon as the organisations running the exit polls announce clearly what the result will be. The two candidates who qualify for the second ballot by leading the poll at the first ballot immediately restart and refocus their campaigns. Those debarred from standing at the second ballot support one or other of the candidates, or oppose both. There are more meetings, posters and television or radio broadcasts and, eventually, a televised debate between the two candidates. When the polls are open, two weeks after the first ballot, both candidates and voters have extreme 'campaign fatigue'.

Since 1962, when the constitution was changed to provide for the direct election of the president by universal suffrage, the organisation of presidential campaigns has been the object of political controversy. Initial fears – not misplaced – that presidents might be 'sold like soap powder', with simple slogans, high-pressure sales techniques and group targeting based on opinion polls, led to a high degree of campaign regulation, particularly in relation to the use of television, the publication of opinion polls and campaign financing. No private advertising on radio or television is allowed, limits are set on campaign expenditure and no opinion polls may be published in the week preceding each ballot. Official election broadcasts take place on the main television channels (France 2, France 3, TF1 and ARTE)

Table 2.1 Interest of voters (%) in parliamentary and presidential election campaigns[4]

	1974 pres.	1978 parl.	1981 pres.
Those who follow the campaign:			
Almost every day	59	30	52
From time to time	32	48	39
Never	9	22	9

Table 2.2 Measures of participation in politics in the 1980s[5]

Belong to a political party	1 200 000	(1989)
Often watch *L'Heure de Vérité* on TV	4 400 000	(1985)
Watched the 1988 Chirac/Mitterrand debate	21 700 000	(1988)
Followed radio/TV political programmes before the presidential election	23 800 000	(1988)

and the public and some private radio stations under the supervision of the regulatory authority, the Conseil Supérieur de l'Audiovisuel. Campaign expenditure is scrutinised by the Constitutional Council.

The results of studies of earlier elections show that campaigns for presidential elections inspire much more interest among voters than those for other elections. Table 2.1 shows that even the campaign for a crucial legislative election like that of 1978 (when the left was expected to win and enforce a period of 'cohabitation' on President Giscard d'Estaing) inspired less interest than those for the presidential elections which preceded and followed.

Table 2.2 confirms this view, since, whereas only 10 per cent of voters watch a current affairs television programme outside election periods, more than half of the voters tune in to political broadcasts during a presidential campaign. Indeed, in 1988 half the electorate even watched the long Chirac–Mitterrand debate before the second ballot.

Despite the rise of television campaigning, traditional forms of electioneering have not been forgotten. Tracts are drafted and sent to all voters by post. Standard-sized posters can be displayed on official advertising hoardings specially erected in every commune. Candidates or their campaign staffs meet with representatives of different interest groups or reply to

Table 2.3 Information sources in presidential election campaigns[6]

	Sources most used by voters 1988 (%)	Sources voters find most useful 1981 (%)
Newspapers	26	43
Radio	17	33
News (TV)	31	—
Political programmes (TV)	25	—
News and political programmes (TV)	—	68
Opinion polls	3	10
Posters	2	3 ·
Tracts	2	4
Official leaflets	5	—
Discussion (family, friends)	25	20
Other	22	6

their questions by post. Candidates hold public election meetings in towns across France and the campaign teams often organise coaches to bring in supporters from country villages. These meetings are intended less to convert the hostile and uncertain than to revive the loyalty of those in the same party or coalition as the candidate and to ensure that they will talk to friends and relatives, raise funds for the campaign and mobilise to turn out voters to the polling stations. Such meetings are also intended to make news: the candidates hope that either the brilliance of their speeches or the sheer size of their audience will 'grab the headlines' not only in the press but also on television news broadcasts. Hence, traditional campaign tools have been used to gain access to television. It is clear, as Table 2.3 shows, that since 1965 television has become both the most used information channel about election campaigns and the means of information most preferred by voters.

Radio and television are major campaign vehicles less because of the official election broadcasts during the two-week official campaigns than because of their reporting of the entire campaign in news broadcasts and their current affairs programmes. In these programmes the candidates, or their supporters, are cross-questioned by journalists or specialists. During presidential election campaigns regular broadcast series (including, in 1995, *Face à la Une* and *Sept sur Sept* on TF1, *Les Quatre Vérités* and *L'Heure de Vérité* on France 2 and *Dimanche Soir* and *La Marché du Siècle* on France 3) are supplemented by special campaign reports. In 1995, even M6, the entertainment channel, created a special programme, *Zone Interdite*, on the presidential campaign.

Current affairs television programmes allow the voters to see the candidates themselves without the trouble of going to election meetings. Voters can also hear the candidates under interrogation by journalists, supposedly on their behalf. Before the second ballot, voters can see the two candidates side by side in a debate and make direct comparisons about the ways in which they argue, analyse and express their ideas. For candidates, television provides opportunities to project their personal qualities as leaders and statespersons, to remind groups of traditional loyalties and the benefits of reaffirming those loyalties and to present their programmes and raise issues.

The impact of personalities is difficult to assess, but television coverage can transform an unknown candidate with television qualities and skills into a significant first-ballot performer (like Jean Lecanuet in 1965), hence compensating for some of the initial inequality inherent in the contest. Similarly, in the debate prior to the second ballot a challenger facing an incumbent president does not need to 'win' the debate, but only to perform as well as the incumbent – to show that he or she is a credible alternative (as Mitterrand did in 1981, but as Chirac failed to do in 1988). All candidates attempt to use television to impose one or two questions on which their positions enjoy majority support as major campaign and electoral issues. For success, voters must consider these questions to be interesting and important (salience), they must have clear opinions and these opinions must be divided unevenly, and they must perceive that the candidates have different positions on the issues in question. Hence, unemployment may have a very high salience to voters and high electoral significance in one election because the voters perceive real differences between the candidates (as in 1981 between Mitterrand and Giscard), but have high salience and very little significance in another election because the voters perceive little difference in the candidates' positions (as in 1988).

Although many voters start the campaign with personal
preferences (reflecting objective and subjective social identities and previous experience), many are far from certain
in those preferences. The success of Mitterrand's 1981 campaign reflected his skill in reinforcing the preferences of
those who started with sympathy for him and in winning
over those who started either with weak preferences for
Giscard or who were undecided. It was television rather than
any of the more traditional tools which contributed most to
that success. Once again, in 1988 Mitterrand's television
performances contributed greatly to mobilising his traditional
supporters and winning-over the hesitant. In both campaigns,
Mitterrand was advised by the advertising guru Jacques
Séguela, whose approach was characterised by messages and
images which were simple, uncontroversial (but not unambiguous) and, above all, positive about the candidate and
the future of France (*La force tranquille* and *110 Propositions
pour la France* in 1981 and *Génération Mitterrand, La France
unie* and *Lettre à tous les Français* in 1988). The failures of
the incumbent government were underlined (in 1988
Mitterrand clearly branded Chirac as head of government
and solely responsible for everything unpopular in the period
of *cohabitation*) and a brighter future in safer, wiser hands
was promised. 'Dirty tricks' were allowed, but only if effective,
guaranteed not to rebound and executed by others. The
television campaign of general messages, aimed at a wide
public was complemented by 'niche marketing' targeted, in
meetings and tracts, at particular interest groups and, notably, at young people.[7]

In previous campaigns, the last few weeks before the election have been the crucial times when those still wavering
finally made their choices. Sometimes those choices were
made in the light of the predictions from opinion polls in
the early phases of the campaign. In 1988, one in five voters
admitted to 'hesitating until the last minute' or 'deciding
during the official campaign'.[8]

In short, election campaigns have influenced the results
of presidential elections in France and especially when no
party or coalition held a position of electoral hegemony in
the country. If television has been the main channel of the
campaign, more traditional tools have been carefully deployed

by candidates in the knowledge that successful speeches, tracts or public meetings would, in turn, be reported by television.

STAGES AND DYNAMICS OF THE 1995 CAMPAIGN

The dynamics of the 1995 campaign were more similar to those of 1988 than those of other previous presidential elections. The main competition was between candidates of the centre-right coalition and the Socialist Party for the presidency, while two first ballot subplots concerned the struggle within the centre-right between the incumbent prime minister and an earlier one and the valiant attempts of the 'small' candidates to gather as many votes as possible. In 1995, as in 1988, the last weeks of the campaign appear to have been critical: one first ballot exit poll revealed that only 53 per cent of voters had made up their minds 'several months ago', whereas 20 per cent had decided 'several weeks ago' and 26 per cent 'in the last days' or 'at the last minute'.[9] There were, however, four important differences in 1995. The first was the absence of an incumbent president. The second was the massive electoral hegemony of the centre-right: the 1993 legislative victory had been so great and the humiliation of the socialists at the 1994 European election so dramatic that in early 1994 the election of a centre-right candidate was widely seen as a foregone conclusion. The third factor was the huge popularity of the incumbent prime minister, Edouard Balladur, throughout 1993 and 1994. The final factor was the possibility of a Jacques Delors candidacy, and in late 1994 the opinion polls showed that the (then still incumbent) President of the European Commission had an exceptionally wide appeal.

In the first pre-campaign phase, Balladur rose to a position dominating all opinion polls in late 1993 and the first nine months of 1994. The second 'open' campaign phase began with the announcements of candidature by Jean-Marie Le Pen, Robert Hue, Dominique Voynet and Chirac and the attempts of many socialists to persuade Delors to stand. In November, Delors took the lead in the opinion polls, but his categorical statement of 'non-candidature' in December 1994 changed the character of the 'open' campaign.

For the next months both Chirac and several socialist would-
be candidates energetically strove to win over those who had
expressed support for Delors. By the time the official campaign phase began, Jospin was at last attempting to build
an effective strategy and Chirac had taken the lead in the
opinion polls from Balladur. From then until the first ballot on 23 April the campaign was marked by Chirac's
unchallengeable lead in the polls and the contest between
Jospin and Balladur to win through to the second ballot.
The surprise of Jospin heading the first ballot poll opened
a final phase of hard campaigning for the second ballot
with the slight (if highly optimistic) possibility that Chirac
would not win.

The phase of Balladurian ascendancy – and the pre-campaign for the presidency – really began in 1992 when Chirac
decided that, in the likely event of a centre-right victory in
the 1993 National Assembly elections, he would not seek
the post of prime minister. Chirac visited all parts of the
country to renew old friendships, establish new ones and,
above all, to build up his electoral machinery, while Balladur
began to govern France with surprising popularity. Balladur's
apparent preoccupation with governing, however, was de-
ceptive: once his popularity in the opinion polls had out-
lived the 'honeymoon' months after the 1993 election, he
started to lay the foundations for a campaign network across
France. While in his own speeches and writings he avoided
even indirect suggestions that he might stand for president,
he did nothing to discourage his friends and allies – and
enemies of Chirac – from publicly calling on him to be a
candidate, or merely commenting favourably on his suitability
and electability. In late 1993 and 1994, rather than campaigning himself, Balladur, like Mitterrand in the 1987
Génération Mitterrand appeal, let others do the work for him.
In theory, this strategy of appearing to respond to a 'call'
should have had the double advantage of contrasting Chirac's
naked personal ambition to be president and overcoming
the criticisms of personal treachery to his former friend and
party leader, which Chirac acolytes would (and did) inevitably voice.

For this strategy to succeed, however, Balladur had not
only to maintain an unblemished record of governmental

achievements (a thankless task with over three million people unemployed, not to mention continuing corruption scandals and an Algerian civil war which was likely to spill over into France at any moment), but also to capture the imagination of voters in competition with other candidates. Balladur was very popular when the alternatives were either Mitterrand or former Prime Ministers Pierre Bérégovoy and Edith Cresson, but that was not the choice for voters in 1995. The humiliation of Michel Rocard in the 1994 European Parliament election and his subsequent ejection from the leadership of the PS meant that he was no longer a credible candidate for the presidency (see Chapter 5). In the absence of any real candidate from the centre-left, Balladur dominated the opinion polls during early 1994. It appeared that Chirac had made a major strategic error by allowing Balladur to establish himself as the 'natural' choice for the centre-right and 'unbeatable' candidate for the Elysée.

At the start of the 'open' campaign phase it was far from clear that Balladur would be eclipsed in the polls. In September, Jean-Marie Le Pen (FN), Robert Hue (Communist), Arlette Laguiller (Lutte Ouvrière) and Brice Lalonde (Génération Ecologie) all announced their candidatures, followed in October by Dominique Voynet (Les Verts) and Chirac. In late 1994 and early 1995 some 40 others (including the poetically named Benoît Frappe of the Natural Law Party, whose presidential platform included the reduction of crime and unemployment by meditation and levitation) announced their presidential intentions, but failed to secure the necessary signatures. Of all the obscure candidates, only one, Jacques Cheminade, leader of the hitherto unknown Federation for a New Solidarity, somehow managed to acquire the essential 500 signatures. Initially none of these posed a threat to Balladur.

Ironically it was a man who refused to be a candidate, Jacques Delors, who transformed the dynamics of the campaign and demonstrated that Balladur could be beaten. Since Rocard's eclipse in June 1994, press and television journalists had increasingly identified the President of the European Commission as the only politician on the left with the stature to have any chance of winning. On 11 December, however, with his presidency of the Commission virtually concluded after the Essen European Council meeting, Delors put an end to the speculation and announced that he would not enter the presidential race. By then, though, he had shown that more attractive and imaginative styles of, and agendas for, ruling France were possible: Balladur was beatable.[10]

The next two months were dominated by socialist attempts to find a candidate and Chirac's efforts to overtake Balladur. While the PS debated, the other candidates got on with their campaigns. The Christmas period saw attempts by both Chirac and Balladur to demonstrate presidential qualities. The first was by Chirac and came in response to the occupation of an empty block in the centre of Paris (rue du Dragon) by homeless people and the call – widely reported in the media – from Abbé Pierre (the father figure of campaigning against homelessness since 1945) for the government to change its policy and start using its existing powers to requisition empty property. There was some surprise when Chirac leapt aboard the populist bandwagon, criticising the government and calling for requisitions. Although Abbé Pierre responded by casting doubt on the track-record of Chirac and his team in this policy area, the Chirac campaign continued to press the case – and, in so doing, differentiated his position from that of the incumbent prime minister who was pushed both to defend his position and to make concessions. Balladur, in turn, had a chance to dominate the media and demonstrate his leadership qualities. When Algerian fundamentalists hijacked a full Air France plane at Algiers airport, Balladur, working closely with the Minister of the Interior, Charles Pasqua, organised the rescue of the plane and most of the passengers. The release of the hijack victims, however, was a one-off success, while the rue du Dragon squat launched a constant – and paying – campaign theme: that a Chirac presidency meant a change for a more fair and caring society. On 10 January 1995, Chirac published his campaign booklet, with, as title, his campaign slogan, 'La France pour Tous'. Although the cover design, a green apple full of ripe red fruit, was vaguely ecological, the message was one of social solidarity – sharing the fruits of prosperity.

While Jospin announced that he was standing for his party's nomination on 4 January, he was not officially nominated by the PS until 5 February. Despite several attempts by his rivals to discredit him, the outcome of the consultation of PS members was clear: Jospin was chosen by 65 per cent of those voting. The starting problems for his campaign, however, were enormous. Eleven weeks before the first ballot, he did not have a campaign team or a platform, or even a united party. He knew from the polls that only by differentiating himself from Mitterrand could he have any chance of winning the presidency, but that if he criticised the president the *mitterrandistes* would try to destroy him. Nonetheless, the publicity in the media about his candidature and the strong boost of winning two-thirds of the votes in the PS gave Jospin's campaign a kick-start. In the second week of February, one opinion poll even showed Jospin ahead of both Balladur and Chirac, but it soon proved a mirage, a short-lived result of the former losing popularity faster than the latter was gaining credibility.

February marked a turning point in the campaign, since Chirac overtook the prime minister in the opinion polls. At the start of the month the polls showed that Balladur, with 30 per cent of voting intentions, had an eight to ten point lead over Chirac, while Jospin trailed Chirac by two to three points. By early March, however, all the polls indicated that Chirac was leading Balladur by two to six points and Jospin by one to three points. Furthermore, during the first half of March Chirac was increasing his poll ratings (up to 30 per cent for CSA) and support for Balladur continued to slide (as far as 16.5 per cent for BVA).

For Jean Charlot, this change in the leadership of the presidential race is explained by a real decline in support for Balladur and the consequent rallying of former Balladur supporters, especially RPR and UDF sympathisers, to the Chirac cause.[11] Furthermore, support drained away from Balladur in response to his handling of two controversial issues, a proposed reform of the University Institutes of Technology (IUT) and a telephone tapping scandal. In the first case, a series of student protests against a measure to prevent IUT students graduating with two-year diplomas from taking further university degrees had already shown the extent of student discontent, when an official report proposed a reduction of student financial aid and an increase in university registration fees. After three days of strikes and mass demonstrations by students, the prime minister withdrew the original plan for IUT diplomas and four days later his Education Minister, François Fillon, announced that the recommendations of the official report on aid and fees had not been adopted. This wave of protests and Balladur's reaction caused concern to many. Among young people the view that the prime minister was out of touch with the problems of youth (which had already been voiced a year earlier when his government had unsuccessfully attempted to introduce a reduced minimum wage for newcomers to the labour market) was again widely shared. Many parents sympathised with the aspirations of their offspring. For others, however, the prime minister appeared too weak and willing to give way in the face of any demonstration or protest (as he had in the Air France and minimum wage conflicts in preceding months).

The telephone tapping incident, known as the 'affaire Schuller-Maréchal', after the names of the two main protagonists, Didier Schuller and Jean-Pierre Maréchal, was equally, if not more, damaging. On 8 February, the Paris Appeal Court dismissed the case against Maréchal of attempting to blackmail Schuller on the grounds of entrapment by the police and invalid evidence obtained by means of illegal telephone tapping. The problem was that Schuller was a close ally on the Hauts-de-Seine departmental council led by Pasqua (the man reputed as most likely to become prime minister if Balladur were to be elected to the Elysée), while Maréchal was the father-in-law of Eric Halphen, the examining magistrate investigating allegations of corruption in the public housing office (HLM) of the Parisian region (including the Hauts-de-Seine). Earlier suggestions that Halphen's family ties implied that he should be replaced at the head of the HLM investigation were at once dropped. Furthermore, on 20 February Balladur had to make a public admission that the telephone tapping had been illegal (although he had made a statement that it had been legal two days earlier). The prime minister continued to affirm his trust in the Minister of the Interior, Charles Pasqua, and, by agreeing to resign, the Criminal Police director became the designated scapegoat of the *affaire*. Charlot's detailed analysis of the opinion polls which followed this débâcle reveals a clearly negative impact both on Balladur's own image and that of Pasqua.[12] From seeming to be a considerable asset, Pasqua's support was becoming a liability. Furthermore, the media concentrated on the scandal, almost ignoring Balladur's press conference on 13 February (which *Le Monde* reported under the title, 'Edouard Balladur ou l'inévitable ennui') and his first big public meeting in Nogent-sur-Marne on 16 February.

In contrast, Chirac grabbed the headlines on 17 February by holding a vast and enthusiastic meeting at the Paris Exhibition Park at the Porte de Versailles with some 15 000 fans brought in by coach. Jospin, weeks behind the other candidates, also gained significant coverage for the announcement of his campaign team on 21 February. His choice of Delors to head the *comité de soutien* and Martine Aubry (Delors' daughter) as his official spokesperson augured well and to avoid any controversy Jospin also published a statement of his personal finances. The platform of the PS candidate, a list of 'Propositions pour la France', followed on 7 March. By that time, however, Chirac was clearly leading the opinion polls and rapidly consolidating support among those who were losing faith in Balladur.

The rest of the 'open' campaign and the entire official first ballot campaign was marked by Chirac's domination of the opinion polls, Balladur's attempts at a come-back and Jospin's efforts to win through to the second round. On 8 March, Balladur had another set-back when *Le Canard Enchaîné* published an article about his personal fortune and profitable financial dealings, revealing the huge salary and profits he had gained by his employment with the GSI company and subsequent sale of its shares. Within a week, not only Balladur but also Chirac and Le Pen followed Jospin's example and made public declarations about their personal wealth. Two weeks later, *Le Monde* persuaded all candidates, except Le Pen, to provide details of their 1994 tax payments. The contrast was marked between the relatively ordinary tax resources of Hue and Jospin and the comfortable upper-middle class fortunes of Balladur and Chirac, but it was the former who suffered most from this episode in the campaign.

The prime minister's attempts to reverse the trend were

many and various. One was to humanise his austere image. On 12 March he used his television appearance on *Sept sur Sept* to exhibit a personal warmth hitherto well concealed in public. Two days later, at a meeting of 300 supporters in Montpellier, the new and friendly approach was again on show: candidate and friends sat down to a paella together, Balladur wandering around the room informally greeting supporters and even climbing on a chair to speak. Over the next days the prime minister became known as 'Edouard' or even 'Doudou'. If his helicopter was forced down by fog, then candidate Edouard hitch-hiked. He dismissed the attacks on his personal wealth as 'campaign stink-bombs'. He made direct attacks on Chirac as an out-of-date demagogue, promising anything to be elected. His campaign team even had some lucky breaks, including *Le Canard Enchaîné 's* criticism of Chirac for his cheaply rented flat in the rue du Bac and Chirac's public altercation with Jean-Claude Trichet, the governor of the newly independent Banque de France, following the publication of the bank's annual report on 11 April.

Huge expense and great efforts went into organising a massive public meeting, the 'Fête à Edouard', for 15 000 fans from all parts of France at Le Bourget on 25 March. The inevitable speech was preceded by a fun fair, tables of food, wine and beer from all parts of France, accordion players and singers, sales of T-shirts bearing the slogan (in English) 'Just Doudou it' and ritual chanting of 'Doudou avec nous' (instead of 'Balladur président' at earlier meetings). These colourful efforts were not fruitless and in late March Balladur's poll ratings again began to rise from the 18 per cent level to which they had sunk. In early April, one poll (admittedly by IPSOS, which regularly over-estimated Balladur's support) showed the prime minister overtaking Jospin and only two points behind Chirac. One poll, however, did not make a trend.

Balladur's difficulties reflected both the effectiveness of Chirac's developing campaign and the steady progress of Jospin. Chirac scored three notable successes, winning support from former critics, the mass meeting for young people in Paris and his official campaign broadcasts on television. First came a visit to the home of his 1981 rival, Giscard d'Estaing, at Chamalières and an explicit display of support when Giscard attended Chirac's public meeting at nearby Clermont-Ferrand on 17 March. One week later, Chirac received similar honours in Bordeaux from the man whom he had helped to defeat in 1974, former Prime Minister Jacques Chaban-Delmas. On 9 April, the Chirac team organised an open meeting for young people at the Bercy sports hall and, to their delight, about 17 000 people came to see and hear the candidate and his friends from the worlds of entertainment and sport (led by Johnny Halliday and Alain Prost). His direct, sensitive speech won headline reports as much as the sheer number of participants. Finally, Chirac ran a highly professional series of official campaign broadcasts on the television, constantly reusing his campaign logo of the apple tree, his theme of 'healing the social divide' and his slogans of 'changing politics', 'changing priorities' and 'sharing'.

Meanwhile, after a slow and late start, the Jospin campaign was picking up speed. If initially Jospin had appeared to many as rather cold, aloof and alone, by late March he was gaining confidence, warmth and weight. The official campaign slogan 'Avec Jospin, c'est clair' (which voters found anything but clear) was *de facto* replaced by 'Pour une France plus juste'. On 13 March Jospin was given the declared support of François Mitterrand. On 6 April over 7000 people came to hear him speak at Montpellier and, after a rousing speech and a rapturous response from his supporters, a radiant Jospin left the stage blowing kisses to his supporters. Two days later a similar number of people, led by former prime ministers Mauroy and Rocard warmly welcomed him to Rennes. The only problem was that, despite the improving reports from the campaign team, the opinion polls seemed stuck at near 20 per cent from mid-March onwards.

As the polls showed, the campaigns of the other candidates were having some impact on the voters. Hue, as *Le Monde* reported, seemed a 'natural' candidate – warm, friendly, funny, even with journalists.[13] His description of Chirac ('the shark from *Jaws* who wants to pretend he is Flipper the dolphin') was widely quoted. Laguiller brought a touch of nostalgia to the campaign. Her 'Robin Hood' themes had changed little since they were last aired in 1988. Both she and Voynet called for bigger roles for women in politics and Balladur led the responsive bids, promising ten female ministers in any future government. Voynet's campaign was marked by the continued divisions of the ecologists. Despite the eloquence and charm she displayed in public meetings, she stayed low in the polls. De Villiers constantly emphasised his anti-Maastricht and anti-Schengen ideas and his criticisms of corruption. Le Pen and the FN were well organised for this campaign, which in many places was run with enthusiasm fired by the thought that gains at the first ballot would prepare the way for victories in the June municipal elections. Le Pen performed very professionally on television and at his rallies. He constantly strove to 'positivise' his message, to discuss issues other than law and order and immigrants, including economics, international relations and European integration, and to show himself as responsible and serious but capable of carrying out major policy changes. He missed few opportunities to remind his large enthusiastic audiences of the long list of former ministers – left- and right-wing alike – who were in jail, awaiting trial or merely removed from office. Le Pen campaigned deliberately against everyone else (dismissing de Villiers as a distraction who had stolen his ideas) but saved his most venomous darts for Chirac.

The surprise result of 23 April showed not only that all the polls overestimated support for Chirac, but also opened the final stage of the campaign with the vague (but hitherto unthinkable) prospect that Jospin might even win. The basic arithmetic of the votes, however, meant that such a victory would require a massive swing to the left, since Chirac, Balladur and the other right- and extreme-right wing candidates, de Villiers and Le Pen respectively, had totalled almost 60 per cent of the vote between them at the first ballot (see Appendix 1). While Le Pen could be relied upon to attack both candidates and encourage his supporters to abstain or spoil their papers (which he did on 1 May), neither de Villiers nor Balladur would do the same. Indeed, Balladur announced his support for Chirac and called on his voters to do the same just a few hours after the close of the polls on 23 April. So too did de Villiers and Pasqua did the same the next day. The major public display of centre-right unity behind Chirac was reserved for a public meeting in Paris at the Bagatelle gardens on 29 April. Chirac was the sole star on the stage, but the front row of spectators included Balladur, Pasqua, de Villiers, Giscard, the senior UDF figure François Léotard and, indeed, all the main first-ballot supporters of both Balladur and Chirac. The rivals of the previous week shook hands as allies (if not friends). The enthusiastic Chirac campaign team claimed 50 000 people attended and even critics suggested over 30 000 people took part. The message here, repeated in all official campaign broadcasts, was that the whole centre-right was mobilised behind Chirac and his platform. Just in case there were any doubts, the campaign closed on 5 May with a public meeting in Lyon where former prime minister Raymond Barre, the one coalition leader absent from the Bagatelle meeting, gave his full support to Chirac.

Jospin had neither the unanimous backing of all the forces on the left nor the real hope of gaining more than a small number of Le Pen's first ballot voters. Hue merely called on his voters to 'vote against Chirac' and Laguiller announced that she would abstain. Le Pen's advice to his voters that 'Chirac was a "social democrat" like Jospin but worse' was unlikely to swing mass support to the socialist candidate. Delors campaigned hard and even hinted that he might become prime minister if Jospin were elected. Jospin's team focused their efforts on the official broadcasts, a number of public meetings across different parts of France culminating on 4 May in a huge public meeting in Toulouse, the candidate's political base, and preparing for the televised debate with Chirac.

For most French voters, the symbolic culmination of the campaign came on 2 May with the debate between the two candidates on the main television channels. The rules of the game were agreed between Chirac's and Jospin's advisers. Led by journalists, Alain Duhamel and Guillaume Durand, the two contestants carefully and courteously explored all the main issues, admitting similarities and marking differences in a calm and measured way for almost two hours. Tension and humour were in short supply and neither candidate clearly dominated the debate. Both were articulate and impressive rather than inspiring. In the absence of published opinion polls, the journalists could only report their impressions of the impact of the debate. Their general verdict was that, although Jospin had shown presidential qualities on a par with those of Chirac, he had not demonstrated the clear superiority of character and policies necessary to swing huge numbers of hesitant voters to support him. Hence, unlike the first ballot result, Chirac's clear but not massive victory caused little surprise on 7 May.

CAMPAIGN METHODS AND RESOURCES

In 1995, as at earlier elections, campaigns were built by candidate-based teams with party support, focusing particular strategies on specific target groups and using the available funds. In comparing the methods and resources of the candidates, and, in particular, the three main ones, we see once again that, although Balladur seemed to start with huge advantages, Chirac had the best resources and most professionally run campaign.

From early February 1995, the official Balladur campaign was managed by Nicolas Bazire, previously the prime minister's chief of staff, from campaign headquarters at 84 rue de Grenelle. The benefits of incumbency at first seemed enormous, notably in terms of media coverage and transport subsidies. However, the problems were numerous. Incumbency itself was a problem, especially when government policies became unpopular. Also, the candidate himself and his closest political allies, led by Pasqua, Léotard, Nicolas Sarkozy and Simone Veil, were all highly occupied by their governmental responsibilities so that, initially at least, campaigning was a part-time activity. That would have been less important had there been an effective party machine to support the campaign, but the UDF remained what it had always been – a loose umbrella organisation – and of its components only the CDS was really mobilised. One hope was that Pasqua would bring part of the RPR machine to work for Balladur but it proved illusory. As Bazire told Jean Charlot, the problem was that the RPR had been strongly '*juppéisé*', a reference to Alain Juppé, the pro-Chirac leader of the Gaullist Party.[14] There was a *comité de soutien* and an informal network of friends in all parts of France, so that neither funds nor well-placed supporters were lacking, but the Balladur team simply did not have the campaigning activity of that of Chirac.

Jospin's team started from even greater disadvantages. It received no hidden subsidies, had no means of easy access to media coverage or free transport and had a highly divided party base at the beginning of the campaign. Daniel Vaillant, aided by Claude Estier (who had campaigned with Mitterrand since 1974), set up Jospin's team at 100 rue du Cherche-Midi, but only at the end of February. The contributions from Delors, Rocard, Mauroy, Aubry and Dominique Strauss-Kahn were considerable, but the PS secretariat nearby, still run by Henri Emmanuelli whom Jospin had defeated to win the party's investiture, only really mobilised with any enthusiasm after the first ballot. Party mobilisation was greater in the provinces, notably in Brittany, the Nord-Pas-de-Calais and the south-west, but in general the PS appeared a much less energetic or effective machine than in any of the three previous presidential contests.

The contrast with the Chirac machine was striking. Already in the summer of 1988, Jean Charlot had performed an 'autopsy' of that year's defeat and in September 1989, at her father's request, Claude Chirac had started to re-examine the grassroots basis for a 1995 victory.[15] In early 1992, a 'presidential group' had established offices at 174 Boulevard St. Germain, where a team composed of Maurice Ulrich, Jean-Pierre Denis, Christine Albanel, François Baroin, Patrick Stefanini, Claude Chirac and, until mid-1994, Nicolas Sarkozy helped Chirac to rethink both how France should be ruled and how the presidential election should be won. Chirac's short book, *Une nouvelle France. Réflexions 1*, presented a synthesis of the new thinking and the campaign booklet, *La France pour Tous*, further developed the main themes. Chirac also had a loyal team of party supporters, led by Juppé, Michel Debré, Bernard Pons and Jacques Toubon, and joined after 1992 by Philippe Séguin. Alain Madelin from the UDF was another close ally. Behind these leaders were the not inconsiderable resources of the RPR headquarters and party apparatus and the Hôtel de Ville of Paris. Advertising experts Goudard and Brochand were responsible for 'communications'. In January 1995 a campaign headquarters – to coordinate the mobilisation of all these resources – was set up at 30 avénue d'Iéna.

In the first ballot campaign, the use of public meetings varied considerably between candidates.[16] The record was held by Dominique Voynet. As befits a candidate proclaiming the merits of popular participation, she spoke at no fewer than 80 public meetings in all parts of the country. Her nearest challenger was the indefatigable Robert Hue with 74 meetings followed by Jospin with 57 despite the shortness of his campaign. Both Chirac (35 meetings) and Balladur (33) preferred fewer but bigger gatherings as did Le Pen (21). Lack of funds meant that Laguiller held only 21 public meetings, whereas de Villiers spoke at 35. All candidates made collections for funds at their meetings, but a distinctive feature of Le Pen's meetings was the entry charge (40 francs per head, minimum) and the sales of Nietzsche's writings. The value-for-money meeting was Balladur's 'Fête à Edouard' where the best free food in Paris was available.

Controversy over campaign financing is a feature of most French presidential elections, despite the legal rules and supervision of accounts by the Constitutional Council, and 1995 was not exceptional in this respect. Once again, criticisms were voiced about the total cost of campaigning, the accuracy of the declaration of expenses made by the candidates and the imbalance of resources between them. The official figures published by the Constitutional Council indicated that the total spent by all candidates at both ballots was 426.91 million francs (over £53 million) – a substantial amount by any calculations.[17] In fact, the law (62–1292 of 6 November 1962, modified by 95–65 of 19 January 1995) set ceilings on expenses which were considerably higher than the actual expenses declared. The two candidates who stood at both ballots were authorised to spend up to 120 million francs in total, whereas candidates who only stood at the first ballot faced a maximum spending figure of 90 million francs. Of all the candidates in 1995, only Chirac (total 116.62 million francs) and Balladur (83.85 million francs) were close to their respective ceilings, whereas the combined expenditure of Laguiller, Voynet and Cheminade was only 23.98 million francs. If all the candidates had spent up to the expenses ceiling, the total would have been 870 million francs

Table 2.4 Official spending figures for the 1995 campaign (in millions of francs)

Candidate	Total	Reim-bursed	Polls	Post	TV (1)	TV (2)	Travel	Meet-ings
Cheminade	4.72	4.69	0.02	0.51	1.43	0.15	0.80	0.02
Voynet	7.91	7.20	—	0.27	2.38	1.00	0.70	0.61
Laguiller	11.35	10.76	0.27	0.02	1.56	0.11	2.12	0.12
de Villiers	24.16	7.20	1.08	4.12	2.68	0.09	0.72	1.14
Le Pen	41.36	32.40	—	4.93	11.33	2.60	2.13	0.74
Hue	48.76	32.40	0.90	2.00	19.36	1.64	2.42	0.50
Balladur	83.85	30.18	1.62	13.69	10.47	0.37	3.54	30.49
Jospin	88.20	43.20	1.82	2.22	37.76	1.31	4.21	16.39
Chirac	116.62	43.29	3.61	25.10	34.32	4.11	10.13	15.63

TV (1) is the figure for total expenditure on the production of election leaflets and TV programmes.
TV (2) is the figure for total expenditure on professional advice on communications and propaganda materials.

(over £100 million). Hence, although the total official cost of the campaign was less than half of what it might have been, it was still a huge bill to pay, even for informing the public about the issues, proposals and candidates before important elections.

Inevitably the questions were asked as to whether Chirac won because he spent the most and where the money came from. As Table 2.4 indicates, the bulk of the taxpayers' money (131 161 510 francs) was devoted to the conception and production of television broadcasts and printed election materials. Over half that total was spent by Chirac and Jospin. The other major expenditure item was that of travel and election meetings by the candidates and in total over 92 million francs were spent. A lot of Chirac's money was spent on leaflets and publications; 15 million copies of the shorter version of *La France pour Tous* were distributed to most homes.

Almost half the costs were met by the taxpayers. In 1995, the Constitutional Council recognised that for all the candidates a total of 211.29 million francs was reimbursable from state funds. This total could have reached 313.20 million francs, but only if all the first ballot candidates had polled the 5 per cent share of the vote needed to qualify for the maximum reimbursement of 32.40 million francs (on the assumption that they had spent more than that sum on their campaigns.

In fund-raising, the Chirac campaign had two advantages over the others. The first was that by starting early the Chirac campaign was able to receive gifts from firms (*personnes morales*) for 2.4 million francs. A new campaign finance law, voted on 21 January 1995, banned such contributions so that neither Balladur nor Jospin received funding of this kind. More importantly, the Chirac campaign ran a well-organised 'Association to Finance the Election of Jacques Chirac', based on carefully studied American techniques, including direct mailings, which produced 160 000 cheques. Hence the total contributions from individuals totalled 69.6 million francs for Chirac, in stark contrast to 21.1 million francs for Balladur and only 6.9 million francs for Jospin.

CONCLUSION

In March 1995, Jacques Séguela (the advertising specialist who had advised Mitterrand in 1981 and 1988) told *Libération* that 'The campaign of images and clips has replaced the debate of ideas and previous election campaigns. The most "televisual" of the candidates will be elected, which Jacques Chirac has clearly understood.'[18] He praised the professionalism of Chirac's campaign (notably his repetition of the slogan 'La France pour Tous', the apple-tree logo, the promises of hope and change and even the dominant use of the colour blue ('the most televisual of colours') in all his election broadcasts. But is Séguela's explanation of Chirac's success adequate and were there distinctive elements to the 1995 campaign in comparison to those of previous presidential elections?

In 1981, when Chirac first stood for the presidential election, he came third with 18 per cent of the first ballot vote. In 1988, Chirac, then prime minister, improved his performance. After coming second at the first ballot with 19 per cent of the vote, he went on to win 46 per cent against Mitterrand at the second. On both occasions it was clear that, if Chirac had a strong party base in the RPR, a coalition partner in the UDF and considerable personal appeal (notably in his two political bases, Paris and the Corrèze), he also had a significant 'rejection impact' on the electorate. In one sense the challenge he faced in 1995 was to hold on to all his 1988 assets, to gain substantial support and to reduce or remove his 'rejection image'. That task was singularly complicated in 1995 by the direct competition from a respected and competent prime minister from his own party who started the campaign with great popularity and whose appeal drew votes from Chirac's 1988 base. However, the Chirac campaign knew that, although Balladur would attract the support of older and more bourgeois voters at the first ballot, these votes could easily be regained at the second ballot.

The real advantages of the Chirac team were the early investigations of the electorate and its varied demands, their long and careful preparations, the professional organisation and sheer determination of their candidate to become president. Nonetheless, despite his many assets and his clearly superior campaigning, Chirac only won a narrow lead over Balladur at the first ballot. He also won less votes than the 'newcomer' Jospin who represented those political forces which had been so humiliatingly defeated by the centre-right in 1993. Despite his inexperience, a late start, a hesitant party base and an ill-fated and sometimes improvised campaign, Jospin proved a surprisingly effective candidate. Jospin himself, on hearing the first ballot score, told Vaillant '... if only we hadn't had a drab candidate, a poor campaign director and bad public relations, we could have won at the first ballot.'[19] Chirac's victory on 7 May was not a surprise, but it was not the huge triumph for which he had hoped.

NOTES

1. Notably *Le Monde* and *Libération* and three books: Bacqué and Saverot (1995), Cotta (1995) and Scrutator (1995). I am also most grateful to Jean Charlot for sending me a copy of his excellent book (1995) straight from the press. My thanks also to Alain Guyomarch, Arnaud Miguet and Pascal Perrineau for helpful comments and discussions.

Curiously, although opinion polls proliferated during the election campaign, much of the data currently available from them is unhelpful beyond the trend charts constructed by Charlot. The published polls provide only globalised figures, whereas the results of private polls, which may or may not have influenced candidates to change their strategies, are not available.

2. Habert and Lancelot (1988).
3. Cayrol (1985); Mayer and Perrineau (1992).
4. Cayrol (1985), p. 386.
5. Mayer and Perrineau (1992), p. 18.
6. Cayrol (1985), p. 386; Mayer and Perrineau (1992), p. 105.
7. Estier (1995).
8. Mayer and Perrineau (1992), p. 104.
9. *L'Election présidentielle. 23 avril el 7 mai 1995* (Paris: *Le Monde*, 1995), p. 50.
10. Duhamel (1995).
11. Charlot (1995), pp. 239–54.
12. Ibid., pp. 244–5.
13. *Le Monde*, 26–27 March 1995.
14. Charlot (1995), pp. 239–54.
15. Ibid., pp. 19–23.
16. Information in this paragraph is from *Libération*, 22–23 April 1995.
17. Official figures from the *Journal officiel*, 19 July 1995, pp. 10710–30.
18. *Libération*, 29 March 1995.
19. *Le Monde*, 26 April 1995.

3 The Institutional Logics of Presidential Elections

Robert Elgie

The study of institutions and the role they play in determining political outcomes is not new. Institutionalism has a long intellectual history which encompasses the work of writers as famous and as diverse as Montesquieu, Bagehot, Ostrogorski and Weber. In France, the institutionalist tradition is exemplified by Maurice Duverger's pioneering work in the early 1950s on political parties, electoral systems and party systems.[1] More recently it may be associated with the 'strategic analysis of institutions' which was developed mainly by Jean-Luc Parodi and Olivier Duhamel.[2] Despite these deep intellectual foundations, it is only in the last few years that political scientists have begun to pay systematic attention to the nature of institutions and to address the question of how and why they affect the political process.[3] The essence of the new institutionalist approach is that institutions help to define the behaviour of political actors. They do so by encouraging people to adopt certain forms of action and by discouraging them from adopting certain others. They provide individuals with resources and constraints. They create incentives and disincentives. They open up certain possibilities and close off others. In short, they establish the rules of the political game. This is not to say, though, that institutions predetermine political outcomes, that they fix behaviour in advance or that they leave political actors with no alternatives. It is simply to say that by studying institutions it is possible to gain insights into the nature of political competition, the distribution of political power and the patterns of public policy-making which occur within individual political systems.

A central element of the new institutionalist approach is that institutions introduce a degree of continuity into the political process. By their very nature, institutions are

51

comparatively stable. They consist of a set of 'formal rules, compliance procedures and standard operating practices',[4] the result of which is that their impact on the political system is at least relatively predictable. In other words, they set in train certain institutional logics which endure over time. At the same time, a further element of the new institutionalist approach is that institutions are heterogeneous entities. They consist of a sometimes bewildering and contradictory set of formal rules, compliance procedures and standard operating practices which create the conditions for a relatively predictable but what may also be a highly complex political game. In other words, they may set in train certain conflicting institutional logics to which political actors have to respond.

This chapter focuses on the 1995 presidential election as a way of illuminating the conflicting institutional logics of the system which is used to elect the President of the French Republic. It will be shown that the conduct of the 1995 presidential election campaign was in part shaped by the nature of this system and the nature of the institution to which it applies. This is not to say that these factors determined the outcome of the election. The outcome was determined by the pattern of party competition, the configuration of electoral support and candidates' responses to the issue agenda (see Chapters 2, 4, 5, 6 and 7). It is simply to say that the institutionalist approach helps us to understand why some of the main events of the 1995 campaign occurred in the way that they did. In this context, the first part of the chapter will outline the formal rules of the electoral system and will identify some of its more immediate effects. The second part will examine the conflicting institutional logics of presidential elections more explicitly and will assess some of the strategies that candidates are encouraged to adopt in order to succeed.

THE ELECTORAL SYSTEM

In the original version of the 1958 Constitution, the President of the Republic was elected by an electoral college consisting mainly of parliamentarians and representatives of local government. In the Fifth Republic's first presidential election on 21 December 1958, Charles de Gaulle received 62 394 electoral college votes, Georges Marrane, the Communist Party candidate, received 10 355 votes and Albert Chatelet, the candidate of the non-communist left, received 6721 votes. In 1962, however, this system was changed. In September of that year, President de Gaulle announced that he was proposing a constitutional amendment whereby, henceforth, the president would be directly elected by universal suffrage. On 28 October 1962, the proposal was approved in a popular referendum by 61.8 per cent of those who voted and the first election under the new system was held in December 1965. (For the results of presidential elections since 1965, see Appendix 1.) Since this time, presidential elections have been the defining moments of the political system. Successful candidates have exercised leadership on the basis of having acquired a popular legitimacy and with the support of a parliamentary majority presidents have been the country's principal decision-makers. In short, presidential elections have been the basis for a system of presidential government.

The rules which currently govern presidential elections are fixed both by the 1962 constitutional amendment and by other complementary laws. These rules determine the conditions which budding candidates have to meet in order to stand at the election and then what they have to do in order to win. The first condition that candidates must meet in order to stand concerns the requirements of eligibility. In order to be eligible, a candidate must be a French citizen, over 23 years of age and, in the case of men, they must have completed their period of military service.[5] More importantly, a candidate must never have been declared bankrupt, or have been found guilty of any offence which would automatically render him or her ineligible, such as any felony or electoral fraud. These rules help to structure the electoral process. For example, in 1974, the Constitutional Council declared that an aspiring candidate was unable to stand because he had been declared bankrupt 14 years earlier. More significantly, in December 1994 the left-wing businessman Bernard Tapie was also declared bankrupt and was deprived of the chance of launching a late presidential bid. In 1995, this situation certainly helped Lionel Jospin's campaign, bearing in mind that at the June 1994 European election Tapie's Energie radicale list won 12.0 per cent of the vote, which helped to split the left-wing electorate and was a cause of the Socialist Party's poor showing (see Chapter 5). In this way, the eligibility requirements had an immediate effect on the outcome of the 1995 presidential contest.

The second condition that candidates must meet concerns the rules of sponsorship (*parrainage*). In order to stand, candidates must be officially sponsored by a certain number of elected representatives. From 1965–74, candidates required the support of only 100 such sponsors. This led to a growth in the number of candidates contesting the election (six in 1965, seven in 1969, 12 in 1974) and, in particular, it led to a growth in the number of little-known candidates who had no chance of winning.[6] To counteract this trend, a law was passed in 1976 which greatly increased the required number of sponsors (see Exhibit 3.1). The result was a reduction in the number of candidates contesting the election (ten in 1981, nine in both 1988 and 1995) and an increase in the number of disappointed would-be candidates. For example, in 1981 Jean-Marie Le Pen was unable to stand because he failed to gain the support of the necessary number of sponsors and in 1995 the same was true of Antoine Waechter, the leader of the Mouvement écologiste indépendant. Needless to say, the candidates who fail to gain the necessary number of sponsors usually represent only marginal political movements.[7] Nevertheless, in the context of an increasingly divided party system where every vote is precious, the fate of 'serious' candidates will at least partly rest on the number of small candidates with whom they have to compete and, hence, the sponsorship requirements will also help to shape the outcome of the election campaign.

Once they have met the conditions which allow them to stand for election, candidates then have to meet certain requirements in order to win. The system for electing the French President is variously known by a number of technical and interchangeable terms. It can be called a majority system with second ballot, a majority runoff system, a two-ballot (or double-ballot) plurality-with-runoff system, or a

> **Exhibit 3.1** Standing for election: sponsorship
>
> Since 1976, in order to stand candidates must be sponsored by at least 500 elected representatives spread across at least 30 different departments with no more than 50 sponsors coming from a single department. In 1995, over 40 000 people were eligible to sponsor a candidate, the majority of whom were mayors (nearly 35 000) and general councillors (nearly 3500), but the list also included deputies, senators, regional councillors and the members of the Council of Paris, the Corsican Assembly, the Territorial Assemblies of the Overseas Territories and the Higher Council of the French Abroad. Sponsorships had to be made on an official form which was available from the departmental prefect. These forms had to be sent to the Constitutional Council no earlier than 16 March and no later than midnight 4 April 1995. In 1995, the Constitutional Council received 13 983 official sponsorship forms and nine candidates received the required amount. The totals were as follows:
>
> | | | | |
> |---|---|---|---|
> | Jacques Chirac | 4097 | Dominique Voynet | 710 |
> | Edouard Balladur | 2425 | Philippe de Villiers | 641 |
> | Lionel Jospin | 2164 | Jean-Marie Le Pen | 591 |
> | Robert Hue | 1025 | Jacques Cheminade | 558 |
> | Arlette Laguiller | 803 | | |
>
> Note that Antoine Waechter received the support of only 405 sponsors, Max Siméoni, the regionalist candidate, received 77, Jean-François Hory, the Radical candidate, received 33 and Brice Lalonde, the leader of Génération Ecologie, only three.

two-ballot majority-plurality system.[8] Whatever the nomenclature (and here it will be called the majority runoff system), the essential components of the system are the same. In order to be elected at the first ballot, a candidate must win more than 50 per cent of the valid votes cast. If no candidate does so, then a second ballot is held two weeks later. At the second and final ballot, only two candidates are allowed to stand, namely those who came first and second at the first ballot, and the candidate who wins the most amount of votes cast (which will necessarily be more than 50 per cent of the valid votes cast) is elected. It should be noted that electors cast only one vote at each ballot and that the number of votes for each candidate is simply totalled up nationally without the intermediation of a US-style electoral college.

Since the first edition of Maurice Duverger's book on political parties in 1951, it has been generally accepted that different types of electoral systems produce different types of political consequences.[9] In particular, Duverger argued that the British-style plurality or first-past-the-post electoral system favours a two-party system and that the French-style majority runoff electoral system, like its proportional representation counterpart, favours a multiparty system, that is a system with more than two parties. Indeed, he argued that the relationship between a plurality system and a two-party system 'approaches most nearly perhaps to a true sociological law'.[10] Since the first edition of Duverger's book, these relationships have been explored more deeply and propositions about the links between the different types of electoral systems and party systems have been adapted and refined in order to account for significant counterexamples.[11] In particular, with the French case in mind, Duverger himself has argued that some of the effects of the majority runoff electoral system are at least partly dependent on whether or not the system in which it operates is presidentialised.[12] Against this background, the rest of this chapter examines three conflicting institutional logics of the majority runoff system as it is used for French presidential elections. These are: the personality/party logic, the multiparty/biparty logic and the populism/centrism logic.

THE CONFLICTING LOGICS OF PRESIDENTIAL ELECTIONS

The personality/party logic

According to the second President of the Fifth Republic, Georges Pompidou, any candidate who is seriously trying to win the presidential election needs to combine three attributes: a national stature, the experience of power and the support of a party.[13] According to two political scientists, Olivier Duhamel and Jérôme Jaffré, E (or election) = N + O + P + X, where N is notoriety, O is popularity in the opinion polls, P is the support of a political party and X is a catch-all category which includes governmental experience and/or charisma.[14] Whichever version is preferred, the observation which is common to both of these formulae is that successful presidential candidates are those who are able to combine personal appeal with party support. Candidates who have considerable personal qualities, but who run a campaign without the backing of a political party, like Michel Debré in 1981, or with the backing of only a poorly entrenched one, like Philippe de Villiers in 1995, are likely to fare badly. Similarly, candidates who have the backing of a political party but who are decidedly uncharismatic figures, like the communist André Lajoinie in 1988 and Dominique Voynet in 1995, are also likely to fare badly by failing to maximise their party's electoral potential. Therefore, the first conflicting institutional logic of French presidential elections is that they encourage a situation in which both personal qualities and party backing are important.

The personality aspect of presidential elections ensures that only a limited number of people are in a position to contest the election seriously. In order to stand a chance of winning, candidates need to have gained a considerable political reputation. In 1995, the list of actual and potential presidential candidates consisted of those who had held high office either domestically or internationally and included former Ministers (Henri Emmanuelli, Lionel Jospin and Jack Lang), former and current Prime Ministers (Edouard Balladur, Raymond Barre, Jacques Chirac and Michel Rocard), a former President of the Republic (Valéry Giscard d'Estaing) and the then incumbent President of the European Commission (Jacques Delors). Indeed, of the six presidential elections since the 1962 constitutional reform, two have been won by incumbent presidents (1965 and 1988), two by former prime ministers (1969 and 1995), one by an incumbent Finance Minister (1974) and one by a candidate who had considerable ministerial experience during the Fourth Republic and who had previously contested the presidential election on two occasions (1981). These examples are illustrative of the fact that successful presidential candidates need a stature. They need a standing. They need to be able to demonstrate that they are capable of assuming the awesome responsibilities which are incumbent upon the head of state. By 1995, Jacques Chirac had acquired such a reputation and he benefited from it (see Chapter 7).

In addition, the personality aspect of presidential elections also ensures that candidates are encouraged to emphasise their personal qualities and to underline what is distinctive about their campaign as opposed to everyone else's. In short, presidential elections encourage personalised campaigns. This means that all candidates, serious or otherwise, have to pay attention both to their media image and to their style of campaigning. As the last chapter showed, candidates emphasise their distinctiveness both to a mass audience by way of their media interviews and campaign advertisements and to a local audience by way of their campaign meetings and rallies, pictures and sound bites which are, of course, also transmitted to a mass audience by the media on news programmes. It is by virtue of this personalised aspect of presidential elections that candidates without the stature derived from the experience of high office can create a popular reputation for themselves and so do well, but it is also by virtue of this aspect that candidates with such stature can tarnish their reputation and so do badly. Jean-Marie Le Pen, for example, falls into the first category. His personal scores at both the 1988 and 1995 elections were greater than those his party has ever achieved at any other national or local election. This reflects his effective campaigning style, his oratorical ability and his populism (see below). Edouard Balladur, however, falls into the second category. His campaign started badly in January and February 1995 as he appeared too haughty, too distant from the people and too much as the incumbent seeking re-election when there was a popular desire for change. His image problem and poor campaigning style, therefore, was at least partly responsible for his first round defeat.

In these ways, then, the nature of the presidential election is such that it personalises the campaign and ineluctably focuses attention on the personal qualities, media image and electioneering style of each candidate. At the same time, though, there is a strong party political element to the election.[15] In part this is because of the sponsorship rules considered above. Many of those who are able to sponsor candidates are themselves members of a political party. Therefore, candidates are likely to be party figures. In addition, though, it is also because parties continue to play an important role in structuring the political process. In recent years, there has been a growing popular discontent with the set of established political parties, and issue movements have emerged to promote causes which have been inadequately treated by them, such as anti-racism, the campaign against homelessness and the Bosnian war (see Chapter 1). Nevertheless, political parties still help to mobilise support and to sensitise policy issues and they provide candidates with their main source of campaign funds and logistical back-up. In these ways, parties are the backbone of any serious campaign. They are a support mechanism without which candidates would be unable to organise a nationwide campaign. Therefore, without the backing of political parties, potential candidates such as the comedian Coluche in 1981 or, more seriously, Raymond Barre in 1995 are unlikely even to stand, or, if they do stand, then they are almost doomed to fail, like the largely incoherent Jacques Cheminade in 1995. However, candidates with the backing of large party organisations, such as Jacques Chirac, Lionel Jospin and Edouard Balladur in 1995 are in a position to compete with the chance of success. As a result, independent candidates have yet to do well in presidential elections and all successful candidates have been associated with party organisations.

The importance of parties in the election campaign is reflected in several ways. First of all, it means that the first campaign hurdle would-be candidates have to cross is a party one. For some candidates, this hurdle is sufficiently low not to be an obstacle. For example, in 1995 Jacques Chirac, Robert Hue, Arlette Laguiller, Jean-Marie Le Pen, Philippe de Villiers and Dominique Voynet were all virtually guaranteed of being selected as their party's official presidential candidate. However, for other candidates, party selection is a potential barrier. For example, at the 1995 election, Lionel Jospin faced a degree of difficulty in this respect (see Chapter 5). For these candidates, internal party politics was an important part of the campaign process. Finally, for yet other candidates, the task consists not so much of gaining the support of one's own party, but of attracting the support of other parties. For example, in 1995 Edouard Balladur tried to win the backing of the various elements of the UDF confederation of parties, even though he was a fully paid-up member of the Gaullist RPR. This was because the RPR was largely dominated by his rival, Jacques Chirac, and so the only strategy left open to the incumbent prime minister was to win the support of the UDF (see Chapter 4). In the absence of its own credible candidate, most of the UDF rallied to Balladur as a way of ensuring that its policies were articulated during the election campaign and that its interests were promoted. What this particular example shows, therefore, is not only that candidates need parties, but also that parties need candidates.[16]

Secondly, the importance of parties is reflected in the programmatic aspect of presidential campaigns. At the election, candidates are obliged to present a project, or manifesto, in which they give an indication of what they would do as president if they were to be elected. Parties are at once associated with such a project and distanced from it. On the one hand, the fact that parties select candidates (or that candidates select parties) means that those standing for election do so as the incarnation of a particular political tradition.[17] Candidates are automatically identified with that tradition's myths, structures and beliefs and, as a result, they have at least to pay lip-service to its concomitant ideological commitments and policy orientations. In this way, the project that a candidate presents is at least in part a reflection of these commitments and orientations. It is at least in part a reflection of long-standing preoccupations with which the party in question is associated. On the other hand, though, the candidate's project must also be a personal statement. It is a personal declaration of integrity and intent. It is the basis for a contract between an individual and the French people which will last for the next seven years. So, in 1995, all candidates adopted projects that broadly reflected the party political traditions with which they were associated and that publicly placed them in context of a particular political family. However, as if to underline the conflicting logics of presidential elections, all candidates also adopted projects that reflected their own versions of these traditions and that emphasised the personal nature of their appeal.

The multiparty/biparty logic

According to the old political adage, at the first round of French elections voters choose and at the second round they eliminate. More specifically, according to Olivier Duhamel, the first round of the election leads to competition and politicisation, whereas the second round leads to a grouping together and unanimity.[18] Both of these statements illustrate the second conflicting logic of French presidential elections. Majority runoff systems produce a tendency towards multipartism tempered by alliances.[19] At the first ballot of the election there is an incentive for multiparty competition to occur. However, at the second ballot there is no room for anything other than binary, or biparty, competition to occur. Indeed, at the second ballot there is a strong incentive for a bipolar form of competition to occur between a candidate of the left and a candidate of the right. The result of this logic is that serious candidates have to respond to the different forms of competition that the two rounds produce. The successful candidate will be the one who responds most effectively and who adopts the strategy which best suits these different forms of competition.

Majority runoff electoral systems are associated with multiparty competition at the first ballot.[20] Duverger believed that this proposition applied to the study of politics comparatively and subsequent evidence has confirmed his argument.[21] For example, in their study of presidential elections, Shugart and Taagepera demonstrated that the average effective

number of candidates was 3.8 under majority runoff systems
compared with only 2.7 under plurality systems.[22] Similarly,
in their analysis of gubernatorial primary elections organised by the Democratic Party in the United States, Wright
and Riker have shown that a higher number of candidates
compete in states where the majority runoff system is used
than in those where the plurality system is used.[23] In France,
the multiparty nature of the first ballot competition confirms these findings. For example, as stated above, the number
of candidates standing at presidential elections since 1965
has ranged from six to 12. The number of candidates winning less than 5 per cent of the vote was two in 1965, three
in 1969, nine in 1974, six in 1981, four in 1988 and three
in 1995. There have been candidates from the same political family (for example, Defferre and Rocard in 1969 and
Lajoinie and Juquin in 1988), as well as candidates from
the same political party (for example, Chirac, Debré and
Garaud in 1981 and Chirac and Balladur in 1995). In short,
the evidence both comparatively and in France suggests that
multiparty, or at least multicandidate, competition is a natural
consequence of majority runoff electoral systems.

Such competition occurs because at the first ballot there
are strong incentives both for candidates to stand and for
voters to vote for them. In the first place, candidates are
encouraged to stand because it takes less for them to 'win'
under majority runoff systems than under single ballot plurality systems. At the first ballot of French presidential elections, a 'winning' candidate does not have to gain either an
absolute majority of valid votes cast (50 per cent plus one),
or even a plurality of votes cast (more than any other candidate). He or she simply has to gain more than the third-
placed candidate.[24] Thus, majority runoff systems encourage
candidates to stand if they believe that they have at least an
even-money chance of coming second at the first ballot.
Secondly, candidates are also encouraged to stand because,
even if they do not expect to come at least second at the
first ballot, they may still hope to win enough votes so as to
be in a position to influence the outcome of the second
ballot as the top two candidates try to build coalitions in
order to win more than 50 per cent of the vote (see below).[25] In this way, as Riker states, majority runoff systems

encourage candidates to stand at the first ballot by allowing them 'to get a bit of political influence with relatively few votes'.[26] Finally, voters are encouraged to vote for the candidates who stand at the first ballot because majority runoff systems reduce the potential for wasted votes. All voters wish to support the candidate who is nearest to their own preferences. However, single ballot plurality systems, like the British one, provide a strong incentive for voters to support not simply the candidate who is nearest to their own preferences, but for the one who stands a chance of winning who is nearest to their own preferences. As a result, voters tend to choose candidates from larger parties, even if such candidates represent their second preference. By contrast, majority runoff systems remove most of the risk of wasted votes because voters can vote sincerely and choose their preferred candidate at the first ballot, even if they have to choose their second (or third or fourth) preference at the second ballot.[27] Nevertheless, the result is that small-party candidates may do well and the incentives for multiparty competition increase.

Whatever the incentives, the consequences of multiparty competition at the first ballot are twofold. Firstly, it encourages two types of candidates: those who compete with the aim of winning through to the second ballot and those who compete without the expectation of ever doing so.[28] In 1995, the first category consisted of Balladur, Chirac and Jospin, whereas the second consisted of Cheminade, Hue, Laguiller, Le Pen, de Villiers and Voynet. None of the candidates from the second category was ever a serious contender for the second round. Instead, their principal aim was to maximise their first-round vote in order to influence events between the two rounds and afterwards.[29] Discounting Cheminade, for Hue, Laguiller and Voynet, the strategy was to try and force Jospin to take on board significant elements of their policy proposals in return for the promise of a declaration of unconditional support between the first and second rounds (see Chapter 5). For de Villiers, the strategy was the same but with regard to Chirac. For Le Pen, the strategy was rather more nuanced. Before the first ballot he hoped that either Chirac or, more likely, Balladur might (covertly) adopt some of the FN's policies, which would allow him to make some sort of declaration of support prior to the second ballot. However, with Balladur eliminated and with Chirac seemingly unwilling to follow his 1988 example of indirectly courting the FN vote, Le Pen's strategy changed. He declared that he would cast a 'Joan of Arc' vote, meaning that he would support neither of the two remaining candidates at the second round. He hoped that this would provoke a high abstention rate and a large number of spoilt ballots both of which would delegitimise the victory of either Chirac or Jospin. In the end, this strategy also failed, but that he should have adopted it is indicative of some of the consequences brought about by the majority runoff system.[30]

Secondly, the nature of the competition at the first ballot means that the campaign is particularly intense between the candidates in the first of the above categories who are competing for second and third place.[31] This is a direct consequence of the fact that 'winning' at the first ballot means arriving either in first or second place. Candidates who arrive in third place, even if only by a small number of votes, find that their campaign comes to an abrupt end and that they may have to spend a considerable amount of time in the political wilderness in order to recoup their strength. By contrast, candidates who arrive in second place, even if they are outdistanced by their first-placed rivals, find that their campaign is still alive, that their reputation is likely to be enhanced and that their chances of winning at the second ballot are still intact. Indeed, it must be remembered that Giscard d'Estaing won in 1974 after arriving in second place at the first ballot, as did Mitterrand in 1981 and Chirac in 1995. Furthermore, in 1995 Jospin's reputation was enhanced not just by his surprising first-round performance, but also by his extremely creditable second-round performance. Whatever the situation, the key task is to come at least second and to avoid coming third at all costs. Consequently, the lowest political blows at the first ballot are traded between the candidates who are fighting to avoid finishing in third place. So, in 1995 competition was more severe between Chirac and Balladur than between Chirac and Jospin. Indeed, the Interior Minister, Charles Pasqua, called the 1995 first-ballot campaign the most 'disgusting' that he could remember. Indeed, it was only at the second ballot that Chirac 'discovered' Jospin and that the competition between the two increased in intensity.

This institutional tendency towards a form of multiparty competition at the first ballot is matched by an equivalent tendency towards a form of binary and bipolar competition at the second ballot.[32] This second tendency is derived from the rule that only two candidates may stand at the second ballot and that, therefore, the winner will be the one who gains more than 50 per cent of the valid votes cast. The result of this rule is twofold: firstly, it means that the two second-round candidates are obliged to build alliances, or coalitions, in order to boost their necessarily insufficient first-round scores; secondly, it means that these alliances are likely to be formed between candidates representing parties or movements from the same political family. That is to say, there is a majoritarian aspect to the second ballot, which creates an institutional tendency for a candidate backed by a coalition of right-wing parties to face a candidate backed by a coalition of left-wing parties. Indeed, it has been argued that the majoritarian, biparty aspect of the second ballot comes before the multipolar, multiparty aspect of the first ballot,[33] or, in other words, that the former is more important than the latter.[34] Evidence for this argument in the 1995 campaign can be found by way of the fact that Lionel Jospin repeatedly reminded potential communist, ecologist and trotskyist supporters to 'vote usefully' and to support him at the first round in order to ensure the presence of a left-wing candidate at the second round (see Chapter 5). Whether or not the biparty logic is stronger than the multiparty logic, what is clear is that there are conflicting logics at work which candidates have to address.

The first consequence of the second-ballot competition is that candidates have to build alliances. Those who aim to win through to the second ballot may begin this process even before the first ballot. For example, at the first ballot of the 1995 election, the big three candidates all tried to enlarge their basis of support so as to include forces from parties other than those with which they were most closely associated. So, Lionel Jospin included dissident ecologists such as Noël Mamère and ex-communists such as Pierre Juquin on his campaign committee, Jacques Chirac courted

the support of UDF figures such as Alain Madelin, Charles
Millon, Hervé de Charette and Valéry Giscard d'Estaing,
whereas Edouard Balladur won the backing of senior RPR
members such as Charles Pasqua and Nicholas Sarkozy.
Whatever the spread of their first-ballot support, though, at
the second ballot the two remaining candidates cannot help
but continue and extend the alliance-building process. They
may feign indifference and simply acknowledge the support
of those who decide to come over to their camp, but if they
do so this is simply a façade. Behind the scenes, contacts
will be made with former rivals and the terms of post-elec-
toral deals will be thrashed out. Indeed, the outcome of the
election will depend in no small degree on the outcome of
this alliance-building process. In 1981, Chirac's equivocal
backing for Giscard seriously harmed the latter's prospects.
In 1988, Barre's rather tardy declaration of support scarcely
helped Chirac's already difficult situation. In 1995, though,
Balladur and his supporters immediately rallied to Chirac
and the outcome of the election was virtually secured.

The second consequence of the second ballot competition is that candidates tend to build alliances with parties
of their own political family. That is to say, socialist candidates look first to the communists, the ecologists, other smaller
left-wing groupings and friendly forces on the centre-left,
whereas Gaullist candidates seek out their centre-right colleagues and vice versa. According to Duhamel and Jaffré,
two candidates from the same political family would only
meet at the second ballot if there was a 'phenomenal
combination of unfortunate circumstances'.[35] In 1969, such
a combination did occur because of de Gaulle's abrupt mid-
term resignation, the aftermath of the events of May 1968
and the disarray on the left.[36] In 1995, it nearly occurred
again because of Delors' decision not to stand, the absence
of a UDF candidate and a similar degree of weakness and
division on the left. Nevertheless, the left/right divide has
been sufficiently strong for competition at the second ballot to have taken the form, and for it to continue to take
the form, of a left/right battle (see Chapter 1). The result
is that voters develop a dual loyalty.[37] On the one hand,
they develop a loyalty to a particular party which can be
expressed by way of a 'sincere' vote at the first ballot (see

above). On the other hand, they also develop a loyalty to a political family which can again be expressed by a 'sincere' vote at the second ballot as a result of the left/right competition. The net result is that at the second ballot communists become used to voting for a socialist as the only remaining representative of the left-wing family and that UDF supporters become used to voting for a Gaullist (and vice versa) as the only remaining representative of the right-wing family. In this way, despite an increasingly fragmented party system (see Chapter 1) and an institutional tendency towards multiparty competition at the first ballot, the second ballot of presidential elections helps both to encourage biparty, binary competition and to reinforce bipolar popular allegiances to left- and right-wing political families.

The populism/centrism logic

The final conflicting logic of French presidential elections contrasts the plebiscitary nature of the vote with the fact that it encourages a centripetal form of political competition. As expressions of popular opinion, presidential elections are the perfect stage for the emotive firebrand. They encourage candidates to whip up popular support and to appeal directly to the public for backing. In this way, presidential elections favour populist candidates. At the same time, though, they make it difficult for populist candidates who are at the extremes of the political system to succeed. Instead, they drive candidates to the centre of the political spectrum in search of the votes of the uncommitted, the undecided and the apathetic. As a result, presidential elections also encourage a form of centrism. The consequence of this conflicting institutional logic is that the successful candidate will be the one who addresses the wishes of the people, but who does so in a way which does not alienate the electorally significant group of political waverers in the middle ground whose support is essential for victory.

The French President is a republican monarch.[38] That is to say, the president can claim to be the representative not of a particular interest group or even a political party, but of the nation as a whole. The president is at once the spokesperson for and the incarnation of the general will, pronouncing on behalf of the people and in the interests of the people. Having said that, there is undoubtedly a sense in which all political leaders in all liberal democracies can claim to be fulfilling the same function. The very nature of their position obliges them to adopt a discourse which emphasises their connection with the national interest. They all maintain that they are doing what is best for the country. Nevertheless, in France the connection between the president and the national interest is particularly strong. In many other systems, leaders come to power by virtue of their party's strength in the legislature. In France, though, the president comes to power by virtue of being directly elected by universal suffrage. As such, the president's authority is derived from a clear, unambiguous and unmediated link with the people. As a result, presidential candidates have to cultivate this link. They have to stress that they know what the people want and that, if elected, they will act in the people's interest. It is in this sense that presidential elections promote populist campaigns.

However, presidential elections promote different types of populist campaigns. In particular, they promote what might be called exclusionary populists and inclusive populists. Jean-Marie Le Pen falls into the first category. He claims that he is not afraid to say out loud what ordinary people think to themselves. He identifies all other candidates and parties as enemies and he is unwilling to compromise his strategy in order to build a wider coalition of support. In this way, he excludes himself from the political mainstream and is excluded by others because of his views. By contrast, Jacques Chirac falls into the second category. In 1995, he stressed that he was aware of the problems with which the French were faced and that he would supply the remedies that they wanted. However, he campaigned in a way which was designed to encourage the support of other political forces (with the exception of the FN) so that they would wish to be included in his electoral coalition. Whatever the nomenclature, presidential elections suit both types of populist candidates. For example, as noted above, it is not coincidental that Le Pen's personal scores at the first round of both the 1988 and 1995 presidential elections were greater than those achieved by his party in any equivalent national election. Instead, these results were brought about at least partly because his demagogy suits the nature of presidential elections. Similarly, in 1995 Chirac's flesh-pressing style was much more suited to the rigours of presidential elections than Balladur's lofty, technocratic pedagogy. The lesson, therefore, is that populism pays.

Having said that, presidential elections ultimately favour inclusive populists who are able to build coalitions more than they do exclusionary populists who are unable or unwilling to do so. In this way, they favour candidates who are situated nearer to the centre of the political spectrum rather than those who are to be found at the extremes.[39] In the last section it was noted that the institutional logic of the second ballot obliges candidates to form broad coalitions of support in order to win more than 50 per cent of the valid votes cast. In so doing, candidates naturally look to the other parties in their own left- or right-wing political family for backing. At the same time, though, there is an equally strong institutional logic for second-round candidates to try and win votes from the group of uncommitted voters in the centre of the political spectrum. For candidates this is because the support of one's own political family may still not amount to the level of support which is needed for victory at the second ballot and for voters this is because they are likely to find moderate candidates less unappealing than extremist candidates. Indeed, similar to the point noted above, serious candidates may be inclined to move to the centre even before the first ballot in order to increase their chances of qualifying for the second ballot. The result is that inclusive populists are much better placed to contest the election successfully than exclusionary populists. The latter may benefit from the populist encouragement that direct elections naturally generate, but the former are likely to benefit both from this aspect of the election and from the need to build broad electoral coalitions which include the support of moderate voters in the centre ground.

This move to the centre has been a regular occurrence at presidential elections. For example, in 1974, despite his formal alliance with the communists, François Mitterrand ran a personalised campaign which was designed to allay the fears of the non-communist, centre-left electorate.[40] In 1981,

Mitterrand again distanced himself from the Socialist party's official policy document and campaigned on a personal programme, the *110 Propositions pour la France*. In so doing, he was able to reconcile the conflicting needs of winning the votes of the left as a whole with that of winning a proportion of both the Gaullist and the ecologist electorate as well.[41] In 1988, Mitterrand's centrist strategy was even clearer. He promoted a policy of '*ouverture*', whereby he explicitly courted the support of senior centrist politicians such as Jean-Pierre Soisson, Olivier Stirn and Lionel Stoléru, all of whom had previously been ministers during the Giscard presidency. By contrast in 1988, Chirac's presidential strategy was ambiguous. At this time he felt that he needed to win the votes of the FN's electorate in order to maximise his chances of winning. This meant that he staged certain campaign *coups* (or at least that he did not prevent them from being staged), such as the bloody storming of a pro-independence stronghold in New Caledonia, the release of French hostages from the Lebanon and the French agent who was convicted of sinking the Greenpeace ship, the *Rainbow Warrior*, in 1985. In the end, this may have won him the support of a proportion of the FN's electorate, but it also lost him the support of an equivalent proportion of the centrist electorate. As a result, he was unsuccessful. In 1995, though, as noted above, Chirac's strategy was different. He eschewed any compromise with the FN and consolidated his position with the centrists. Consequently, he was able to reconcile the conflicting needs to be both populist and centrist and succeeded where before he had failed.

CONCLUSION

From this brief analysis, it is apparent that presidential elections create the conditions for a complex political game. In order to be successful, candidates have to be aware of the rules of the game and they have to adapt their campaign strategies accordingly. Presidential elections produce serious candidates and marginal candidates. They produce exclusionary populists and inclusive populists. They require candidates to emphasise their personal qualities at the same time as they associate themselves with a political party. They oblige candidates to run individual campaigns at the first ballot and then build a wide-ranging coalition of support at the second ballot. Moreover, they compel candidates to build a coalition which includes the support of either left- or right-wing voters as well as the support of uncommitted voters in the centre-ground. Finally, they encourage candidates to adopt a populist discourse but one which is not extremist. Needless to say, most candidates are unable to meet all these requirements. Some aspiring candidates, such as Michel Rocard, fail to gain the support of their party and are unable even to stand. Some actual candidates, such as Dominique Voynet and Robert Hue, fail to achieve the stature of a serious candidate and can only hope to affect the outcome of the second ballot. Some serious candidates, such as Edouard Balladur, fail to win through to the second ballot and have to rebuild their political careers. Some second ballot candidates, such as Lionel Jospin, fail to mobilise sufficient support to win there and have to hope that the electoral conditions will be more favourable the next time around. In this context, it is hardly surprisingly that those candidates who are eventually successful at the second ballot, such as Jacques Chirac, immediately derive a stature and a respect which create the conditions for them to exercise executive leadership. It is on the basis of how he now exercises such leadership that Chirac will decide whether he wishes to take part in the next political game of this sort which is scheduled for the year 2002.

NOTES

1. Duverger (1967) is an updated version of his 1951 text.
2. See, for example, Parodi (1980, 1983a and 1985) and Olivier Duhamel (1985, 1986a, 1986b, 1987 and 1993b).
3. Given the French tradition, it might be more correct to argue that it is only in the last few years that non-francophone political scientists have begun to pay systematic attention to the nature of institutions. Nevertheless, the 'new institutionalism' is generally said to begin with March and Olsen (1984) and is fully treated in Steinmo, Thelen and Longstreth (1992).

4. Hall (1986), p. 19.
5. Alain Krivine stood at the 1969 presidential election before he had completed his military service.
6. In 1974, six candidates won less than 1 per cent of the vote.
7. This was true of the National Front in 1981.
8. These terms have been used by Duverger (1967), Shugart and Taagepera (1994), Fishburn (1986) and Lijphart (1994) respectively.
9. Although Duverger's analysis is based on electoral systems for legislative elections, his points concerning first-past-the-post and majority runoff systems are also applicable to presidential elections.
10. Duverger (1967), p. 247.
11. The best overview of this topic is Grofman and Lijphart (eds) (1986).
12. Duverger (1986), p. 81.
13. Quoted by Thomas Ferenczi in *Le Monde*, 9 March 1995, p. 1.
14. Duhamel and Jaffré (1987), p. 68.
15. See Sylvie Pierre-Brossolette, 'La revanche des partis', in *L'Express*, 23 May 1995.
16. See the remarks in Colliard (1995), pp. 69–70.
17. Alain Duhamel (1987), p. 13.
18. Olivier Duhamel (1993a), p. 307.
19. See Duverger (1986), p. 70.
20. This hypothesis has been defended by many writers, for example Parodi (1973), p. 60 and Olivier Duhamel (1993a), p. 414.
21. Duverger (1967), pp. 269–75.
22. Shugart and Taagepera (1994), p. 333.
23. Wright and Riker (1989), p. 161.
24. An analogous argument is found in Riker (1986), p. 21.
25. See the argument in Parodi (1978), p. 193.
26. Riker (1986), p. 29.
27. This argument is treated by Lijphart (1994), p. 120.
28. See Shugart and Taagepera (1994), p. 338.
29. Jean-François Hory and Brice Lalonde dropped out of the race before the first ballot partly because their predicted scores indicated that they would have had little influence at the second ballot.
30. It might be noted, though, that as a result of the number of spoilt ballots Chirac was the first President to be elected by less than 50 per cent of the total number of votes cast (including spoilt ballots), even if, of course, he won more than 50 per cent of the valid votes cast.
31. Shugart and Taagepera (1994), p. 341.
32. See Guettier (1990), pp. 71–5.
33. Parodi (1981), p. 26.
34. Parodi (1973), p. 68.
35. Duhamel and Jaffré (1987), p. 54.
36. Parodi (1983b), pp. 1–2.
37. Parodi (1989), p. 149.
38. This approach to the presidency may be found in Morabito (1995).
39. Parodi (1981), p. 33.
40. Blondel (1975), p. 54.
41. Machin and Wright (1982), p. 9.

4 Candidates and Parties of the Right

Peter Fysh

This chapter does not offer a complete narrative of the activities of candidates and parties of the right before and during the 1995 presidential contest. In accordance with the analytical framework established in Chapter 3, party programmes, campaign issues and the attitude of the electorate are identified only when they illustrate the ways in which parties and candidates are constrained by the tension between three pairs of opposites – party and personality, the multiparty and bipolar characteristics of the party system, populism and centrism as approaches to campaign strategy. The aim here will be to test the degree to which the 1995 campaign – at least as far as the right was concerned – illustrated this triple 'institutional logic' and to examine and account for the respects, if any, in which 1995 diverged from the theoretical model. Not all the 'institutional logics' apply to all candidates. The strategies of the 'fringe' candidates, Jean-Marie Le Pen and Philippe de Villiers, were almost by definition exclusively focused on the first ballot; for them a populist discourse and behaviour appropriate to a multiparty system are almost axiomatic. Most attention is therefore devoted to the two mainstream candidates, Jacques Chirac and Edouard Balladur, who had the most choices to make, albeit in a context partially shaped by their extremist rivals. The chapter falls into two main parts. A survey of party fortunes during the second Mitterrand *septennat* of 1988–95 identifies the factors which structured the emergence of certain candidatures and the 'non-emergence' of others, leaving the two mainstream conservative parties, RPR and UDF, apparently weaker than ever in relation to the extremes now personified not only by Le Pen but also by newcomer Philippe de Villiers. The rest of the chapter offers an interpretation of party and candidate

73

strategies during the 1995 contest in terms of each of the three dimensions already identified.

1988 TO 1995 – THE STRATEGIC CONTEXT VIEWED FROM THE RIGHT

During Mitterrand's second term both French conservative parties were faced by the same set of four interlinked strategic problems. First, both parties faced a crisis of leadership legitimacy and internal democracy as a result of the second successive failure of their existing elites. Second, both were destabilised by some of the indirect consequences of the collapse of the Soviet Empire. For the UDF this was limited to the way in which the changed strategic context affected the planned deepening and enlarging of the European Union negotiated at Maastricht at the end of 1991. For the RPR, a more wide-ranging internal debate covered the balance sheet of the ultra-liberal policies of the mid-1980s, Maastricht, the Gulf War and doubts about the relevance of the independent nuclear deterrent. Within the UDF the Maastricht issue led eventually to the resignation of Philippe de Villiers and his emergence as a presidential candidate, but the rival candidacies of Balladur and Chirac in the RPR owed nothing to such policy disagreements for the two were on the same side in all the major debates. Thirdly, there was a two-part problem of alliance strategy: what attitude to take to the Front National? how to choose a single presidential candidate to represent a coalition which for 30 years had worked perfectly well at local and parliamentary level but failed to work at the pinnacle of the political system? The fourth major strategic problem was the same as the one that some influential conservatives believed had been badly handled in 1986–88: on winning the parliamentary elections in 1993, should the conservative coalition accept office under President Mitterrand? If so, who should be prime minister and what effect would that decision have on the subsequent presidential chances of the various conservative contenders?

Leadership and party democracy

Jacques Chirac's career as three-times presidential candidate is directly linked to his position as leader of the Gaullist party, which he refounded as the RPR in 1976. His and the party's fortunes have been a perfect illustration of the observation that the profile gained in a presidential election campaign prepares the ground for later parliamentary success – the party elite 'need' Jacques Chirac as much as he needs them to support his presidential ambitions and the RPR has long been seen as the 'creature' of its founder[1].

Chirac's standing within the party was at an all-time low, however, following his second successive defeat in 1988. Many activists blamed the rivalry between the men of the 1970s, Chirac; the former President of the Republic from 1974–81 Valéry Giscard d'Estaing; and Giscard's prime minister from 1976–81 Raymond Barre, for the failure of the RPR and UDF to agree on a single candidate capable of beating Mitterrand, a failure which was all the starker given the minimal ideological differences between the two parties and the long record of amicable cooperation at local level. The European elections of the following year, 1989, provided the best ever chance of ditching the old leaders for good; almost all the best-known 'young Turks' of both parties for a few weeks actively discussed forming their own list of candidates independently of the official investiture committees, but the mutiny auto-destructed when one or two key RPR members at the last moment drew back from abandoning their places in Chirac's power network.[2]

Chirac rode out the crisis over two years by a change of general secretary, promises of more internal elections to local party posts and acceptance of the right to organise factions. Ahead of the 1990 party congress his former right-hand man and Minister of the Interior from 1986–88, Charles Pasqua, actually suggested that he ought to resign as leader 'for his own good' to escape the wear and tear of day-to-day politics. But at the congress itself, a motion critical of the leadership presented by Pasqua and Philippe Séguin – itself an earth-shattering event in the history of Gaullism – was easily defeated and Chirac's position emphatically restored. Subsequently, in 1992, the party was split even more seriously

when Pasqua and Séguin led a campaign against ratification of the Maastricht Treaty on European Union, in opposition to Chirac's line. But this time, although gaining the
support of a majority of Gaullist parliamentarians, they avoided
a direct attack on the leader, claiming that the movement
was able to reforge its unity after vigorous internal debate
and that many of their policy preferences had been taken
on board by the leadership for the 1993 elections. After
1990 Chirac's leadership was not questioned again, no one
has ever opposed him in a leadership election, and it was
axiomatic that he would again be a presidential candidate
in 1995, either directly or in whatever form of conservative
primary might be organised. But if leadership of a major
party, as suggested in Chapter 3, is usually a sufficient condition for *présidentiable* status, so also is a major office of
state. Though not formally challenged within the party, Chirac
would later find his path obstructed outside it by his own
former close colleague and fellow Gaullist, Edouard Balladur,
who took advantage of his role as prime minister to launch
a bid for the presidency.

The crisis in the Union pour la Démocratie Française (UDF)
arose from the centrifugal tendencies inherent in the ram-
shackle confederation, along with the feeling that the existing leader, Valéry Giscard d'Estaing, was a has-been who
ought to retire. Giscard indeed took a long time to recover
from the personal trauma of his failed campaign for re-election in 1981, control of his Parti Républicain (PR) passing
to the ambitious young deputy François Léotard. The *raison
d'être* of the UDF, the confederation built around the PR in
1978 to back Giscard's bid for presidential re-election in
1981, was visibly weakened when the PR leaders competed
with those of the Centre des Démocrates Sociaux (CDS),[3]
the second-largest and Christian Democratic wing of the UDF,
for posts in Chirac's 1986 government, from which Jean
Lecanuet, the formal leader of the UDF, was left out. The
most popular UDF politician in the country became Simone
Veil, who successfully led a joint RPR-UDF list for the European elections in 1984, and it was Raymond Barre who
emerged as the UDF's only realistic presidential contender
for 1988.

In the wake of Barre's defeat Giscard struggled to revive

his presidential ambitions by walling up the crumbling confederal structure. In the 1989 European elections he re-established his national status by leading the official joint RPR-UDF list to a comfortable victory over Simone Veil's 'dissident' list, ultimately dependent largely on the CDS, the most ardently pro-European of the conservative factions. Three years of efforts were crowned in the autumn of 1991 by the organisation of a 1600 strong *conseil national* of the UDF, at which Giscard became its first president to be elected (un-opposed) by secret ballot. He was again an uncontested fig-urehead but the UDF remained essentially a 'cadre' party, a grouping of patronage networks rather than a mass or-ganisation bound in defence of a distinct ideology. Giscard had been powerless to prevent the CDS from forming its own group in the National Assembly in 1988 in order to take an independent line in relation to socialist government policies. Worse, the semi-desertion of the ambitious young 'Léotard gang' in 1986 had been followed by the more com-prehensive betrayal of a number of *giscardien* former minis-ters from the 1970s (Jean-Pierre Soisson, Lionel Stoléru, Michel Durafour) who rallied to Mitterrand's 'presidential majority' and took posts in Michel Rocard's largely socialist government.

The Maastricht factor

But potentially the most serious sign of the disintegration of Giscard's 20-year project to create a centre-right 'Euro-pean and social' pole in French politics – affecting not only its organisational but soon also its ideological coherence – got under way in the summer of 1991 when a young Cath-olic PR deputy from the Vendée, Philippe de Villiers, launched the Combat pour les Valeurs, a new movement intended to defend the Catholic, small-town and traditionally conserva-tive values typical of the rural west. A year later de Villiers' nationalist, protectionist and anti-immigrant sentiments were made known to millions as he campaigned hard against ratification of the Maastricht Treaty. Giscard himself was heavily criticised by de Villiers and others for agreeing to appear on the same platform as socialists in defence of the European Union. For the first time the UDF lost its pretention

to be the most solidly pro-European force in French politics. De Villiers returned to the charge in 1994 when his
movement ran a successful campaign in the European elections, winning 12.34 per cent of the vote and securing a
number of seats at Strasbourg. While he no longer attracted
as much support among Gaullist and UDF *notables* as he
had at the launch of his movement, he had secured important financial backing in the shape of the Anglo-French entrepreneur Jimmy Goldsmith and the endorsement of a
high-profile 'moral' figure from civil society, Thierry Jean-
Pierre, a magistrate who had made a speciality of pursuing
cases involving the sale of public contracts and money laundering in the financing of the (then) ruling Socialist Party.
De Villiers' electoral threat, furthermore, seemed substantial. Significantly, he had made little headway in the polls
and was dismissed as a splinter movement as long as he
limited himself to criticising the federalist vision of Europe
implicit in the Maastricht Treaty, but he made a breakthrough
during the last two weeks of the campaign when he posed
aggressively as the majority's alternative leader on European
policy.[4] This seemed to show that there was a potentially
rebellious constituency of opinion among conservative voters
motivated by the fear of loss of sovereignty inherent in a
single European currency, common defence policies and the
further liberalisation of world trade, issues on which Pasqua
and Séguin had also campaigned, although neither seemed
interested in testing their own popularity in a presidential
contest. Analyses of de Villiers' 1994 electorate in terms of
geography, age and class, furthermore, showed that it was
similar in make-up to the pro-European conservatives who
had voted for the RPR-UDF list headed by Dominique Baudis
in the same election, and rather dissimilar from the younger
and more masculine electorate of the FN.[5] In November
1994, less than six months before the presidential poll, de
Villiers effectively declared his candidacy by resigning from
the PR and transforming his *combat* into something more
like a political party, the Mouvement pour la France, with
local federations and a skeleton national decision-making
body. His actions underlined the divided and weakened state
of the UDF, at the same time leaving room for the emergence of a candidate who was not even a member of the

party but who declared himself the defender of traditional UDF policies – Edouard Balladur.

Alliance strategy – the problem of the Front National

In the seven years since 1988 the two mainstream conservative parties made no headway in their attempt to ward off the electoral threat posed by the FN which Le Pen skilfully led through a number of set-backs. The decimation of the FN's parliamentary group, thanks to the abandonment of proportional representation in 1988, was compensated by a 10 per cent share of the vote in the 1989 European election, the same as in 1984, and by the party's ability to field more and more candidates at successive rounds of local elections, a sure sign of steady implantation at the grass roots.[6] Party fortunes were harmed neither by the profound but short-lived national shockwave set off by the desecration of a Jewish cemetery in Carpentras in 1990, nor by Le Pen's vociferous opposition to the deployment of French troops in the Gulf crisis of 1990–91, nor by the publication of a hard-line new programme which attracted blanket condemnation by the liberal press. In reaction to their 1988 defeat the mainstream parties agreed to ban any future electoral pacts with the fascists of the sort which had helped legitimise them in Dreux in 1983 and Marseille in 1988. Nonetheless the FN made a significant breakthrough in the 1993 parliamentary elections, increasing from about 30 to over 100 the number of constituencies in which they passed the barrier of 12.5 per cent of registered voters on the first round, the condition for participation in the second. This result, little commented on at the time, seriously increased the danger that at some time in the future the conservatives would be damaged by FN participation in three-cornered runoffs. It also made it very likely that Le Pen would once again stand in the presidential election in 1995 and by doing so would in the first round once again divert a battalion of voters who would somehow have to be dragged back into the conservative camp in the second.

The ban on electoral pacts with the fascists was largely adhered to; a bright media spotlight turned on the results of the 1992 regional elections induced a number of

conservative winners to accept office as regional president
only if they still had a majority after deducting from the
votes cast in their name a number equal to the number of
FN councillors who might have voted for them. But if the
conservative leaders had learned that electoral deals only
served to increase the credibility of Le Pen and his friends,
they could not resist imitating both their rhetoric and their
policies. Within a few months of each other in the autumn
of 1991 Giscard and another UDF heavyweight, Michel
Poniatowski, compared immigration in France to an 'inva-
sion' and even to the 'occupation'.[7] Chirac, meanwhile, was
pursued in the courts by an anti-racist movement for a speech
in which immigrants were caricatured as noisy, smelly and
polygamous, keeping up to 20 children on social security.
When returned to power in 1993 the RPR and UDF together
lost no time in passing a battery of new laws restricting rights
of residence and asylum and tightening up on the acquisition of French nationality by birth or by marriage.

The voters' reaction – giving Le Pen a larger share of the
vote in 1995 than he received in 1988 – seemed to vindi-
cate the fascist leader's own oft-repeated prognosis: faced
with a choice between the original and a poor copy, his
supporters continue to choose the original. Paradoxically,
however, in 1995 the impact of Le Pen's campaign on the
issue agenda was small. At the first round, convinced that,
whether or not they won the FN's votes, the socialists could
not win, Chirac and Balladur focused their critical attention on each other studiously ignoring their extremist rival.
With Le Pen left to make the not unusual claim that he was
the victim of a deliberate media conspiracy to silence him,
his supporters found other ways of making the news. Shortly
before the first round of voting FN campaigners in Marseille shot dead a young Arab who had disturbed them while
they were sticking up posters. Between the rounds, during
the FN's annual march in commemoration of Joan of Arc,
more heavies set upon another unfortunate, beat him up
and threw him in the Seine where he drowned. The imme-
diacy of these events was so great that Chirac – this time
spared the presence in his campaign team of Charles Pasqua
– was not tempted to court Le Pen's now homeless voters
in the way that he had in 1988. During the crucial face-to-

face debate on the eve of the second round of voting he was in any case let off the hook by Jospin's astonishing opening statement that the drowning incident was of no importance for the wider democratic process. All in all, thanks to the socialists' weakness, in terms of his impact on the outcome of the election if not in terms of the FN's murderous potential, Le Pen's campaign played a less influential role in 1995 than in 1988 despite the fact that he won more votes in this election than in the previous one.

Alliance strategy – the great primary debate

Following the aborted revolt over the 1989 European election list, the spring of 1990 saw more unrest among the layer of ambitious fortyish would-be ministers now condemned to seven years of opposition, with a group of PR and RPR deputies jointly calling for the holding of a conference to refound a single right-wing party, a Force Unie to match the France Unie of Mitterrand's presidential majority. Instead, Giscard and Chirac sanctioned discussions in theory aiming at either a fusion of the two main parties so that only one presidential candidate would be nominated, or a sort of primary election in which voters or members would have a chance to choose the standard-bearer of the right. Enthusiastic discussions took place during 1990 and 1991 but they ran into the sand in the face of conflicting objectives and technical difficulties. The pressing need for agreement seemed to dissipate somewhat during 1991 and 1992 when the disastrous Cresson premiership, succeeded by that of the ill-fated Bérégovoy, led the socialists to resounding defeats in the 1992 and 1993 regional and parliamentary elections. By the end of 1994, however, the schemes were revived when a new and perilous possible socialist candidate appeared on the horizon in the shape of Jacques Delors.

The technical problems, on their own close to insuperable, revolved around four key questions: who should vote? who should stand? who should pay? and who would control any election which did take place? Restriction of the primary electorate to RPR and UDF councillors, whose allegiance could be determined accurately, was open to the objection that candidate selection would be confiscated by a relatively narrow layer of party *notables*. An electoral college composed entirely of party members would tip the advantage distinctly in favour of the RPR, who had a more systematic attitude to membership than did the UDF, as well as opening up the danger of all too easily manipulable mass recruitment drives. Throwing the election open to RPR and UDF voters raised the question of how to distinguish them from machiavellian socialists and communists who would turn out to vote for the candidate judged to present the least danger to their own side. Accepting this risk and allowing all citizens to vote would turn the primary into a virtual third round of the presidential election, an interference in public matters likely to be disqualified by the Constitutional Council. Furthermore, unless the Council ruled otherwise, the parties could have no possible sanction (other than expulsion, which is not a very powerful weapon) against any member of their own (Philippe de Villiers for instance) who chose not participate in a primary but insisted in presenting him or herself in the first round of the election proper. Finally, the larger the electoral college decided on, the more expensive the election would be, imposing either a severe strain on party finances or the need to turn to the state or local government for assistance, itself far from sure to be forthcoming.

These technical issues notwithstanding, the 1990 attempts at agreement on the dual question of party fusion and primaries foundered on the rival leaders' conflicting interests. Giscard was more interested in a larger party within which he could seek wider support but he was afraid of primaries, particularly those open to rank-and-file voters, among whom his patrician image and lack of organised support would put him at a disadvantage. Chirac, reluctant to liquidate his faithful band of militants into a larger structure, was more favourable to primaries, though aware of the danger to his own chances should Pasqua decide to enter the fray. On 18 May 1990 came the announcement of a formal RPR-UDF confederation, to be known as the UPF, Union Pour la France, flanked by a complicated primary system in which there would be two colleges, local councillors having multiple votes but only gaining a decisive influence if they turned out in sufficient numbers to outweigh the rank and file. The Union was to be of the most superficial kind, with no president and no general secretary, merely a *bureau confédéral* made up of 15 UDF and 15 RPR members. Operational in mid-September, the plan stalled badly in November over Giscard's refusal to endorse primaries in the event of an emergency presidential election (likely to be caused, he believed, by Mitterrand's death in office). A big media launch of the agreed procedures, for which 4000 invitations had already been sent out, had to be scrapped at the last moment. Further committee meetings produced a new draft 'charter' in April 1992 but it was not formally ratified by all interested parties until the eve of the 1993 elections.

By mid-1994 it was apparent that the best-placed (if so far undeclared) candidate if a primary were to take place was Edouard Balladur who could count on solid supporters in both the RPR and UDF. The *chiraquiens* accordingly preferred to avoid the subject but Balladur's camp made no great play of it either since it was part of their strategy to delay an official announcement of candidacy until as late as possible in order to get the maximum benefit from Balladur's position as prime minister 'above the fray'. At the national council of the PR in June, party spokespeople limited themselves to recording the party's formal support for the idea. Others doubted if a primary could be made to work; Hervé de Charette, Giscard's loyal spokesman as organiser of the UDF's Club Perspectives et Réalités, regretted ever having signed the charter in the first place.[8] It was left to Charles Pasqua, still perhaps dreaming of a possible role for himself in the future contest, to draft a bill to give the Minister of the Interior power to provide public funds to help parties who wished to 'associate the electorate' in their choice of candidates for the presidential election.[9] The draft was never taken up by the government but, in the face of the Delors danger, Pasqua returned to the charge in November, this time urging all conservative deputies and county councillors to get hold of the electoral rolls and form local committees to organise a primary in their own offices. This time the appeal was heeded and a score or so local parties produced a variety of formulae involving different degrees of popular participation. The RPR and UDF general secretaries, Alain Juppé and François Bayrou respectively, even met and agreed to form a national committee to organise a primary financed by the parties themselves.[10] Soon, however, Delors announced his intention not to stand, the committees were disbanded and everyone breathed a sigh of relief; 1995, after all, saw no new additions to the formal rules governing election to the presidency of the Republic.

Cohabitation – graveyard or nursery of presidential ambition?

For many months prior to the event it was taken for granted by all who had an interest in the matter that Edouard Balladur would be the new prime minister appointed by François Mitterrand after the right's landslide win in the spring 1993 election. With no political future after 1995, Mitterrand had little incentive to make a machiavellian choice which would turn his second experience of governing with a conservative majority into the same tactical battle which the first had been. So soon after the narrow ratification of the Maastricht Treaty, his sole condition – which Balladur was able to satisfy – was that prime minister and government should share his own preference for closer European union. The leaders of the various factions in the UDF seemed happy to take office again with the man who had been the highest ranking member of the team in which most of them had served from 1986 to 1988. Probably they preferred seeing an RPR member at Matignon to a party colleague whose new status would mean promotion to the rank of 'first among equals' within the UDF itself. Above all, the promotion of Balladur met Jacques Chirac's desire to avoid another two years of responsibility without power possibly ending, as in 1988, with his being obliged to defend a government balance sheet from which his rivals were able to dissociate themselves. This time he would spurn the poisoned chalice, let his loyal friend and adviser take on the ungrateful role of safety valve, retire to the Paris town hall, play down his links with the government and polish his campaign strategy, ready to spring back into the limelight when the time was right! Balladur himself seemed to confirm that the two had agreed a private pact by predicting that the key to a successful future *cohabitation* was that the right's prime minister should on no account be seen as a possible contender for the presidency.[11]

But the pact was not to last: whatever the emotional shock, Chirac would not have taken long to realise that the betrayal of his 'friend of thirty years' was for real. He better than anyone understood, as Balladur's candidacy would now illustrate to perfection, that one of the keys of French politics is patronage, the lure of office certain to provide the prime minister with a large collection of hitherto unsuspected admirers. Nor did insiders make the mistake of believing that Balladur's ambition was unexpectedly nurtured by his spell in the prime minister's office. The five-year preparation to which he subjected himself in order to be a candidate for Matignon was an equally good preparation for the Elysée along with the conviction, confirmed by Chirac's second defeat, that he was the best man for the job. Balladur did not return to business after leaving government in 1988, instead being successively elected member of the National Assembly and Paris councillor. But he hardly used the sumptuous office Chirac put at his disposal in the town hall, preferring instead the premises of his own newly founded Mouvement pour le Libéralisme Populaire. From here he organised seminars, edited a newsletter, sent articles to the press, published three or four books, participated in RPR committee meetings, had lunches with leaders of the different UDF factions (whom he invited to join him in study groups on European issues) and undertook foreign and provincial tours to meet world leaders and the grassroots activists of the RPR. In short, he did everything necessary to make himself the obvious candidate for the prime ministership (he was not just propelled into it by Chirac), and in doing so equipped himself with the friends, the staff and the notoriety necessary to run for president. While he signalled no major difference with Chirac, he had in effect founded his own independent political enterprise long before 1993. An indication of the balance of power in their relationship was that, while Chirac continued – as he had since the early 1980s – to send Balladur drafts of his speeches and articles for Balladur's comments and approval before they went public (and Chirac continually telephoned 'Edouard' if he was not present at a drafting meeting), Balladur never consulted Chirac on anything that he himself wrote. So clear was Balladur's deliberate independence that Alain Juppé warned Chirac as early as 1989 to beware of his ex-minister's ambitions. Chirac usually dismissed such warnings on the ground that Balladur was too stiff and remote a personality ever to become popular with the public.[12]

It was certainly true that Balladur would never be able to replace Chirac, at least in the RPR activists' eyes. A necessary condition for his ambition to be converted into a credible candidacy was, therefore, that the UDF should not produce a candidate of its own. Balladur was given an early opportunity to win favour with his coalition partners, at the same time exploiting intra-UDF rivalries to his own advantage, in the composition of his government, on which Chirac was barely consulted.[13] Although the RPR was the largest party in the National Assembly, it had only 13 full ministers to 16 for the UDF. Interior and Foreign Affairs went to the Gaullists but Justice, Defence, Finance, Industry, Education and an enlarged Social Affairs ministry including responsibility for Urban Affairs went to important UDF leaders. CDS deputies, much fewer in number than their PR colleagues, received a disproportionately high share of the posts, Balladur no doubt mindful that with their regularly reasserted distinctive 'social' and 'European' profile they had formed the core of support for Raymond Barre's presidential candidacy in 1988. One of the new government's early policy initiatives – unsuccessful as it turned out – was an attempt to increase the scope for local authority funding of private Catholic schools, a pledge of Balladur's willingness to borrow from the CDS policy agenda. His candidacy became an open secret, acknowledged by everyone but himself, by December 1993 when two of the highest-ranking members of the government, Veil and Léotard, informed the press of their conviction that the prime minister had all the right qualities for a good president and a good 'unitary' candidate of the right.

By this time there was no longer any doubt about the CDS' *balladurisme,* but the PR leaders were more preoccupied by the danger that Giscard might decide to run. While his chances of winning were remote, his candidacy alone would seriously harm Balladur's chances and for this reason it had to be prevented. June 1994 saw a curious episode when 27 PR deputies, apparently inspired by Léotard, tried to form an independent parliamentary group, citing their desire to emancipate themselves from the UDF, from Giscard, from his determination that there should be a UDF candidacy and from the regime of dual membership with the Club Perspectives et Réalités, the last remaining section of the UDF which still professed total loyalty to its founder. The crisis was smoothed over when a National Council meeting voted to 'do everything for a single candidacy of the majority' – a formula which became a convenient cover for all those, Gaullists and UDF alike, who wanted to show their support for the 'candidate' who was best placed in the polls (Balladur) without openly condemning the others.[14] It was no accident that the three leading personalities in the PR, Léotard (honorary president), Longuet (president) and Madelin (secretary general) were all government ministers who could look forward to new opportunities – for one of them, perhaps even Matignon[15] – should their patron make it to the Elysée and to a fight for survival should Giscard gain the upper hand. An intra-UDF feud continued throughout the autumn of 1994 and into the new year, with Balladur's supporters trying to convince a reluctant Giscard to call a meeting which would officially endorse their favourite's candidacy. Charles Millon, formerly Barre's campaign organiser and now leader of the UDF in the National Assembly, significantly the only major UDF figure who had not found a place in government (he was said to have three times refused the poisoned chalice of Agriculture), announced that he himself would stand if neither Giscard nor Barre were willing to do so. Failing to live up to this promise, he eventually threw his support behind Chirac, gaining the handsome reward of the Defence ministry after Chirac's election. Six weeks before the poll it was left to Giscard to deliver the last cut to the shredded unity of his own 'party', not sparing even the Club Perspectives et Réalités, which he had founded 30 years before. While two of its stalwarts, Alain Lamassoure and Jean-Pierre Fourcade were rapturously welcomed at a meeting organised by the CDS and PR to support Balladur, the Club met to endorse Chirac, its organiser Hervé de Charette pouring out his bile against 'those who have prevented the emergence of a candidate from the UDF ranks'.[16] Obscure resentment nursed against Balladur since the days of the Pompidou presidency? Belief that Léotard and company had wrecked his own chances of a credible candidacy? Memories of the young Chirac who had himself betrayed the Gaullists to their mutual advantage in 1974? Whatever Giscard's motives for backing the man who had been his constant rival for two decades, his camp soon collected a share of the spoils of victory. In April 1995 Hervé de Charette was the obscure Minister of Housing in Balladur's government; a few weeks later he was Chirac's Minister of Foreign Affairs.

If Balladur was encouraged to mount his candidacy partly by what seemed to be a 'demand' coming from the UDF, his treatment at the hands of some RPR colleagues soon provided the justification for tearing up whatever agreement may have existed between himself and Chirac. In June 1993 Philippe Séguin, the new President of the National Assembly, launched a blistering attack on the government's handling of the unemployment crisis, likening its social policy to the defeatism of Munich in 1938. A few weeks later Balladur had to deal with a serious bout of speculation against the franc which effectively broke its parity with the German mark and severely damaged the timetable for monetary union agreed at Maastricht, of which Balladur was a firm supporter and Séguin a determined opponent. On both occasions Balladur complained that Chirac failed to support strongly and publicly enough both Balladur himself and French monetary policy, allowing the press to speculate that a future Chirac presidency might adopt the 'alternative economic policy' based on devaluation and protectionism, developed by Séguin in a series of speeches, some later published in book form.[17] This scenario became all the more plausible when Séguin himself turned up at the young Gaullists' summer school in September with a call for Chirac to 'show the way' by standing for the presidency in defence of a 'political project'.[18] While Chirac refrained from explicitly endorsing all of Séguin's programme, it was clear that appearing to propose a 'project', however vaguely defined,[19] rather than merely defending the balance sheet of the past two years' government, was implicit in the strategy of encouraging

Balladur to go to Matignon in the first place. During the year and a half remaining before the election he went back on his commitment to some of the items contained in the Maastricht Treaty (taking account of the close result in the 1992 referendum and of the anti-European campaigns of his rivals Le Pen and de Villiers), hinted that the fight against unemployment was not incompatible with a generalised pay increase and, as Mayor of Paris, orchestrated some spectacular requisitions of empty properties in favour of the homeless.

From the beginning of 1994, therefore, it was clear that the personal collaboration between Chirac and Balladur was at an end even though neither of them was yet officially a candidate; each refrained from attacking the other by name but the press gleefully reported each phrase of Chirac's which implied less than total support for the government. The lure of office took over, provoking the same intolerable tension within the RPR that it had in the UDF; Balladur's supporters made thinly veiled accusations of 'demagogy' against the Chirac camp, which cried 'immobilism' in return. Throughout all of 1994 Balladur remained ahead in the polls and by the end of the year had been clearly endorsed by as many as two-thirds of the Gaullist parliamentarians, Chirac's backers being reduced to Séguin plus a hard core of three succeeding RPR general secretaries whose loyalty had never wavered during three presidential campaigns (Bernard Pons, Jacques Toubon, Alain Juppé). The crucial bastion of the party organisation was kept in hand by newcomer Jean-Louis Debré (who also turned out to be a combative and effective television performer), drafted in as Juppé's assistant general secretary while the latter was occupied with the Foreign ministry. The party was getting ready to give a dramatic and bizarre twist to a contest in which the socialist candidate had been regarded as dead and buried before the campaign even started; it would go into the election with two candidates, Balladur the prime minister and 'legitimate' leader of the majority, and Chirac the founder and inspirer of the movement in which he was now paradoxically reduced to the rank of outsider.

THE 1995 FRENCH PRESIDENTIAL ELECTION – AN INTERPRETATION

Party versus personality

As far as the 'party/personality' dichotomy is concerned, the 1995 campaign provided three innovations, one clarification and one confirmation of a rule, each of which tells us something interesting about how French politics works. Firstly, the UDF, one of the major players in the system since it was founded by Giscard d'Estaing in 1978, was unable to field a candidate. This can be understood in the context of the gradual break-up of the symmetrical bipolar pattern of French politics, at its sharpest in the period 1977–81, when four parties of roughly equal strength made up two two-part coalitions. The demise of the Communist Party as a possible coalition partner for the socialists led directly to Mitterrand's search for another pattern of alliances in 1988, which in turn encouraged the CDS to adopt its position of semi-independence within the UDF. This was both an expression and a reinforcement of a traditional style of behaviour typical of the 'cadre' parties of the French right since the days of the Third Republic. Rather than evolving formalised rules governing leadership selection and internal democracy, they have depended on – usually revelled in – the delights and poisons of factionalism, patronage and personal rivalry. The fate of the UDF in 1995 illustrates that these tendencies are again as strong as they have ever been in the Fifth Republic.

The dual RPR candidature was the second innovation – at least in so far as the two candidates were both serious presidential runners evenly matched in terms of support, for the party has always contained defenders of what they regard as the purity of the Gaullist tradition and fielded no less than three candidates in 1981. In 1995 the way in which the split came about illustrated two things in particular: firstly, the strong streak of loyalty towards existing leaders which French political scientists have dubbed 'legitimism' and which encourages the Fifth Republic's prime ministers – even, as in Balladur's case, with little party background – to aspire to the highest office; secondly, the extraordinary flexibility of Gaullist ideology which over two decades has allowed Chirac to swing wildly in different directions in policy terms to suit the tactical needs of the particular election he was contesting.

The third innovation arose from conservative fears that disunity would once again let in the left, as it was thought to have done in 1981 and 1988. As a result the 1995 election became the first in which the conservatives for a while seriously considered the practicalities of organising an American-style primary election to decide who should be their standard-bearer in the first round of the contest proper. Even the brief discussion for which there has been room here will have shown that the American example was ultimately not transferable. Primaries in the USA are a hangover from the pre-democratic era which have survived partly because they help integrate the regional dimension into a continent-wide party system. French parties have other ways of coping with regionalism and the French constitution already allows for a two-ballot presidential election. The first ballot has traditionally (except in 1969) and effectively had the function of selecting a single right-wing candidate from among two or more rivals so that it was ultimately incongruous to think of adding a third. The frequency with which the issue was raised in the run up to the 1995 contest had more to do with tactical considerations than any kind of malfunction in the French political system.

If primaries were a bit of red herring the campaign did provide a useful clarification of a feature of French politics usually partially obscured by the party system with its trappings of ideology and interest representation. Balladur's campaign, since it could hardly be the campaign of a party, established beyond doubt that one of the rules of the political game is that it is a spoils system; it is not always or only the party which binds candidate and supporters together, but often an implicit deal in which personal loyalty is offered in exchange for the hope or the promise of office. Nevertheless, and in confirmation of another rule, while Chirac was abandoned by two-thirds of his own party's parliamentarians, he managed to keep enough of a grip on the party central office and grass roots to see off his upstart rival. In the face of the immense attractive power of Balladur's office, party still counted.

The French party system – multipolar or bipolar?

The usual tension between the multipolar and bipolar tendencies of the French party system was modified in five ways in 1995. The multipolar aspect was strengthened by the active presence of de Villiers and Le Pen. Although their electorates are different, these two were sufficiently aware of the similarity of their programmes to devote part of their attention to denouncing each other, Le Pen accusing de Villiers of 'sterilising' a number of votes which could usefully swell his own anti-system total, while de Villiers maintained that it was Le Pen's effort which was really wasted for he, de Villiers, was truly a part of the majority and that a future conservative president would have to take account of his views.

However, multiparty politics was weakened as far as the main candidates were concerned for four reasons. The absence of a UDF candidate implied that neither Chirac nor Balladur need pay much attention to stressing their own party's identity and values for, on the right at least, whatever else happened the RPR would win. Furthermore, if the remote possibility of a socialist victory were ignored, the potential winner would have no need to prepare his party either for an early general election or a subsequent bout of coalition-building, for the massive right-wing majority in the National Assembly still had three years to run. Next, the 'personal' nature of Balladur's candidacy dictated that he should seek support in conservative ranks generally rather than defend the particular identity or mission of the RPR, a strategy which corresponded with his vision of the way in which politics in the Fifth Republic ought to operate.[20] Ironically the RPR did not find an overt champion in Jacques Chirac either; shunned by a majority of his own parliamentarians, he spoke neither as party leader (as he had in 1981) nor as spokesman of the conservative coalition (as he tried to do in 1988), but rather from a position outside and above parties in the manner of de Gaulle, a posture which also served to mute the left–right bipolarity which had been at its most evident in 1974 and 1981.

Populism and centrism

The third institutional logic, the tension between populism and centrism, potentially has two aspects. On the one hand, the need to adopt a fairly populist discourse on the first round in order to please a particular party or camp must be balanced by a more responsible 'centrist' message on the second round to appeal to voters who do not strongly identify with either right or left. In this respect the 1995 election was rather untypical; neither Gaullist candidate chose to 'rally' the RPR, nor did they seek to turn the election into a strongly polarised left–right contest, given the nature of the socialist challenge. But populist currents may over-flow into the second round in another way; in this respect 1995 produced the same strategic configuration as 1988: a sizeable vote for the eliminated extremist Le Pen inevitably challenged the surviving mainstream right-winger (Chirac) to give a between-the-rounds hint that some of the extremist voters' concerns would be taken care of in the event of victory. In 1988 Chirac's relative weakness *vis-à-vis* Mitterrand ensured that the hints were given; in 1995, however, he had a much stronger position in relation to Jospin and could afford to dispense with Le Pen's good opinion.

Irrespective of these calculations, however, Chirac's 1995 campaign resolved the potential populist/centrist dilemma in innovative fashion. Written off by the political class and the opinion polls he devoted several months to a lonely 'tour de France' in search of the average voter, making contacts which he claimed revealed to him the importance of the *fracture sociale* currently afflicting the country. This gave him the excuse for adopting those of Séguin's ideas, and striking the poses, which were necessary to distinguish his campaign from Balladur's. In short Chirac himself moved to the left, adopting a centrist populism valid for both rounds of the election which, by relying on his temporary absence from major national responsibilities, allowed him to ape the classic Gaullist pose of *rassembleur*, appealing to voters of all parties and of none in the higher interests of the nation. The role of outsider, even to an extent of 'victim', fitted perfectly with the self-effacing strategy which Chirac followed during the 1993–95 *cohabitation*. The implicit condemnation of the 'immobilism' of Balladur's government sat uneasily, however, both with the record of Chirac the deputy, who from 1993 to 1995 loyally voted for the core elements of Balladur's legislative programme, and with the fact that some of his key backers (Madelin, Juppé) held important posts in that same government. The candidate's conventional partisan career, moreover, stretching over 28 years, 18 of them as Mayor of Paris, including a second spell as prime minister from 1986–88 in which he followed Thatcherite policies deliberately designed to widen the gap between rich and poor, ill fitted him for the pose of anti-system crusader. Demagogic populism was certainly an important ingredient and arguably a winning formula in the 1995 presidential election.

CONCLUSION

Reflexes and traditions embedded in French politics throughout the Fifth Republic and beyond were the most influential factors determining the emergence and performances of the candidates and parties of the right in 1995. In the case of the UDF, the cadre-party tradition and, in the case of the RPR, legitimism and the ambiguous and flexible Gaullist nationalism were the factors which made both parties vulnerable to splinters and leadership rivalries. However, contemporary policy dilemmas have not been absent. Unemployment, corruption, the difficulties of urban life and multi-ethnic cohabitation have continued to nourish the authoritarian and xenophobic message of the FN. As for the mainstream parties, the intellectual form in which their fractures came to be expressed display the difficulty which today's parties have in managing the financial and foreign policy issues connected with European Union, themselves constrained by wider trends and events such as globalisation and the collapse of the Soviet empire.

NOTES

1. Lawson (1981); Shonfeld (1981).
2. Bresson and Thénard (1989).
3. The CDS has since changed its name to Force Démocrate.
4. *Le Monde*, 14 June 1994.
5. *Le Monde*, 19 November 1994.
6. Ysmal (1992).
7. Giscard in *Le Figaro Magazine*, 21 September 1991; Poniatowski in *Le Monde*, 15 October 1991. See also *Le Monde*, 18 October 1991 and 26 October 1991.
8. *Le Monde*, 28 June 1994 and 30 June 1994.
9. *Le Monde*, 2 July 1994.
10. *Libération*, 22 November 1994.
11. *Le Monde*, 13 June 1990. See also Nay (1994), pp. 330–1.
12. This and other details of Balladur's activities in Nay (1994), pp. 307–42.
13. Nay (1994), pp. 356–7.
14. On the crisis in the PR see *Le Monde*, 17 June 1994, 23 June 1994 and 28 June 1994.
15. Their prime ministerial ambitions were openly paraded at the party's summer school a few weeks later; see *Le Monde*, 6 September 1994.
16. *Libération*, 13 March 1995.
17. Séguin (1994); Fysh (1995).
18. *Le Monde*, 7 September 1993.
19. Chirac (1994).
20. Balladur (1990), pp. 61–74.

5 Candidates and Parties of the Left

Steven Griggs

The institutional logics governing French presidential elections impose competing pressures upon the management of political parties during electoral campaigns. Each candidate must mobilise internal party support while simultaneously meeting the conflicting but requisite demands of personalisation and wider inter-party alliances (see Chapter 3). This chapter examines how candidates on the left managed such competing pressures at the presidential elections of 1995. The first section analyses the evolution of the left from the victory of François Mitterrand in 1981 to the beginning of the 1995 campaign. The second then illustrates the mechanics of candidate selection and the party processes that dictated which candidates emerged or failed to emerge. The final section analyses the dynamics of inter- and intra-party competition on the left throughout the first and second rounds.

THE EVOLUTION OF THE LEFT, 1981–95

Throughout the Giscard presidency (1974–81) the French party system was best understood as a bipolar quadrille of four similar sized political parties organised into rival two-party electoral coalitions of the left and right.[1] At the 1978 parliamentary election, on the left the PCF (with 20.6 per cent of votes cast at the first round) lined up with the PS (24.7 per cent including the left-radical MRG) against the right-wing coalition of the RPR (22.6 per cent) and the UDF (21.5 per cent).[2] Indeed, the dominance of these four parties, collecting almost 90 per cent of votes between them, marginalised all other political parties.[3] The MRG was subsumed within the orbit of the PS, but the ecologists and diverse movements of the left such as the trotskyite Lutte Ouvrière (LO) were relegated to the sidelines.

The election of François Mitterrand in 1981 and the arrival of the PS in government brought to an end the apparent balance of the French party system. The left as a whole won more than 50 per cent of the votes at the 1981 National Assembly election with the PS alone winning 37.5 per cent of votes cast in the first round. The single-party majority which it gained enshrined it as the dominant party in France and confirmed the accelerated decline of the PCF whose share of the vote fell to 16.1 per cent. In fact, this shift in the relative party strength on the left had been under way throughout the 1970s. In 1978, the relative balance of the PS and PCF masked the rise of the PS which, with the MRG, won more votes than the PCF for the first time since its formation in 1971.

However, the premise of competing bipolar coalitions remained valid at least until 1984. In 1981, the PS, with its independence guaranteed by its single-party majority, entered into a governmental coalition with the PCF and four communist ministers entered the Mauroy government. The alliance between the PS and the PCF had always been 'troubled'[4] as the two parties adjusted reluctantly to the bipolarisation of the majority runoff electoral system of the Fifth Republic. The renewed cooperation of 1981 collapsed in 1984 as the PCF refused to participate in the Fabius government with recriminations over the economic realism and failures of the Mauroy government. With the withdrawal of the PCF, the coalition of the left finally collapsed and with it the foundations underlying the bipolar quadrille.

The PS remained the largest party in France throughout the National Assembly elections of the 1980s, despite its setbacks in European and local elections. After the introduction of proportional representation, which minimised its losses at the 1986 parliamentary election, PS support actually rose in 1988. However, its dominance at the polls could not disguise the weakening foundations of its support and its internal conflicts. First, the PS in office failed to satisfy the aspirations of its electorate, locking itself into economic realism and the maintenance of a strong franc from 1983. Second, after the break-up of the PS/PCF coalition in 1984, the PS was unable to find a satisfactory replacement for its alliance with the PCF. It veered from openings to the centre to potential alliances with the emerging Verts, 'big bang' redefinitions of alliances on the left and back towards alliances with the communists when the needs of the majority runoff electoral system dictated. Finally, the PS was beset by internal rivalries as Mitterrand's hold over the party lapsed and it was torn by a fratricidal battle between Lionel Jospin and Laurent Fabius, both loyal *mitterrandistes* who rose to prominence under his tutelage in the 1970s. This rivalry peaked at Rennes in 1990 when the PS left its party conference more divided than ever.

After the warning of the 1992 regional election, the PS was finally punished for its misdemeanours at the 1993 parliamentary elections. Its share of the vote fell to 17.39 per cent at the first round and it won a total of only 53 seats in the National Assembly. Following this defeat, the left-wing Socialisme et République faction, formerly known as CERES and led by Jean-Pierre Chevènement, dissolved in April 1993. Chevènement subsequently launched the Mouvement des Citoyens (MDC) in December 1993. His list at the European election in 1994 scored 2.54 per cent. It was the same election which was to see the electoral nadir of the PS. Its list led by Michel Rocard crashed to merely 14.5 per cent. Put simply, the PS was no longer the dominant party of France.

Significantly for the overall balance between the left and right, the decline of the PS was not met by a resurgent PCF. The decline of the PCF continued throughout the 1980s and 1990s as it came to rest upon a residual electorate bordering around 10 per cent. Indeed, the PCF became reliant upon pockets of local support for its continued survival at national elections. Its decline elicited little response from the leadership of Georges Marchais, who squashed opposition from *contestataires* within the party, thereby aiding and abetting the development of dissident communist movements. At the 1988 presidential elections, the ex-communist Pierre Juquin, stood against the official PCF candidate, André Lajoinie. However, the retirement of the conservative Georges Marchais and the appointment of Robert Hue as National Secretary in January 1994 brought the PCF out of its isolation on the left. Hue, looking personally to embody change within the PCF, launched in April 1994 the prospect of a

Pacte Unitaire pour le Progrès (PUP) on the left taking in movements from the centre through to the far left.

In fact, from the opening of the second Mitterrand *septennat* in 1988, electoral behaviour in France was marked by rising abstentions and the further emergence of a protest vote. This evolution profited marginal parties who were equally favoured by the system of proportional representation used for European and regional elections. On the left, this evolution was marked by the rise of the ecologists who won 10.7 per cent of the vote at the 1989 European election and 14.7 per cent at the 1992 regional election. It signalled the weakening hold over the party system exercised by traditional parties. Indeed, at the 1989 European election, the 'big three' of the PS, UDF and RPR could muster only 60 per cent of the vote, a proportion which fell to 50 per cent at the 1992 regional election.

Most recently, the MRG under the presidency of Jean-François Hory has flexed its muscles and considered leaving the orbit of the PS. In November 1994, it relaunched itself as Radical, with the aim of developing into a large and independent federation of the centre-left. The then MRG was encouraged in its plans by the score of Bernard Tapie's Energie Radicale list at the 1994 European election. Tapie, the Marseille football chairman and businessman, had been courted by the PS after its switch in the mid-1980s to the values of enterprise and the delights of the market. He joined the MRG in February 1993 and engaged in a symbiotic relationship with Jean-François Hory in which the notoriety of Tapie and his status as a *présidentiable* were exchanged in return for the party political base that Tapie lacked. Both sought to exploit the decline of the socialists, Tapie himself having benefited from the decline of the young and popular socialist vote at the 1994 European election.

However, the primary challenge to the dominance of the PS has come from the Verts, albeit if, after much initial promise, the ecologists have failed to consolidate their early inroads. At the 1993 parliamentary election ecologists polled 10.7 per cent at the first round, but the vote was split between three movements. Rival factions, not to mention rival egos, have persistently dragged ecology from the hard left where it marries environmentalism with anti-productivism

through to the pragmatic centre where it invites cooperation from both the left and the right via its own autonomous electoral strategy where it claimed to be 'above' the
traditional left–right cleavage. In November 1986, the Verts
came under the hold of Antoine Waechter as they moved
towards a neither left nor right electoral strategy centred
on ecology. However, Waechter's control of the Verts was
overturned in November 1993 by Dominique Voynet who
firmly anchored the party on the left with a platform of
environmental and social concerns. Indeed, Voynet brought
into the Verts' orbit the dissident left of ex-communists within
the Alternative Rouge et Verte (AREV) group. Waechter
subsequently left the Verts in September 1994 to form the
Mouvement écologiste indépendant (MEI). However, further
competition came from the centrist environmentalism of Brice
Lalonde, Minister for the Environment in the Rocard government. Lalonde formed Génération Ecologie (GE) in December 1990. GE, which began life as a haven for disgruntled
socialists, has veered from centre-left to centre-right as the
opportunism of Lalonde dictated endorsements of the
Balladur government and then Chirac's presidential candidacy. Noel Mamère, looking to cement GE on the left of
centre, departed the party on the heels of others following
accusations of leftism to found Convergence Ecologie
Solidarité.

Consequently, at the beginnings of the campaign for the
1995 presidential election, the system of party alliances and
party management on the left were in a state of flux and
were no longer subsumed within the traditional confines of
PS-PCF relations. The PCF had declined from the early 1980s
and then stagnated. The PS remained a pivotal actor on
the left, but was no longer the dominant party that it had
been. The MRG was threatening to spread its wings and
the ecology movement, albeit fragmented, had emerged as
a challenger on the left. Such marginal parties had fed on
the emerging protest vote. Even Lutte Ouvrière, a relatively
insignificant observer at the last three presidential campaigns,
was waiting in the wings to mop up the support of disgruntled
socialists. However, all parties on the left were fighting over
a reduced core of left-wing voters. From the balanced left–
right electorates of the late 1970s and the dominant left of

the early 1980s the electorate had clearly swung to the right in the 1990s. As the left entered the 1995 presidential elections, the talk was of the 1969 presidential election when no left-wing candidate made it through to the second round.

PARTY MANAGEMENT AND THE EMERGENCE OF CANDIDATES

The emergence of candidates at presidential elections depends not simply upon the formal gathering of 500 sponsors or the avoidance of bankruptcy, but also upon informal requirements such as the acquisition of that elusive profile of a *présidentiable* likely to win the election or meet the expectations of the party faithful. The primary hurdle facing prospective candidates is that of party selection which provides candidates with the essential support mechanisms upon which to base a nationwide campaign for the presidency. Not least, political parties guarantee all candidates a core of loyal first-round support (see Chapter 3). However, in the run-up to the 1995 presidential election, there was no single path leading to, or guaranteeing, participation in the opening round on 23 April. Candidates faced their own constraints and followed their own particular routes. Indeed, candidates emerged after having successfully mixed their own cocktail of requirements combining with varying degrees of difficulty the obligations of 500 sponsors and formal eligibility with those of party support and the requisite status of *présidentiable*.

Viewed within the narrow confines of the 1995 presidential election, party selection was something of a foregone conclusion for the likes of Arlette Laguiller (LO), Robert Hue (PCF), Dominique Voynet (Verts), Antoine Waechter (MEI) and Brice Lalonde (GE). The leadership that they exerted over their respective parties effectively reduced the nomination process to one whereby it was left to the candidates themselves to decide whether or not they wanted to stand. The perennial Arlette Laguiller had been the candidate of Lutte Ouvrière since 1974 and possessed the notoriety of three presidential campaigns to legitimise her claims. Robert Hue had sealed his nomination in January 1994 when he replaced Marchais at the head of the French Communist Party. He was subsequently elected candidate by the national conference of the PCF with only three abstentions against him in early November.[5] Similarly, Voynet, who was formally elected as a candidate in October 1994 by the membership of the Verts and its hard left partner AREV with 78.5 per cent of the vote, had already effectively assured her candidacy when ousting Waechter from the leadership of the Verts in November 1993. Indeed, despite continued opposition to her left-wing environmentalism at the 1994 conference, her rivals were unable to contest the legitimacy of her election as candidate.[6] Finally, both Waechter and Lalonde stood at the head of parties that were effectively vehicles for their own ambitions. The 400-strong membership of MEI elected Waechter as a candidate with 90 per cent of the vote in early January 1995.[7] GE endorsed Lalonde in a conference at Laval in December 1994 with a motion supporting him gaining 72.7 per cent of the conference vote.[8] The anti-Lalonde faction, which sought to push the party towards support for Jacques Delors in the presidential election, simply walked out of the party as a result.

The prospect of three ecology candidates and the fragmentation of the ecology vote at the first round led Lalonde to call for a common ecology candidate. His calls were ignored by his rivals, but the process of natural selection eventually dictated that only one candidate was to participate in the first round of the presidential elections. In the first instance, Waechter was eliminated by his failure to gain 500 sponsors. In 1988, the Verts, represented by Waechter, only gained their 504 sponsors with the help of communist politicians.[9] In 1995, they faced similar problems with only a handful of mayors and approximately 200 regional councillors and competition from other minority candidates.[10] In such a scramble for sponsors, the existence of local party networks of *notables* was determinant and counted against Waechter and his embryonic MEI. Indeed, in this race the LO had established networks in place and even the Verts complained that they were often coming off second best to the team of Laguiller. Despite her difficulties, though, Voynet could call upon the Verts' party organisation to contact between 25 and 30 000 mayors and dissident communists in the search for sponsors. GE had one official per department working upon the task of collecting signatures and at first sought to exploit its ministerial contacts and those officials who supported Lalonde or Waechter at the 1981 and 1988 presidential elections respectively.[11] However, from the outset, it was apparent that Waechter was simply unable to meet the requirements of 500 sponsors. At the end of January 1995, Voynet claimed 350 sponsors, Lalonde 190 but Waechter only 100.[12] On 4 April, as the deadline for gathering sponsors passed, Waechter had failed to gain the required amount and was unable to contest the election.

Lalonde was always a reluctant candidate for the 1995 presidential election. He repeatedly called for a single ecology candidate as well as urging Raymond Barre to stand, ready to withdraw in that eventuality. The GE list at the 1994 European election had performed poorly, winning only 2.01 per cent and opinion polls offered Lalonde the prospect of another drubbing at the presidential election, estimating his support at 0.5 per cent.[13] In mid-February 1995, Lalonde recognised the failure of his proposition for a single ecology candidate. Subsequently, Barre announced his decision not to stand and Lalonde, having stopped collecting sponsors, was left without the necessary support to pursue his candidacy. He formally withdrew from the race on 15 March 1995. His failure to promote a single candidate, coupled with his insignificant rating in the opinion polls, explained his decision not to stand.

This lack of presidential status also ended the campaign of Jean-François Hory for Radical. Hory announced his decision to stand somewhat belatedly on 23 February 1995. His late entry into the campaign was dictated by the ineligibility of Bernard Tapie and developments within the PS which saw Lionel Jospin win the PS nomination at their primaries at the beginning of February (see below). Tapie, who had carried the Radical colours in the 1994 European election, was rendered ineligible for the presidential elections by being declared bankrupt as his business empire and football chairmanship collapsed under scandals of bribery and corruption. After the nomination of Jospin by the PS, Hory met informally with Jospin on 19 February, but was unable over subsequent meetings to agree an acceptable compromise with the PS candidate.[14] In fact, Hory placed a veto on the candidacy of Jospin, declaring in mid-January that Jospin was not an identikit photo of their ideal candidate[15] and that if designated Jospin would only lose the elections and consequently Radical would present its own candidate.[16] Hory briefly launched former socialist minister Bernard Kouchner as a possible candidate in mid-January, but then supported the PS's First Secretary, Henri Emmanuelli, with the prospect of a common candidate and organisational ties with the PS. With the victory of Jospin and the removal of Tapie, Hory was pushed into standing himself.

However, Hory was never a credible alternative to Tapie. Opinion polls estimated support for Hory in the first round at only 0.5 per cent. His opponents within Radical refused to take part in such 'a suicidal undertaking'.[17] The old guard of Michel Crépeau, Roger-Gérard Schwartzenberg and Emile Zuccarelli called for Hory to stand down.[18] Even Tapie, an opponent of Jospin, switched his support at the beginning of March to the PS candidate, for whom he acknowledged a 'préjugé favorable'. By 20 March, Tapie was back on board supporting Hory.[19] Yet, the internal opposition to Hory persisted as his candidacy failed to find an echo in the public domain. Bowing to the inevitable, Hory dropped out of the race at the end of March.

Indeed, the perception of *présidentiable* status played a pivotal role in the selection process of the PS. As far back as 1990, approximately two-thirds of PS delegates argued that Michel Rocard would make a good presidential candidate, placing him over 30 points ahead of his nearest challenger, Laurent Fabius.[20] Indeed, by July 1992, he was generally acknowledged as the PS's 'natural' presidential candidate. However, following the failure of the PS list which he led at the 1994 European election, Rocard was summarily replaced as First Secretary after failing to win a vote of confidence from the party leadership. With the removal of Rocard and his replacement by Emmanuelli, the PS leadership progressively mobilised behind the possible candidacy of Jacques Delors, the President of the European Commission and former PS Finance Minister. The support for Delors was founded upon his status as a *présidentiable* and the belief within the PS that it could actually win the presidential election with Delors as its candidate. Polls showed that the range of his support within the electorate satisfied the demands of the presidential election coupling the necessary standing on the left (in the second round against Balladur 93 per cent of communist supporters would vote for him) with an appeal to the more moderate electorate of the centre (44 per cent of UDF supporters placed Delors in the centre, centre-right or plainly on the right).[21] By the beginning of November 1994, with little overt campaigning on his behalf, polls indicated that Delors would beat Chirac with 54 per cent in the second round and run close to Balladur with 48 per cent.[22] By the end of November, polls indicated that he would beat both Chirac with 56 per cent and Balladur with 52 per cent in the second round.

The emergence of Delors demonstrated the informality of the selection process within the PS. As it tried to force Delors' hand, the PS entered into a period of stasis whereby notions of internal party democracy were subservient to the need for a successful candidate and the desire of the party leadership to win the election. It withdrew from any role in the selection process of its own candidate, having to rely instead on the personal decision of Delors. As such, the PS leadership was transformed into a band of sycophants, exemplified by Emmanuelli who announced to Delors from the rostrum at the Liévin conference in November 1994 that 'I believe that I have the right to tell you that it's your duty [to stand].'[23] In contrast, Jospin and the PS left-winger, Marie-Noëlle Lienemann, voiced concerns that the elevation of Delors as saviour of the PS would rid the party of its identity and any effective role in the selection of its candidate.[24]

The pleas came to little when Delors announced, live on television on 11 December 1994, that he would not stand as the PS candidate. He cited a mixture of personal reasons (his age, the concerns of his wife and his desire not to hamper the political career of his daughter and senior socialist figure, Martine Aubry) as well as his desire to avoid a period of *cohabitation* as the motivations behind his decision. Delors believed that he would not possess a governing majority, particularly as his preferred partners in government, the centrists, were successfully tied into the right through their participation in the Balladur government and the mechanics

of the majority runoff electoral system.[25] As for the PS, it
fell head first from the informal process of nomination surrounding Delors into a formal system of primaries, primaries that the right had accepted but failed to organise
(see Chapter 4). All party members of at least six months'
standing and up to date with their membership fees would
vote for their preferred candidate in a secret ballot within
each local branch. The vote would take place on 3 February 1995 with the result ratified on 5 February at a special
congress in Paris.

The first to declare himself candidate for the PS nomination was Lionel Jospin, First Secretary from 1981 to 1988
before entering the Rocard government as Minister of Education. Having lost his seat at the 1993 National Assembly
election, he effectively retired from politics and his faction
fragmented in June 1994 as Emmanuelli, accompanied by
part of the *jospiniste* membership, was appointed as First
Secretary with the support of the *fabiusiens*. Nevertheless,
with future battles in mind, Jospin declared in October 1994
that he would be a candidate if Delors did not run.[26] Despite appeals from Emmanuelli to delay any announcement,
when Delors eventually announced his decision Jospin forced
the pace of the nomination process, expressing concerns
over the 'void' created by Delors' withdrawal.[27] He declared
his candidacy at the meeting of the party's *bureau national*
on 4 January 1995. His only advantage was that as an 'outsider' he could present himself as the moral candidate for
change who had taken a certain distance from the record
of the PS in office.[28]

Jospin's candidacy reopened his fratricidal battle with the
former *mitterrandiste*, Laurent Fabius. The dominant *fabiusien*
leadership feared that Jospin would use the presidential
elections to relaunch his support within the party. To prevent
such an outcome, it sought a rival candidate to Jospin. Fabius
himself was ineligible due to his implication in the HIV-
contaminated blood scandal. Wild cards, such as the former
PS Minister of Justice and President of the Constitutional
Council Robert Badinter, or the former PS Minister of the
Interior and President of the Cour des Comptes Pierre Joxe,
were either unsuitable or unwilling to stand. Finally, on
17 January 1995, Jack Lang announced his intention to

stand in the party's primaries, although he declared that he was prepared to withdraw if a more appropriate candidate of unity emerged. Lang, the former Minister of Culture, had the advantage of being both an anti-*jospiniste* and the popular choice in the opinion polls. However, his apparent willingness to step aside was soon to be tested as the Fabius clan threw its support behind Emmanuelli, the First Secretary. Emmanuelli announced his decision to stand on 18 January 1995, just one day after Lang, having been convinced to stand by Julien Dray and Jean-Luc Mélenchon, the leaders of La Gauche Socialiste, a left-wing faction in the party.[29]

Emmanuelli drew upon his responsibilities as First Secretary to legitimise his decision to stand. He had been endorsed in November 1994 with 87 per cent of votes at the Liévin conference and could further point to the fact that Mitterrand had stood in 1981 when First Secretary. Emmanuelli campaigned upon a ticket of left-wing unity and a future PS-Radical federation, warning that should Jospin stand, the absence of a common candidate would mean that the left would fail to get through to the second round. Radical publicly vetoed Jospin as a common candidate of the left, declaring that a Jospin candidacy would lead Radical to present its own rival candidate (see above). Emmanuelli met with representatives of Radical on 11 January 1995 to agree increased organisational ties between the two parties. In a deal with Hory, Emmanuelli was to be the common candidate of the left and Hory was to preside over a federation of PS-Radical parties.[30] Such a platform enabled Emmanuelli to side-step attacks of internal party politics as the motivation behind his campaign and asserted his distinctiveness from Jospin. Jospin opposed any moves towards organisational cooperation between the PS and Radical as signalling the end of the PS of Epinay, with his supporters preferring to widen the alliances of the PS beyond the narrow cooperation with Radical.

The emergence of Emmanuelli put Lang under increasing pressure to withdraw as the Fabius clan wished to avoid a fragmented anti-Jospin vote. He received little support from *notables* within the PS and his suggestion to replace the system of primaries with a 'committee of wise men' was ignored.

Ségolène Royal, who was one of the few to pick up on the Lang proposal, subsequently resigned her presidency of the party's *conseil national* when her and Lang's calls were ignored.[31] Although Lang delayed any decision over his possible withdrawal, it was always on the cards once he declared that he would move aside if another candidate able to unify the left were to appear. The suspense, or rather the lack of it, ended on 25 January 1995 when Lang officially withdrew from the race and gave his support to Emmanuelli. Ironically, Lang was the only prospective candidate likely to get through to the second round. His 19 per cent support in the opinion polls guaranteed his place in the second round unlike Jospin and Emmanuelli who could only muster 15 and 11 per cent respectively.[32]

There was little campaigning *per se* as the rival candidates relied more on the public parading of their supporters. Mitterrand refused to choose between Emmanuelli and Jospin, but the PS *éléphants* engaged in almost daily declarations of support. Both Emmanuelli and Jospin were ex-*mitterrandistes* and, in fact, Emmanuelli had previously been a fierce anti-Fabius and pro-Jospin supporter. He remained a committed *mitterrandiste* who viewed the failure of the PS as a result of its move away from its socialist principles and endorsed a return to the left as the solution to the electoral problems experienced by the party. In contrast, Jospin had moved towards the positions more typical of Rocard, espousing the need to endorse an 'ethic of responsibility' and to be wary of the differences between promises and government action.[33] As such, Jospin tied himself to the modernising wing of the PS. Indeed, the boundary was effectively drawn between Emmanuelli backed by Fabius and Jospin who drew support from the modernising faction of Aubry and Mauroy, the *rocardiens* and the Agir en Socialiste faction brought together for the Liévin congress.

However, such issues turned out to be secondary, as the campaign was dominated by the question of which candidate was most likely to get the PS through to the second round of the presidential election. Throughout the campaign, Emmanuelli could not counter the charge that he was the least *présidentiable* of the two prospective candidates, further weakened as he was by the threat of legal action

Table 5.1   First-round opinion poll rating (%) for Emmanuelli and
            Jospin (January 1995)

Polls[37]	*19–20*	*19–23*	*24–25*	*24–26*	*30–31*
Emmanuelli	11	13	13	14	13
Jospin	15	15.5	18	17	15.5

against him from his time as party Treasurer. Jospin gained
support from his decision to be the first to announce his
candidacy and from the distance that he took from the failures of the PS in government, reinforced as it was by support from the modernisers within the PS.[34] Indeed, polls
continually placed Emmanuelli behind Jospin at the first
round (see Table 5.1). More significantly, among the general
public, 45 per cent thought Jospin would be a good socialist
candidate against only 27 per cent for Emmanuelli.[35] It was
this issue that was to decide the vote on 3 February 1995.
The PS militants, ignoring the advice of their leaders, did
no more than vote for the candidate who was the most *présidentiable*.[36] In such a competition, Jospin was the clear winner,
gaining 64.85 per cent of votes cast against Emmanuelli's
35.15 per cent.

As such, the emergence of candidates on the left in 1995
was dependent upon issues relating to party management,
the formal rules of eligibility and the elusive status of
présidentiable. Four left-wing candidates made it through to
the first round. Hue, Voynet and Laguiller were all expected
to be candidates exploiting, to varying degrees, control over
their party to assert their candidacy. Most candidates had
to resolve issues of party management, even if it meant, like
Waechter, creating one's own party so as to try to stand as
a candidate. The local networks of party support were subsequently determinant in the battle to find 500 sponsors
which ended Waechter's challenge. The formal rules of eligibility also eliminated Tapie because of bankruptcy. However,
it was the absence of that informal status of *présidentiable*
which led Hory and Lalonde to drop out of the race and
which lay at the heart of the defeat of Emmanuelli (although
Jospin was far from a clear *présidentiable* before his 1995
campaign). Its presence for Jacques Delors permitted him

to bypass altogether any formal nomination process within the PS. Indeed, the acquisition of the status of *présidentiable* had much to do with the expectations of the party faithful. Rocard lost his status as a *présidentiable* at the 1994 European election and promptly lost control of the PS. Voynet was never a *présidentiable*, but had taken control of the Verts in 1993. In short, the candidate selection process was a function of a cocktail of concerns associated with the institutional logics of presidential elections.

PARTY ALLIANCES AND THE DYNAMICS OF A PRESIDENTIAL CAMPAIGN

Having analysed the emergence of candidates on the left in 1995, we now turn our attention to how these candidates dealt with the issues of party leadership and party alliances. The rules governing presidential elections impose competing pressures upon candidates (see Chapter 3). In the first instance, the multiparty competition of the first round necessitates the mobilisation of a distinct party electorate. This multiparty competition, however, gives way in the second round to a bipolarised contest which necessitates the creation of multiparty alliances and the accentuated personalisation of campaign strategies as candidates are obliged to unite their own camp while trawling in the centre for additional support. Indeed, in the personalised arena of French presidential elections, campaign strategies are driven throughout the two rounds by the requirement to remain somewhat 'above parties' while exploiting the support mechanism provided by political parties throughout the campaign.

On the left in 1995, the constraints imposed upon candidates by the conflicting institutional logics of presidential elections only fully applied to Jospin. Jospin was the only candidate on the left who was expected by the party faithful to get through to the second round. The target of Voynet was 5 per cent, that of Hue the 6.7 per cent won by Lajoinie in 1988 and that of Laguiller the 2 per cent averaged in her three previous campaigns. As such, all three were engaged in a pure first-round vote-maximising exercise with no concerns over appealing to the centre or forging future multiparty alliances for the second round. In contrast, Jospin had not only to defend himself on the left without alienating potential support for the second round but also take on Chirac and Balladur in the fight over the centre ground.

With no expectations to deliver on their campaign commitments, the three 'first-round' candidates on the left could simply undercut Jospin's left-wing credentials. All three tied Jospin into the failures of the PS in the 1980s, alleging that he lacked the political will to impose change. Voynet married environmentalism with anti-liberalism to produce a package of proposals which offered the decommissioning of nuclear power stations, legislation on air quality, a reduction in the working week to 35 then to 30 hours and a minimum income for students with the extension of the *revenu minimum d'insertion* to 18 year-olds not in education.[38] For his part, Hue took stances against youth unemployment and the financial corruption of a society where 'money was king', issues that Jospin, he alleged, could not address as long as he accepted the straitjacket of the Maastricht Treaty. He proposed an emergency plan to tackle youth unemployment, a quadrupling of the tax on fortunes and the introduction of a tax on speculative capital gains. Finally, the trotskyite Laguiller, lumping Jospin into the same pro-capitalist class as Balladur and Chirac, offered workers across-the-board wage increases of 1500 francs with increased taxes on firms to finance jobs and build homes.[39] All firms that made profits while making workers redundant were to be expropriated without compensation.

Jospin did put forward a balanced programme of measured change under the inappropriate banner of social democracy (inappropriate given both the content of Jospin's manifesto and the history of the socialist movement in France). His manifesto included measures such as the reduction of the working week, three public investment programmes, a five-year presidential mandate and a new practice of government encapsulated in the slogan 'citizen-president'. However, in contrast to Voynet, for example, he proposed only the negotiated reduction of the working week to 37 hours in 1997 and the introduction of only a 'dose' of proportional representation at legislative elections. In contrast to both Hue and Laguiller, for example, he proposed a 'little push in the right direction' to the minimum wage and no across-the-board wage increases. Such relative timidity points both to Jospin's conversion to the realism of the modernisers and *rocardiens* within the PS as well as the future requirement of his campaign to trawl in the centre.

In fact, the three 'first-round' candidates focused primarily on a different pool of voters than Jospin, that of former socialists and the protest vote. Indeed, the persistent 5 per cent support in the opinion polls for Laguiller saw increasing attacks on her policies by both Hue and Voynet. As the first round approached, Voynet attacked Laguiller, describing support for her as the 'vote défouloir', or crazy vote. The co-president of her campaign support committee, the former communist minister Charles Fiterman, went as far as to describe Laguiller as a Tibetan monk.[40] Hue identified the vote for Laguiller as short-lived, suggesting that while Laguiller appeared as a candidate every seven years, the PCF was an ever-present force in national politics.[41] In her defence, Laguiller assured her supporters that Hue in no way incarnated a radical protest vote, underlining that in the second round Hue would support Jospin without concessions.[42] In an act of pure electoral politics, she betrayed the 'one-upmanship' of the campaign, pointing out that she proposed a 1500 francs across-the-board wage increase while Hue was limited to 1000 francs.[43]

The main weapon employed by Jospin against his competitors on the left was that of tactical voting. Calls to 'vote usefully', rebaptised the 'responsible vote' by Emmanuelli in mid-April,[44] appealed to voters to unite behind Jospin in order to guarantee the presence of the left in the second round. As such, the Jospin campaign was haunted by the spectre of the 1969 presidential election. The issue of tactical voting was driven by the uncertainty of the opinion polls which two weeks before the first round could not confirm Jospin's place in the second round. It amounted to a confidence trick as to who on the left could best convince voters that they held the future in their own hands. At the beginning of April, with the gap in the polls between Balladur and Jospin narrowing, Hue hammered home his belief that Jospin was bound to win through to the second round. He thereby denied allegations that a vote for Hue would be a 'wasted' vote that would cause the left to lose out on the second round.[45] Voynet adopted a different tack attacking the principle of tactical voting which she assured had the 'after-taste of hegemony and the totalitarianism of those who refuse debates'.[46] She contested the appeal of a 'responsible vote' concluding that, if Jospin did not reach the second round, then he only had himself to blame.[47] Laguiller simply said that the real 'useful vote' was one for her, as significant support for her policies would worry the business class and the government.[48]

Parallel to tactical voting, Jospin was able to exploit the personalisation of presidential elections to try and dissociate himself from the record of the PS in government. Indeed, Hue employed a similar campaign strategy with regard to his own party, using the individual pronoun 'I' instead of the standard PCF collective 'we' at campaign meetings as well as personifying the renovation of the PCF with his assertions that the party was wrong not to have separated from the Soviet model earlier than it did.[49] For his part, Jospin, following the example of Mitterrand in 1974 and 1981, set up his campaign team in its own headquarters in the Rue du Cherche-Midi rather than at the PS's headquarters in the Rue Solférino. Likewise, he campaigned upon a personal programme, which although not exploited as overtly as François Mitterrand's *110 Propositions* in 1981 or his *Lettre à tous les Français* in 1988, was in no way a simple validation of the PS manifesto that had been endorsed by the party at the beginning of February.[50] Indeed, Jospin sought to employ the launch of his personal manifesto at the beginning of March as the springboard for the whole of his campaign as he withdrew from overt campaigning to let his nomination by the PS create its own 'demand' within the electorate. In these early stages, he personalised his campaign, fronting the campaign himself and not exploiting the talents of his wider team as Chirac had done with Séguin and Balladur did with Sarkozy.

Throughout his campaign, two strategies labelled Jospin a candidate of renovation and change within the PS. First, as in his campaign for the PS nomination, Jospin packed his campaign team with the post-Mitterrand generation and known modernisers within the PS, bringing to the fore the likes of Martine Aubry, Pierre Moscovici, Jean-Christophe Cambadélis, Dominique Strauss-Kahn and Daniel Vaillant. As his senior statesmen, he relied upon Rocard and Delors,[51] who presided his *comité de soutien*. Second, Jospin acknowledged the mistakes committed by the PS under Mitterrand, taking his distance with the incumbent president throughout the whole of the campaign. In the first round, Mitterrand supported Jospin, although he criticised his lacklustre campaign.[52] In the second round, the rumoured presence of Mitterrand at a Jospin campaign rally was reduced to a letter of support read out at the meeting.[53] Indeed, as the campaign moved on, Emmanuelli was mandated by the PS to ask Mitterrand to intervene in support of Jospin.[54] However, for Jospin, such apparent lack of support from Mitterrand was perceived far less as a electoral hindrance and more as an integral part of his campaign strategy.

However, the PS could not be permanently distanced from the Jospin campaign. Despite his early rise in the opinion polls, the Jospin team became concerned from mid-March onwards that the rise in support for Chirac was not accompanied by a decline in the support for Balladur which would guarantee Jospin's place in the second round (see Table 5.2). In many ways, his initial first-round strategy was to let Chirac and Balladur fight it out among themselves and benefit from the fall-out of the right's own fratricidal battle.[55] His first target on the right was Balladur who was leading the polls at the beginning of February.[56] At this stage of the campaign, Jospin was ahead of Chirac and was assured of his place in the second round. The fall of Balladur and the rise of Chirac on a populist ticket made it increasingly necessary for Jospin to change his line of attack.[57] At the same time, the PS leadership pressurised Jospin to adopt a more 'muscular' campaign against Chirac and Balladur, a proposal which was supported by the Jospin team as the PS became more involved in his campaign.[58] Jean Glavany and Daniel Vaillant, spokespersons for the PS and Jospin respectively, were ordered to harmonise the PS-campaign team relations.[59] Subsequently, Jospin, supported by Emmanuelli, met with PS politicians on 9 April to mobilise the party and to urge them to employ local networks in support of his campaign rather than withdraw to the narrower concerns

Table 5.2 Opinion poll ratings for Balladur, Jospin and Chirac

Poll[60]	7–9 Feb.	21–23 Feb.	8–9 Mar.	11–13 Mar.	21–22 Mar.	25–27 Mar.	4–5 Apr.	8–10 Apr.	13–14 Apr.
Jospin	22.5	24	21	20	22	21	22	21	21
Balladur	28	23.5	20	20	17	18	20	19	18
Chirac	17.5	19	24	27	26	26	24	26	26

of particular local election campaigns. Indeed, the senior leadership of the PS, even Fabius, Jospin's long-term rival, began to take on a more prominent role in the campaign as the *éléphants* were dragged out for the large campaign meetings.

With the increasing focus on Chirac from mid-March, Jospin was able to revert to the basic rule of the first round which requires candidates to unite their own camp. Although the rise of a 'social' Chirac posed a threat to Jospin's populist electorate, it legitimised the campaign and values of Jospin and forced him to appeal more directly to his own electorate.[61] His attacks on Chirac reasserted the cleavages between left and right and sought to demystify Chirac's economic and social policies. Indeed, Jospin and his supporters lumped Chirac and Balladur together as the 'Dupond et Dupont' of French politics, highlighting Chirac's support of the Balladur government. Equally, he raised the alleged insincerity of Chirac and his fluctuating policy commitments over his 20 years at the head of the RPR (noting, in particular, his Thatcherite-Reaganite inspired proposals in the mid-1980s). As if to bear witness to the change in his campaign, a new slogan was introduced which replaced the banal 'Avec Lionel Jospin c'est plus clair' to 'Pour une France plus juste'.

The surprise first-round victory of Jospin with 23.30 per cent signalled a period of 'Jospin-mania' fuelled by the fact that the PS had not only won through to the second round, but had done so in first place. Explanations of Jospin's support pointed to the significance of tactical voting, his rupture with *mitterrandisme* and his adoption of a 'social democratic' platform.[62] Laguiller with 5.30 per cent successfully tapped the protest vote of the working class in the traditional bastions of the left, scoring over two-and-a-half times her average score in the three past campaigns. In contrast, Voynet with 3.32 per cent won less than Waechter in 1988, throwing doubts on the capacity of the Verts to build an alliance between the far left and moderate ecologists.[63] Hue with 8.64 per cent beat the score of Lajoinie in 1988, but was found lacking if compared to the combined 8.86 per cent of Lajoinie and Juquin in 1988, and the 9.18 per cent for the PCF in the first round of the 1993 legislative elections. Indeed, Jospin's own first round score was only surprising in light of the disastrous 1994 European election result. As he embarked upon his second-round strategy of uniting the left, his pool of votes on the left was such that he was dependent upon defections from Balladur's and Le Pen's supporters if he was to have any chance of winning against Chirac.

The absence of pre-existing electoral alliances somewhat hampered Jospin's moves to unite the left in the second round. Following the collapse of the coalition with the communists in 1984, the PS had failed to redefine its electoral strategies. However, at the 1995 presidential election, Jospin benefited (with Cambadélis) both from his management of the meeting of the left in February 1994 at the *Assises de la transformation sociale* and from conjunctural resources inspired by the electoral timetable. The municipal elections were to follow the presidential elections in June and the need for PS support in these local elections could not be ignored by other parties on the left, particularly the PCF. Indeed, in the approach to the presidential elections, relations between the PCF and the PS had warmed against the background of the forthcoming municipal elections, with Hue's PUP initiative in April 1994 and tentative meetings between the leadership of the two parties.

In the first round, Jospin had already begun to lay the foundations of the multiparty alliances for his second-round campaign. He found places in his *conseil politique* for both Noel Mamère and André Buchmann from Convergence Ecologie Solidarité, as well as for Georges Sarre, Béatrice Patric and Paul Loridant from the MDC and for the 1988 presidential candidate Pierre Juquin. The MDC, after Chevènement's decision not to stand, had overcome, with reservations, its anti-European opposition towards Jospin's programme.[64] Indeed, despite the opposition between Hory and Jospin, four members of Radical eventually joined the Jospin campaign.

In addition, Jospin sent far from coded messages to the PCF, proposing on 2 April that if elected he would include PCF ministers within his government. His offer, at this stage in the campaign, cannot be divorced from the issue of tactical voting. His proposal signalled to the PCF electorate that to vote for Jospin was to vote usefully as PCF concerns would be taken into account in the formation of any future government. After somewhat mixed messages, Hue replied that the question of PCF ministers was not yet on the agenda, but, more open to collaboration than Marchais, he also confirmed that in future the PCF would play a role wherever it could.[65] In the second round, Jospin called upon the PCF to join his campaign. However, with no wish to alienate the centre, he attached no concessions to his offer nor did he seek a formal agreement with the PCF.[66] In response, the PCF leadership, meeting on the 26 April, called upon their supporters to block the right in the second round. They did not express support for Jospin, although in a carefully worded statement it was made clear that communist opposition to the right was, of course, to be expressed through voting for Jospin.[67]

The Verts met on 29 and 30 April to decide whether they would support Jospin in the second round. Voynet had earlier laid out the shopping list of concessions with which Jospin could expect to buy the endorsement of the Verts.[68] Jospin had gone some way to meeting these demands with his commitments against the Somport tunnel, the Superphénix nuclear power station and the Rhine–Rhône canal project. Furthermore he proposed the creation of 'green jobs', environmental taxes and 'polluter-pays' policies as well as the move towards a 37-hour working week and the introduction of a dose of proportional representation. Indeed, Voynet readily admitted that the Verts had not achieved such important policy commitments from a candidate since Plogoff and Larzac in 1981 and that the race between Jospin and Chirac 'was not a photo-finish'.[69] However, Jospin's endorsement of proportional representation left him open to attacks from Chirac's supporters who, seizing upon Le Pen's praise of Jospin's honesty and uncorrupted reputation, argued that Jospin was 'belly-dancing around Le Pen to lure him under the pretext of seducing Voynet'.[70] As if to force the message home, Lalonde rallied to Chirac as the best defence against the rise of the FN.

The compromise that came out of the Verts' meeting was that the party would give no formal *consigne de vote* to their supporters, arguing that Jospin had still not made sufficient commitments towards the introduction of proportional representation, the 35-hour week and the dissolution of the Pasqua laws on the entry and residence of foreigners in France. In Jospin's favour, the anchoring of the Verts on the left since November 1993 obliged them to demonstrate their left-wing allegiances in the second round in order to remain consistent with the first-round campaign. Indeed, there was minority support, particularly from delegates from the Nord-Pas-de-Calais region including Marie-Christine Blandin, co-president of Voynet's *comité de soutien*, who wanted to make a direct appeal to vote for Jospin in the second round. Like the statement of the PCF, it was an endorsement of the candidate in all but name.

Such coded support was not forthcoming from Arlette Laguiller. Throughout the first round, Laguiller, in line with her anti-system ideology, equated the policies of Jospin with those of Chirac and Balladur. Indeed, she used her refusal to endorse Jospin in the second round as a means of attacking Hue. In the second round, faced with the choice of Jospin or Chirac, she said that she would prefer personally to abstain. However, to the advantage of Jospin, she offered her supporters no advice on how to vote and did not call upon them to abstain. In fact, much of the far left did rally behind Jospin with support coming from the Alternative Démocratie et Socialisme, Ligue Communiste Révolutionnaire, and the *communistes refondateurs*. Thus, as the second round progressed, Jospin was able to content himself with support from individuals as far removed from one another as Charles Fiterman, the former communist minister and co-president of Voynet's *comité de soutien*, Alain Minc, the political commentator and Balladur supporter, and the former actress turned lover of animals, Brigitte Bardot, who had supported Chirac in the first round.

Jospin's second-round campaign built upon the themes

of the first, attacking Chirac's inconsistencies not only of policy, but also of his strategy caught as it was between Balladur and Le Pen. Equally, he tapped the theme of an RPR-state, Chirac's difficulties with Europe and the inadequacies of his social policies. Throughout, Jospin stressed the differences between his and Chirac's manifestos, supporting his intention to represent himself as the true candidate of change. However, Jospin was always facing an uphill struggle to prevent Chirac from winning a comfortable victory. Whatever the apparent indecision of the electorate, the left could not mobilise a sufficient pool of voters. In the first round, the whole of the left, including the virulent anti-socialist Laguiller, polled only 40 per cent of votes. Chirac, however, without the support of Le Pen, could muster a potential electorate of over 44 per cent. With such an imbalance of support, his victory on 7 May was never truly in doubt: 'defeat was expected, in any case, inevitable'.[71]

CONCLUSION

Throughout both rounds of the campaign, the institutional logics of presidential elections only fully applied to Jospin. By contrast, Hue, Laguiller and Voynet were able to engage in first-round vote maximisation strategies. The logic of presidential elections encourages such first round populist campaigns, although such exclusionary populists are equally penalised by the majority runoff electoral system. Its bipolarisation rewards candidates, such as Jospin, who are more able to move towards the centre ground. Indeed, the institutional logics of presidential elections contributed to the apparent revival of the PS under Jospin. Like Hue, he exploited the personalisation of the campaign to distance himself from the record of the PS and the Mitterrand inheritance. However, with the reorientation of his campaign in the first round, the PS took on a more prominent role as Jospin tried to exploit its networks of local support to boost his campaign. Jospin's appeal to local PS politicians illustrates the ambiguity of the relations between parties and candidates during presidential elections. The reorientation towards attacks on Chirac signalled the need for a typical first-round campaign strategy which mobilises core party support aided by appeals for tactical voting. As required in the second round, Jospin switched to forging multiparty alliances, answering in particular the demands of the Verts. Although he received only coded support in return and even rejection from Laguiller, the institutional logics of presidential elections once again facilitated his task. However, whatever the ability of the left to deal with the institutional logics of presidential elections, it was never realistically in a position to win the election against the right. The left entered the campaign fearing a repeat of 1969, which explains the celebration of Jospin's victory at the first round. In short, there is more to winning elections than complying with institutional logics.

NOTES

1. For an overview of the evolution of the French party system, see Ysmal (1989).
2. Machin (1990), p. 34.
3. Grunberg (1993), pp. 395–9.
4. Wright (1989), pp. 215–53.
5. *Libération*, 7 November 1994.
6. *Libération*, 14 November 1994.
7. *Libération*, 9 January 1995.
8. *Libération*, 9 December 1994 and 12 December 1994.
9. *Libération*, 26 January 1995.
10. *Libération*, 26 January 1995.
11. *Libération*, 26 January and 17 February 1995.
12. *Libération*, 26 January 1995.
13. Poll published by SOFRES-*Le Nouvel Observateur*, 11–13 March 1995.
14. *Libération*, 20 February 1995.
15. *Libération*, 9 January 1995.
16. *Libération*, 11 January 1995.
17, André Sainjon, *Le Monde*, 5–6 March 1995.
18. *Libération*, 4–5 March 1995, p. 14; for Zuccarelli, *Libération*, 17 March 1995, p. 15.
19. *Libération*, 20 March 1995.
20. *Le Monde*, 25–26 March 1990.
21. *Libération*, 12 December 1995.
22. A poll for IFOP-*L'Express*, carried out on 9–10 November 1994 with 935 people interviewed; *Libération*, 16 November 1994.

23. *Libération*, 21 November 1995.
24. *Libération*, 31 October 1994.
25. Delors had allegedly entered into discussions with the centrists who had given no signs that they would support Delors. See *Libération*, 13 December 1994.
26. *Libération*, 31 October 1994.
27. *Libération*, 6 January 1995.
28. *Libération*, 6 February 1995.
29. *Libération*, 26 January 1995.
30. *Libération*, 18 January 1995.
31. *Libération*, 24 January 1995.
32. Poll by IFOP for *L'Express*, 19–20 January 1995, 937 people interviewed; see *Libération*, 25 January 1995.
33. See T. Ferenczi, 'Les deux cultures du socialisme français', in *Le Monde*, 2 February 1995.
34. See *Le Monde*, 5–6 February 1995 and *Libération*, 6 February 1995.
35. Poll by SOFRES-*Le Nouvel Observateur*, see *Libération*, 2 February 1995.
36. *Le Monde*, 5–6 February 1995.
37. All polls in *Libération*, 25 January 1995, 28–29 January 1995 and 2 February 1995.
38. For a summary of Voynet's manifesto, see *Libération*, 17 March 1995.
39. *Libération*, 6 March and 13 March 1995.
40. *Le Monde*, 20 April 1995.
41. *Le Monde*, 14 April 1995.
42. *Le Monde*, 18 April and 21 April 1995.
43. *Le Monde*, 18 April 1995.
44. *Le Monde*, 14 April 1995.
45. *Libération*, 3 April and 19 April 1995.
46. *Le Monde*, 20 April 1995.
47. *Le Monde*, 1 April 1995.
48. *Libération*, 14 April 1995.
49. *Libération*, 8 February 1995 and 21 February 1995. In fact, Hue had expressed his critiques of the Soviet model as far back as February 1994 (see *Libération*, 7 February 1994).
50. *Libération*, 2 February 1995.
51. *Libération*, 14 March and 21 March 1995.
52. *Libération*, 13 March 1995.
53. The meeting was that at Mont-de-Marson. See *Libération*, 29–30 April 1995.
54. *Libération*, 12 April 1995.
55. *Libération*, 6 March 1995.
56. In a television interview just after a week after his nomination, Jospin concentrated his attacks on the prime minister. Jospin appeared on *Sept sur Sept* on 13 February 1995.
57. *Libération*, 20 March 1995.
58. *Libération*, 16 March 1995.
59. *Libération*, 16 March 1995.
60. Source SOFRES.
61. This argument is developed by Serge July in *Libération*, 25 April 1995.

62. Pascal Perrineau in *Le Monde*, 25 April 1995.
63. *Le Monde*, 25 April 1995.
64. *Libération*, 25–26 February and 13 March 1995.
65. *Libération*, 11 April 1995.
66. *Libération*, 26 April 1995.
67. *Le Monde*, 28 April, 1995.
68. *Le Monde*, 26 April 1995.
69. *Libération*, 2 May 1995; *Le Monde*, 3 May 1995.
70. *Libération*, 29–30 April 1995.
71. Pierre Moscovici in *Libération*, 9 May 1995, p. 8.

6 The Issue Agenda in Perspective

Sonia Mazey

Presidential election campaigns provide observers of French politics with valuable insights into the changing nature of the policy agenda in France.[1] As Lipset and Rokkan argued, significant social cleavages and conflicts in West European societies are often manifested in the political system, where they form the basis of ideological cleavages and conflict between political parties.[2] Prominent campaign issues, public opinion polls and debates together with the programmes put forward by candidates and their parties therefore constitute important indicators of current sociopolitical problems, public concerns and competing policy agendas.

Bearing in mind this link between campaign issues and the underlying political climate, this chapter examines the central issues and debates which dominated the 1995 presidential election campaign. The purpose of this discussion is twofold. Firstly, it seeks to highlight the principal themes of this election campaign. Secondly, by placing the 1995 election campaign in a wider historical perspective, the following discussion seeks to explain how and why the issue agenda has changed in France in recent years. In particular, what do these developments illustrate about value/ideological change? In reality, election campaigns themselves are rarely influential in setting the issue agenda. Rather, like geological fault-lines, campaign agendas are largely determined by a much longer-term process of sociopolitical change and, as such, bear the hallmarks of previous conflicts and policies. As argued below, the 1995 campaign agenda was largely shaped by sociopolitical and economic developments during the 1980s and early 1990s. The response of candidates to this agenda highlights the degree to which the nature of the campaign debate was shaped by ongoing 'structural' problems, prevailing policy fashions, political events/ideology

123

and the increasing Europeanisation of French domestic policies.

The discussion is divided into two parts. The first part introduces the conceptual framework drawn from literature on public policy and agenda-setting which underpins the following analysis of the changing French political/issue agenda. Using this framework, the second part seeks to explain the central issues in the 1995 presidential election campaign agenda by reference to the changes which have taken place in France since 1981. No attempt is made to address all issues raised during the campaign. Rather, the focus is upon three key issues, namely socioeconomic policy, race and immigration, and Europe.

THE DYNAMICS OF POLITICAL CHANGE IN FRANCE: AN EXPLANATORY FRAMEWORK

As highlighted below, there is no single dynamic which explains the changing nature of the French political agenda as reflected in presidential campaigns. Broadly speaking, there exist two categories of actors involved in the determination of the campaign agenda: endogenous agenda-setters (parties and candidates involved in the election) and exogenous agenda-setters (perceived problems and actors who indirectly influence the campaign agenda). First, all election campaigns provide political parties and candidates with important opportunities to set the policy agenda or shift it in a preferred direction. However, as Robert Elgie in Chapter 3 explains, the institutional logic of the majority runoff presidential electoral system is particularly important in this respect. Small parties and single-issue candidates stand in the first ballot not as serious presidential candidates but as 'policy entrepreneurs',[3] hoping to push their issue to the forefront of the national political agenda. For serious candidates, however, the election is a more complex 'nested game',[4] involving not just one but two elections. In consequence, major candidates can rarely afford to ignore the issues raised by so-called 'protest' candidates since both their candidacy and ultimate success in the second ballot may depend upon the transfer of votes from supporters of minor candidates. At the same time, however, leading candidates need, from the outset of the campaign, to build a broad-based coalition capable of defeating their opponent in the runoff ballot. In short, all electoral constituencies and lobbies must be courted.

The institutional logic of the presidential election, thus, has important implications for this analysis of the 1995 campaign agenda. Firstly, it provides minor parties with an important window of opportunity to set the campaign agenda. Secondly, it forces leading candidates to engage in two inter-related games: to respond effectively to issues raised by minor candidates; and to devise a winning campaign strategy/manifesto for the decisive runoff ballot, where the binary nature of the contest tends to produce a left versus right challenge. This task necessarily involves a rational calculation on the part of the leading candidates as to the likely nature of the opposition in the second ballot. In the 1995 presidential election campaign, for instance, Chirac's promotion of 'social Gaullism' as a campaign issue had much to do with his (in the event mistaken) belief that his opponent would be the conservative Balladur rather than the socialist Jospin. In this context, Chirac would have been the better placed of the two Gaullist party candidates to attract centrist/left-wing votes.

As rational actors, all presidential candidates attempt to set and manipulate the campaign agenda both by promoting certain issues in an attempt to maximise their voter appeal and/or to embarrass their opponents and by remaining silent on other issues which damage their own image and/or benefit that of their opponents. In the 1995 presidential campaign, for instance, both Balladur and Chirac took great pains to stress their commitment to improving the political representation of women. The somewhat surprising emergence of women and politics as a campaign issue was not unrelated to the electoral significance of female voters. However, election campaigns do not take place in a political vacuum. To paraphrase Marx, men may make their own history, but not in circumstances of their own choosing. As Kingdon has argued, public policy-makers are constrained by and forced to respond to three 'process streams flowing through the [political] system – streams of problems, policies and politics', which together play a major role in shaping the political agenda and range of politically feasible policy options.[5] Each of these three processes – problem recognition, generation of policy proposals and political events – can serve as an impetus (promoting items to higher agenda prominence) or as a constraint (preventing issues from rising on the agenda).

This analysis of agenda setting and public policy-making in the United States is pertinent to this discussion of the changing nature of the French issue agenda. Firstly, it suggests that campaign agendas are influenced by 'the inexorable march of problems pressing in on the system'.[6] Thus, in the 1995 campaign, all candidates were obliged to address the pressing 'problems' of unemployment, immigration, social exclusion and European policy. In contrast, the environment failed to become a high-profile campaign issue, despite the strong performance of the ecologist parties in the 1992 regional elections and Voynet's energetic presidential campaign. In part, this reflects the degree to which mainstream parties (notably the socialists) have stolen the ecologists' clothing in recent years. However, the relatively low importance attached to environmental issues during the campaign also reflects the primacy in the voters' minds of the socioeconomic cleavage in French presidential (and parliamentary) elections. Moreover, as indicated earlier, the majoritarian logic of the electoral system used to elect the French president reinforces this tendency for a left–right campaign. In this context, it proved difficult for the ecologist candidate to push the environment up the issue agenda.

Secondly, the *nature* of the campaign debate – the way in which issues and problems are defined and the parameters of policy solutions proposed – was in 1995, as in 1981 and 1988, to some extent shaped by 'policy streams' – a set of a few prominent policy alternatives based upon the recommendations of specialist policy communities and prevailing intellectual fashion. Other public policy analysts have also stressed the important role played by knowledge in the policy agenda-setting process.[7] 'Epistemic communities', defined by Haas as a 'network of professionals with recognised expertise and competence in a particular domain and an authoritative claim to policy-relevant knowledge within that domain or issue-area'[8] can, at times of policy uncertainty, be influential in providing policy paradigms and in diffusing specialist knowledge and ideas among policy-makers and political institutions. The effect of this process is the creation of new policy orthodoxies and path dependencies in the generation of policy alternatives. The relevance of this material to this particular discussion is obvious. In formulating their campaign manifestos, presidential candidates are undoubtedly influenced by the ideas of epistemic communities, transmitted to them via policy advisers, image consultants and party aides. Moreover, over time, once favoured policy options may be displaced following the generation of new orthodoxies (e.g. the replacement of Keynesianism and public ownership by monetarism and the market as the basis of French economic policy during the 1980s). More generally, in France as elsewhere in Europe, intellectual assumptions regarding the capacity of elected governments to solve problems such as unemployment have been seriously challenged in recent years. This shift was reflected, for example, in the rather modest proposals put forward by the leading candidates in 1995 to reduce unemployment levels.

Finally, the French policy agenda is influenced by the ebb and flow of the 'political stream' – political events such as elections, interest group activity, ideological conflict and 'swings in the national mood'.[9] Political changes such as the decline of French communism, the internal politics of the Socialist party, recent tensions in the Franco-German alliance,[10] industrial disputes, economic recession and political corruption scandals were independent variables influencing the 1995 presidential election campaign agenda and the 'tone' of the political discourse surrounding the election. Sabatier has also argued that 'advocacy coalitions' based upon shared normative values play an important role in bringing about policy change.[11] Whereas epistemic communities are based upon knowledge, advocacy coalitions are shared together by shared belief systems. As Radaelli observes, the advocacy coalition approach to understanding policy dynamics provides an important link between policy and politics since 'there is an implicit model of adversarial democracy – and it explains policy change as the result of the confrontation between different coalitions'.[12] In the context of the French political agenda, the construction and mobilisation during the 1980s of an anti-immigrant coalition has been influential in bringing about changes in nationality and immigration laws. In a similar vein, the emergence of an anti-Maastricht coalition within the French political elite has begun to challenge the long-standing assumptions of French European policy, a development reflected in the reluctance of the major candidates to debate this issue during the 1995 campaign.

Thus, a comprehensive explanation of the dynamics of political change in France needs to take account of the complex interrelationship in recent years between policy problems, changing policy fashions and the policy-learning process, and the wider political context of the policy-making process. Presidential election campaigns provide useful 'windows' through which to view this process. The campaign issue agenda, the candidates' election programmes and the nature of the campaign debates (or non-debates) highlight the interaction between changes in the underlying socio-political culture and the policy agenda.

THE 1995 PRESIDENTIAL ELECTION CAMPAIGN AGENDA IN CONTEXT

The picture of the French issue agenda which emerges from recent presidential election campaigns is (predictably) one of continuity and change. Issues such as macro-economic policy, the problem of unemployment and the escalating cost of welfare provision are hardy perennials which typically feature prominently. The 1995 presidential contest proved to be no exception to this rule. Unemployment was generally regarded by candidates and voters alike to be the priority issue (see Chapter 7), closely followed by social exclusion, personal income, immigration and social protection. However, as indicated below, the *nature* of the debate surrounding these 'core' socioeconomic issues had changed considerably since 1981. In particular, the sharp left–right ideological cleavage which then characterised French politics has diminished following the 'centering'[13] of the three major (i.e. presidential) political parties, namely the PS, RPR and UDF, since the late 1980s. Although the left–right divide in French politics remains electorally important, debate between the major parties on socioeconomic issues has become less polarised and policy agendas have converged.

Paradoxically, however, the gradual *recentrage* of the three major French parties has been accompanied by a declining political consensus in France, a development reflected in the emergence since the mid-1980s of new political issues and increasing fragmentation of the party system. As several observers have noted, France now has a hybrid party system.[14] Minor parties which have no chance of winning control of the presidency have become vehicles for the representation of new populist issues in French politics. In the context of national electoral politics, such parties, along with pressure groups like the anti-racist SOS-Racisme, have become increasingly vocal agenda-setters, ensuring that issues such as the environment, immigration and, more recently, European integration are debated during election campaigns. Electorally and programatically, left-wing parties and their presidential candidates, especially the PS, have been affected by the growing support for the various ecology parties and other 'new' social movements promoting the rights of women, immigrants and the homeless. Meanwhile the republican right-wing parties and presidential contenders have, since the mid-1980s, been challenged by the persistent success of the extreme right-wing, anti-immigrant FN. Immigration featured less prominently in the early stages of the 1995 presidential campaign than in the 1988 contest, but quickly moved up the issue agenda after the first ballot as attention focused upon how Le Pen's supporters would vote in the second ballot.

A more recent cleavage which has emerged in the 1990s concerns attitudes towards further European integration. For most of the Fifth Republic there has been a prevailing consensus (or tacit acquiescence) among French voters in favour of European integration – a consensus which, with the exception of the Communist Party and the FN, was broadly shared by all French parties.[15] This consensus no longer exists. The 1992 referendum result on the Maastricht Treaty (supported by just 51.05 per cent of those who voted) revealed just how deeply the issue of Europe now divides the French electorate. De Villiers' anti-European integration candidacy reflected this divide in 1995. Within the mainstream right-wing parties also, European integration has become a contentious subject and a source of internal disunity. Although the three leading presidential candidates (Balladur, Chirac and Jospin) all expressed their support for European integration during the campaign, they were keen to stress the need for realism in this area and were noticeably reluctant to debate the issue.

Socioeconomic issues in context: from reform to realism

Economic issues, broadly defined, dominated the 1995 presidential campaign debate. Within this category, the pivotal issue was unemployment, cited by 29 per cent of the voters as the single most important issue in determining how they voted in the first ballot[16] (see Chapter 7). Inevitably, this issue was closely linked during the campaign to the related policy problems of social exclusion and the escalating cost of welfare provision. These policy problems were neither new nor peculiarly French. However, the scale of these problems in terms of the numbers of people unemployed and/or homeless and the indebtedness of the social security budget was, by 1995, massive when compared to the French situation in 1981 or to the situation in other EU countries such as Germany. By December 1994, 3.3 million people (12.6 per cent of the workforce) were unemployed, giving France the highest unemployment rate of the G7 countries.[17] Moreover, the bulk of French unemployment is structural and long-term in nature: in 1994 nearly 1.5 million people had been unemployed for more than a year.[18] The impact of lengthening dole queues upon the budget deficit (which soared to a record of 410 billion francs in 1993) and the social security budget deficit merely underlined the seriousness of the economic situation. An annual economic growth rate of 2.9 per cent in the third quarter of 1994 seemed an unlikely cure, on its own, for French unemployment. Yet, notwithstanding the pressing nature of these problems, the parameters of the 1995 campaign debate on socioeconomic policy were much narrower than they had been in 1981 or 1988.

Whereas at the 1981 presidential election voters had been presented with a clear choice (budget austerity, international competition and counter-inflationary policies versus state intervention, social reform and protectionism), at the 1995 election there were few differences between the leading candidates' socioeconomic policy proposals. In part, this policy convergence reflects the apparent failure of more radical economic strategies (Keynesian and monetarist) pursued by successive governments during the 1980s and 1990s to resolve these problems. Ideological and political change – the decline of socialism and increasing support for market-based economics – were also important factors in the emergence of a new attitude among policy-makers in France (as elsewhere in Europe) towards state–economy relations. However, a major factor influencing the 1995 presidential campaign debate on economic policy was the increasingly problematic encroachment since the late 1980s of the EU into domestic policy-making.[19] In particular, completion of the Internal Market and Economic and Monetary Union (EMU) have significantly reduced the range of feasible economic policy strategies available to parties and presidential candidates. For example, state subsidies and nationalisation (key features of French macro-economic policy during the Fifth Republic) run counter to EU competition policy. Similarly, the declared commitment of leading candidates in the 1995 contest to meeting the EMU convergence criteria effectively committed them to pursuing a *franc fort* monetary policy and reining in public expenditure.

A retrospective glance at the changing nature of the economic policy debate in France since 1981 is essential to understanding the significance of this 'core' issue during the 1995 campaign. In particular, this historical analysis highlights the inexorable march of problems pressing in upon successive governments since 1981, the impact of new 'policy streams' upon economic policy during this period and voters' increasing disillusionment with mainstream parties. The central point to emerge from this overview of the economic policy agenda is the degree to which elected governments in France (as elsewhere in Europe) have in recent years become increasingly hemmed in with regard to socioeconomic policy options. Economic recession, financial orthodoxy and European integration have everywhere narrowed the range of feasible policy options available to governments. The increasingly apparent failure of successive governments since 1981 to solve French economic problems prompted a gradual build-up of social and political frustration. These tensions were clearly exposed during the 1995 campaign in the proliferation of protest parties and movements and in the widespread public disillusionment with mainstream candidates.

Unemployment levels in France began to increase sharply in the early 1970s, rising from 400 000 in 1973 to 1.4 million in 1980. When the socialists came to power in 1981, 2 million people (7 per cent of the workforce) were unemployed, the annual inflation rate was 11.1 per cent and the balance of payments deficit was 4.7 billion dollars.[20] High and rising unemployment throughout the 1970s was a central issue in the 1981 presidential election campaign and a major factor in the unpopularity of the outgoing regime. The salience of these issues and of the left–right cleavage sin French politics at this time was reflected in the polarised nature of the 1981 campaign debate on the economy. Mitterrand's personal manifesto, his *110 Propositions pour la France*, and the PS's own *Projet socialiste* offered voters a radical alternative to the budgetary austerity and counter-inflationary policies which had been pursued by the Barre government during the 1970s.

Once elected, Mauroy's socialist government sought to bring down unemployment, reduce social inequalities and extend welfare provision by means of an expansionary fiscal policy, nationalisation and increased public expenditure. In 1981, a variety of innovative schemes were introduced to combat employment including the creation of public sector jobs, early retirement schemes, a reduction in the length of the working week from 40 to 39 hours and youth training schemes. Welfare payments and the minimum wage (SMIC) were increased and all privately owned banks were nationalised along with leading industrial groups. These measures, taken together, increased public spending in 1981 by 28 per cent to a level of 788 billion francs. They were to be paid for by higher taxes on high earners and corporations and by allowing the public sector deficit to double to 2.6 per cent of GDP. It was hoped, moreover, that the above initiatives would give a much-needed boost to economic growth rates, thereby creating a virtuous circle of expanding tax revenues and diminishing unemployment and welfare costs. The impact of the French socialist experiment is well documented and no attempt will be made here to reproduce this material.[21] Suffice to say that the experiment was short-lived, increasingly unpopular and, economically speaking, unsuccessful. By October 1981, the government was faced with unemployment edging towards 2 million, inflation rising above 15 per cent, interest rates of 16 per cent, a budget deficit of 2.9 per cent of GDP and a widening balance of payments deficit.[22] Currency devaluation and a policy of *rigueur*, introduced in the summer of 1982, failed to resolve the crisis. In March 1983, Mitterrand abandoned his 1981 pledge to keep unemployment below 2 million, the franc was devalued for the third time since the socialists came to power and a major deflationary austerity programme was introduced.

Many factors contributed to the failure of the socialists' economic strategy. However, one of the most important was the constraints imposed upon the French reflationary strategy by EC membership and the prevalence of deflationary economic strategies among France's trading partners. The French government was swimming against the economic and intellectual tide. Moreover, it had proved impossible for the government to restrict EC imports into France, while French membership of the EMS was incompatible with a weak currency and high inflation levels. By 1983 it was clear that if France wished to remain within the EC, then French firms would have to be made competitive, the economy would have to be deflated and the budget deficit would have to be reduced. The abandonment of the socialists' reflationary economic strategy thus marked an important turning point in French politics and the policy debate on the economy. First, it represented a clear choice on Mitterrand's part in favour of Europe; henceforth French economic policy would have to take account of EC policies. Secondly, this policy change heralded the emergence of a new ideological context for the political debate on the French economy. The 'policy stream' which had dominated left-wing thinking on the economy since the early 1970s (Keynesianism and protectionism) rapidly waned. As the French economist, Michel Pébereau, put it: 'The lesson was very hard, but it was well understood. No important [French] political leader still believes that international competition is a myth fabricated to justify hardline salary policies, nor that a policy of sweet insouciance towards inflation can in the long run promote growth and full employment.'[23] Thereafter, the Mitterrand administration and the PS steadily moved towards a more market-based economic policy. Thus, it was a socialist government which between 1984 and 1986 relaxed controls over nationalised industries so that they could lay off workers and become more competitive, cut state subsidies, held down public sector wages, reduced corporate taxes, began to deregulate private capital markets and embarked upon the painful process of industrial restructuring and rationalisation.[24] These measures were presented as the only sensible option by a socialist government which now talked in terms of the 'mixed economy' and viewed high unemployment as a necessary evil.

The right-wing coalition elected in 1986 extended and intensified these measures. Influenced by the diffusion of 'new right' ideas from Britain and the US, the Chirac administration adopted a strident market rhetoric which it sought to implement. Inspired by Margaret Thatcher, the French government set about rolling back the frontiers of the state. Between 1986 and 1988 priority was given to reducing inflation rather than unemployment. The budget deficit was reduced and emphasis was placed upon tax cuts rather than public spending measures. Price and rent controls were lifted and regulations limiting lay-offs were repealed in an attempt to free the housing and labour markets. The centrepiece of the Chirac government's 'new economic programme' was, however, its plan to privatise over a five-year period 65 state-owned companies and banks employing 800 000 people. Although the programme was halted by the global stock exchange crash of October 1987, the government managed to sell off eight major corporate groups. Finally, the Chirac government pursued the programme of financial deregulation initiated by the socialists, increasing the capacity of banks to offer a range of financial services and relaxing international exchange controls.

In part, the above measures reflected the new-found enthusiasm of the RPR (and elements of the UDF) for the market. However, as Hall argues, the fact that many of these policies were continued after 1988, when President Mitterrand and a socialist government were re-elected, suggests that there were also deeper trends at work pushing French economic policy in the direction of neo-liberalism.[25] By the late 1980s, there seemed little prospect of reversing the trend: during the 1988 presidential election campaign, Mitterrand promised to a 'ni-ni' policy – no more privatisations and no more nationalisations. As Tiersky observes, Mitterrand's 'neither-nor' formula 'ushered in or perhaps merely recognized the "postnationalization" era in French politics, in which privatization is not, *ipso facto*, a right-wing proposal nor nationalization, *ipso facto*, a left-wing proposal'.[26] Although the pace of privatisation increased again after the return to power in 1993 of Balladur's right-wing coalition government, the policy did not seem to be motivated by a conservative desire for revenge. Nor was there during the 1995 election campaign any call from Jospin for a renationalisation programme. In other respects also the period 1988–95 confirmed the emergence of a new consensus in France on economic policy. For example, successive governments – of left and right – sought to cut public expenditure, to maintain low inflation rates and to reduce the burden of taxes and social insurance on French firms. The adjustment of the French economy to the Internal Market and international competition has, however, been a painful process associated in voters' minds with rising unemployment and high interest rates. The pace of change has, therefore, been uneven. Witness, for instance, the government's decision in October 1993 to shelve plans to make the ailing state-owned Air France and Air Inter companies axe thousands of jobs following industrial action by their employees.

Indeed, despite recent privatisations, the French public sector remains one of the largest in Western Europe. This is not simply a legacy of the French socialist experiment. It is also a throwback to the Gaullist and Giscardian industrial policy of 'national champions' and to the French *étatiste* economic policy style which is also characterised by a large public administration. Since the mid-1980s, the financial burden of the French public sector – invariably portrayed as inefficient and bloated – has become an important and increasingly salient political issue, not least because of EU pressure upon the government to reduce state subsidies to French firms. As indicated above, government attempts to rationalise the public sector by means of privatisation and deregulation have typically been opposed by workers. Moreover, trade unions, though weak generally in France, are more strongly organised within the public sector and have become increasingly militant in recent years in defence of their salaries. This fact, together with the generous welfare and pension provisions secured by public sector workers in the 1970s, has created important labour-market rigidities in France. This problem has been further exacerbated by the minimum legal wage and steep increases in employers' social security charges (triggered by rising unemployment). As governments finally sought to address these structural economic difficulties, the resultant sociopolitical tensions became an increasingly prominent political issue. Thus, by the 1995 presidential election, the maintenance of jobs, workers' social rights and public sector salaries were salient campaign issues for both candidates and voters.

French government policies since the mid-1980s have undoubtedly brought gains such as greater economic competitiveness, low inflation (2–3 per cent) and an increasingly solid currency. The disaster is unemployment. As indicated above, the socialists' Keynesian strategy failed to reduce unemployment between 1981 and 1983. Since then, the priority given to reducing inflation and to defending the French franc – the so-called '*franc fort*' policy – have further contributed to rising unemployment. Successive governments have tried to lower unemployment by means of job training schemes, government subsidised apprenticeships and tax reductions to businesses hiring young people. The impact of these initiatives has, however, been minimal. Significantly, though, unemployment was scarcely debated by the major candidates during the 1988 presidential election campaign, even though opinion polls indicated that it was a major concern of voters. In part, this reflected the higher political salience at that time of race and immigration issues (see below). However, it also reflected an acknowledgement on the part of the major candidates of the intractability of the problem and a recognition that none had a convincing policy alternative. Moreover, recommendations from the august epistemic communities such as the OECD for reducing French unemployment regularly prescribe tax cuts for business investment, more labour market flexibility and additional job training and apprenticeships. In short, more of the same orthodox measures which have come to dominate public policy on this issue in most European countries.[27] Since 1988, completion of the Internal Market and low economic growth have pushed unemployment to the top of the French political agenda again. The high unemployment rates of the past decade have also had increasingly visible social and political costs, manifested in widening disparities between the poor and the well-off, homelessness (especially among young people), periodic outbursts of urban rioting and increased support for the FN which attributes unemployment to the presence of immigrants.

Given the developments outlined above, it was hardly surprising that unemployment – and the related issues of social inequality and social protection – emerged in 1995 as the pivotal campaign issue. The issue was also pushed up the campaign agenda by candidates (notably by Chirac who presented himself as the champion of the homeless and the unemployed) and by the mobilisation during the campaign of the *exclus* themselves who, with Chirac's blessing, occupied empty buildings in the rue du Dragon in Paris. Yet, although each of the three main candidates sought to distinguish their programme from those of his rivals, there was, in fact, little to distinguish them in terms of specific policy commitments. Nor were the policies they proposed particularly innovative or radical. On the right, for instance, both of the two Gaullist contenders put unemployment at the top of their list of priorities, both called for cuts in employers' social security contributions, both advocated special measures to help the long-term unemployed and both promised to reduce the public sector deficit, then standing at 5.2 per cent of GDP. Where Chirac differed from Balladur was in his (somewhat contradictory) call for wages to be increased to boost demand and growth and in his promise to increase spending on welfare and education, while nevertheless promising to reduce income tax. Both said they would stick to the *franc fort* policy and both said they were in favour of a single currency, although Chirac was noticeably more luke-warm on the issue.

Chirac's attempt to present himself as a reformist candi-date, capable of transcending the left–right divide, was un-dermined by Jospin's manifesto. This called for a reduction in the working week from 39 to 37 hours (with the crucial question of pay left to employers and workers to negotiate), the abolition of homelessness within two years and the im-position of taxes on speculative capital movements and pol-luting industries. Yet, although these proposals appeared left-wing in the context of the 1995 campaign, they were a far cry for Mitterrand's *110 Propositions* in 1981. More-over, Jospin also accepted the need for the public deficit to be cut to defend the franc, ruled out a public spending boom, accepted the need to 'contain' increases in health spending and promised not to renationalise privatised firms. He too affirmed his commitment to a single currency, although he expressed doubts as to whether 1997 was a suitable date.[28]

This policy convergence between the major presidential candidates can only be explained by reference to the seis-mic shifts which have occurred within the French economy since 1981. Since then, successive governments have been caught in a pincer-like movement of structural weaknesses and Europeanisation on the one hand and a transnational conventional wisdom with regard to economic policy-mak-ing on the other. Together these pressures have steadily eroded French particularism, bringing France into line with other West European economies.[29] The 1995 presidential election debates merely confirmed the degree to which mainstream parties are now reconciled to this fact. How-ever, voters have become increasingly frustrated and disillu-sioned with the failure of these parties to solve problems such as unemployment. This disillusionment was clearly il-lustrated in the first round of the election where some 40 per cent of voters supported populist candidates such as de Villiers (anti-Maastricht), Laguiller (anti-capitalist) and Le Pen (anti-immigrant), all of whom promised more radical (albeit simplistic) solutions to these problems.

Race and immigration issues: the legitimisation of the unacceptable

The emergence during the 1980s of race and immigration as a major cleavage in French politics cannot be dissociated from the meteoric rise in the electoral fortunes of the FN. Of course, this merely begs the question as to why this populist, anti-immigrant party should have flourished during the 1980s. After all, the FN had been established by Jean-Marie Le Pen back in 1972 and as late as 1981 he had been unable to obtain the 500 sponsors necessary to stand as a candidate in the presidential election. Yet, just three years later, the FN polled 11.1 per cent of the vote in the European election. Two years later, in the legislative election, the FN polled 9.9 per cent and gained 35 National Assembly seats (due to the use of proportional representation). In the first round of the 1988 presidential election Le Pen polled 14.4 per cent of the vote and in the legislative elections that year his party once again obtained 9.9 per cent of the vote, although this time it only gained one seat (due to the use of the majority runoff system). The FN polled 13.9 per cent (and gained 239 seats) in the 1992 regional elections and 12.7 per cent (and no seats) in the 1993 legislative election. Finally, Le Pen gained 15.0 per cent of the first ballot vote in the 1995 presidential election. This success has been achieved on the basis of a populist programme which links social problems, such as unemployment, crime and poverty, to immigration and (to a lesser extent) excessive state interference, a corrupt political elite and 'Euroglobalism'. During the 1995 campaign Le Pen proposed to repatriate three million immigrants over his seven-year presidency, to exclude immigrants from welfare benefit, to give preference to French nationals seeking jobs and public housing, to reintroduce the death penalty and to reverse French ratification of both the Maastricht Treaty and the Schengen Agreement.

The rapid rise of immigration to the top of the French issue agenda during the 1980s provides an excellent example of the agenda impact of the interaction of 'problems', 'policy streams' and 'political streams'. The FN's success is in large part attributable to the political developments and difficult socioeconomic conditions which characterised France during the 1980s. The coming to power in 1981 of a social-ist government, the weakness of the established right-wing opposition parties, rising unemployment, European integra-tion and the increasing assertiveness during the 1980s of second-generation children of immigrants (*les beurs*) together constituted fertile conditions for the cultivation of anti-immigrant sentiment. This situation was skilfully exploited by the FN which offered populist solutions to intractable economic and social problems. Moreover, the FN actively cultivated an influential advocacy coalition by establishing close links within organisations such as trade unions, the Catholic church and youth clubs. FN policies were also dif-fused through a range of pamphlets from the Institut de Formation Nationale, the FN's think-tank, which was launched in 1989, and through publications such as *National Hebdo, Présent, Le Choc du Mois* and *Minute*. Thus, the FN was not merely a political party, it was also a social movement and core of an advocacy coalition. As such, it became an influ-ential agenda-setter during the 1980s, placing issues such as immigration, public morality and *sécurité* (law and order) onto the French political agenda. In this task, the FN was assisted by political events such as frequent elections, which provided the party with valuable publicity, electoral success and political legitimacy, and the demise of the PCF, which enabled the FN to assume the mantle of a right-wing coun-ter-revolutionary force.[30] The increased pace of European integration after 1986 constituted an important exogenous agenda-setter, which further benefited the FN by pushing to the forefront of the French political agenda sensitive is-sues such as national sovereignty, citizenship, asylum policy and the abolition of border controls.

Clearly, the success of the FN cannot be explained simply in terms of anti-socialism. However, the failure of socialist economic policies – notably the failure to reduce unemploy-ment and the introduction of higher taxes and interest rates – was undoubtedly important in heightening voter suscepti-bility to the populist solutions offered by the FN. Equally significant, however, was the failure of the traditional right-wing parties to capitalise on the increasing public hostility to the left. In part, this failure was due to crippling divisions within the so-called 'republican' right during the 1980s, which were exacerbated by the inability of the RPR and UDF to agree on how to respond to the electoral challenge posed by the FN (see Chapter 4). However, surveys suggest that in the 1980s the French public became generally disaffected with the established political class. A SOFRES poll taken in 1991 confirmed that 71 per cent of French voters believed that politicians did not care what the ordinary French citizen thought and 72 per cent thought that once in power politicians quickly forgot the promises they made.[31] The FN's claim to represent the concerns of the 'ordinary' person struck an important chord in French politics. Thus, in France as elsewhere in Western Europe, the failure of established parties to respond effectively to citizens' concerns has stimulated alternative channels of political activism including interest groups, right-wing populist parties such as the FN, single-issue movements and dissidence within party ranks.[32]

The dynamics of party competition during the 1980s were also important in pushing the politics of race and immigration to the top of the French political agenda. In opposition, the RPR and UDF adopted an aggressive discourse in an attempt to narrow the ideological ground between them and the FN. In so doing, they helped to legitimise the FN's policy agenda by anchoring opposition debate around themes such as immigration, anti-communism and law and order.[33] Mitterrand's tactical manipulation of the FN, designed to debilitate and divide the traditional right-wing coalition, merely reinforced this trend. In particular, his decision to introduce proportional representation for the 1986 legislative election ensured that the FN and its agenda featured prominently in French national political debate. The presence of 35 deputies in the National Assembly between 1986 and 1988 also endowed the FN with political legitimacy. Equally, at the level of public policy the FN has been influential in setting the agenda since the mid-1980s. For example, successive governments have stressed their commitment to reducing crime, strengthening family values and stamping out illegal immigration. The 1986 Pasqua laws imposed new restrictions on the entry of foreigners into France, while the French nationality code was changed in 1993, limiting access to French citizenship for certain categories of

immigrants and making it more difficult for French born
children of foreign parents to become citizens.

As indicated above, race and immigration *per se* featured
less prominently in the 1995 campaign than they did in 1988.
Then, law and order, nationality and immigration were central
themes of Chirac's campaign. In a thinly disguised appeal
to FN sympathisers he criticised the 'abuses' of the right to
asylum in France and stressed the need to protect French
'identity', French 'values' and French 'culture'. In terms of
specific commitments he proposed to increase resources for
the police and to reform the nationality laws.[34] Meanwhile,
his principal opponent, Mitterrand, based his campaign on
an appeal for national unity and the defence of traditional
republican values. The fact that in 1995 employment re-
emerged as the dominant campaign issue does not mean,
however, that race and immigration are no longer important issues in French politics. Indeed, a recent CSA poll indicated that two out of three French people admit to having
xenophobic or racist feelings and 59 per cent think that
immigrants are a burden to the French economy.[35] The same
poll found that immigration was cited by 13 per cent of
voters as the most important factor determining their vote
in the 1995 contest. Rather, as highlighted above, the issues
raised by the FN, once regarded as shocking and politically
controversial, have been internalised and institutionalised
within the political system. The response of other parties to
the FN, both at the level of rhetoric and public policy, have
reduced somewhat the high political salience of these issues.
However, the FN has given rise to an important advocacy
coalition and together with the values it represents the party
has effectively penetrated the French political system and
French political culture.

France and Europe: an increasingly problematic relationship

Arguably, the most important new issue to appear on the
French political agenda during the period under discussion
is the debate on European integration. Historically, France
has played a leading role within the European Community
and, as Morris observes, 'much official energy is devoted to

promoting the idea of France's commitment to a "European ideal" of economic and political integration'.[36] National and European electoral campaigns throughout the 1980s suggested that with the exception of the FN and the PCF all French parties were then in favour of European integration, a sentiment which *Eurobarometer* polls indicated was shared by most French people. However, in the national referendum held in September 1992, only 51.05 per cent of those who voted supported ratification of the Maastricht Treaty. Moreover, the intense political debate which preceded the vote revealed the degree to which European integration had become a divisive issue within and between parties and within the French electorate. Briefly, parties are divided along two axes: intergovernmentalism versus political integration and deregulation versus European protectionism.[37] In the 1995 presidential election campaign, Europe was, for the first time, an important 'position issue' for candidates, though there was significantly little serious discussion about European issues. This is notwithstanding de Villiers' candidacy. All three leading candidates, with varying degrees of enthusiasm, stressed the importance of Europe and declared their commitment to maintaining the Franco-German alliance and to introducing monetary union, although in November 1994 Chirac had floated the idea of holding a referendum on EMU. The proposals put forward by minor candidates reflected the cleavages mentioned above. Le Pen, for instance, advocated the abrogation of both the Maastricht Treaty and the Schengen Agreement and the introduction of protectionist policies. Meanwhile, de Villiers opposed EMU and proposed the introduction of protectionist industrial and agricultural policies based upon the principle of Community (rather than national) preference.

There are several interrelated reasons for the shift in French party and public attitudes towards Europe since the late 1980s. At the level of political events, the pace of European integration has accelerated and the scope of European policies widened following the 1986 Single European Act and the 1992 Maastricht Treaty. In consequence, French governments have experienced a significant loss of autonomy with regard to economic, industrial, regional, social and environmental policy. The deregulatory thrust of the Internal Market has also created a more competitive and more difficult environment for French industry. Moreover, as indicated above, the French *dirigiste* model of industrial management, based largely upon public ownership and state subsidies, has been challenged by both EC competition policy and the convergence criteria agreed to in the Maastricht Treaty.[38] Thus, it has become increasingly difficult for French governments to conceal the growing contradiction between their professed commitment to further European integration and EMU on the one hand and to interventionist domestic economic and industrial policy-making on the other. Mitterrand's decision to hold a referendum on the Maastricht Treaty thus triggered a public debate within France about whether the Union should become a deregulated, free market or whether it should be interventionist and protectionist. Meanwhile, the related issues of EU enlargement and institutional reform set in motion by the Maastricht Treaty gave rise to a parallel political debate between those who favour intergovernmentalist EU decision-making structures more in line with de Gaulle's *Europe des Patries* and those who favour more supranationalist structures. An important factor in this debate is the growing concern among French policy-makers that, given the development of the EU, they are no longer able to control the EU decision-making process so effectively as in the past.[39]

The ongoing French debate over European integration has been further complicated by the collapse in 1989 of the Soviet Union and the subsequent unification of Germany. In particular, German unification has significantly altered the balance of power within the Franco-German alliance, giving rise to renewed anxieties in France about the power of a united Germany. In this context, further European integration – notably EMU and maintenance of the Franco-German alliance – appear to many French policy-makers to be the best means of controlling German economic and political power. Thus, paradoxically, changes in the geopolitical situation in Europe since the late 1980s have both weakened France's position within Europe and pushed her yet further in the direction of European integration. Yet, as Menon argues, this 'solution' is itself problematic in the context of the domestic political debate given Chancellor Kohl's commitment to political integration and Eastern European EU enlargement.[40]

Lack of space precludes a detailed analysis of the contours of the complex French debate over Europe during the 1990s. However, for the purposes of this discussion, what has been important is the fragmentation of the political consensus between and within French political parties. Briefly, in the 1994 European election the socialists defended an interventionist and supranationalist EU, the RPR-UDF coalition campaigned for deregulation and intergovernmentalist decision-making structures, while Philippe de Villiers, the communists and the FN, all favoured loose, intergovernmentalist EU structures. Whereas the communists supported greater EU funding of public investment, de Villiers and the FN both favoured protectionist policies.[41] Moreover, during the Maastricht referendum campaign several leading figures within the RPR parliamentary party together with considerable numbers of activists rallied to the anti-Maastricht, pro-national sovereignty campaign led by the senior party and government figures Philippe Séguin and Charles Pasqua. The fact that they enjoyed the support of respected elder statesmen including former prime ministers Michel Debré and Pierre Messmer and de Gaulle's Minister of Foreign Affairs, Maurice Couve de Murville gave added credibility to the anti-Maastricht campaign. In the PS, the nationalistic former minister and deputy Jean Pierre Chevènement also campaigned against the Maastricht Treaty and in 1994 finally left the PS to create his own Mouvement des Citoyens which advocated national protectionist policies in the 1994 European election (see Chapter 5). Disagreements between and within political parties over Maastricht were accompanied by the proliferation of competing advocacy coalitions on Europe as highlighted by the direct action taken by farmers during the GATT negotiations, the formation of the Chasse-Pêche-Nature-Traditions movement (which was opposed to EU policies regulating such activities) and lobbying by the French employers' association, the CNPF, in favour of EMU.

Since the mid-1980s, European integration has, thus, become an influential exogenous agenda-setter in French domestic politics. In particular, integration has progressively undermined the *étatiste* model of French economic development, bringing France more closely into line with its EU counterparts. In addition, European integration and German unification have both weakened the influence of France within the Union. These developments have prompted public disquiet and uncertainty among French politicians about the future of French European policy. Yet, given overriding French economic and political objectives, credible presidential candidates had little choice but to embrace European integration. These conflicting political pressures and uncertainties regarding the future of France's position in Europe explain the conspicuous absence of a serious discussion on Europe during the 1995 presidential election campaign.

CONCLUSION

The central purpose of the above discussion has not been to provide an exhaustive list of the policies advocated by presidential candidates standing in the 1995 presidential election, but to place the 1995 presidential election campaign agenda in a wider historical and political context. Throughout, the aim has been to explain the 1995 campaign agenda by reference to the much longer-term changes which have occurred in the French political/issue agenda since 1981. This study is based upon a conceptual framework drawn from the literature associated with the analysis of agenda-setting and public policy, which seeks to explain the dynamic between socioeconomic developments, changing political issue agendas and public policy responses. The value of this approach lies in its capacity to integrate and explore the agenda impact of the complex interaction between underlying structural problems, policy streams and political events (exogenous and endogenous).

The central point to emerge is the degree to which French governments have become constrained by the increasing weight of underlying problems (notably unemployment), prevailing policy fashion (favouring deregulation and market solutions) and exogenous political events (notably European integration). The combined impact of these pressures has been to reduce the scope for 'heroic' decision-making (see Chapter 8), a trend reflected in the increasing ideological and policy convergence between the mainstream French political parties, for example on macroeconomic policy-making and European policy. French exceptionalism has been largely eroded. The 1995 manifesto commitments and public pronouncements of the three leading presidential candidates on socioeconomic policy and Europe confirmed the degree of consensus which now exists on these core issues. This consensus reflects a tacit acknowledgement by both left and right of the constraints facing national policymakers. The perceived 'failure' of successive governments during the 1980s to solve social and economic problems has, in turn, prompted widespread public disaffection with the established French political parties and growing support for right-wing populist/protest parties, single-issue movements and dissident candidates from the major parties, who have themselves become influential agenda-setters.[42] This process of partisan dealignment and political fragmentation – mirrored in most West European countries during the 1980s – has further reduced the capacity of established political parties to control the domestic political agenda, forcing them instead to respond to issues raised by single-issue movements and protest parties. Other important exogenous influences shaping the French political agenda during the 1990s include German unification and European integration. The latter, especially, has been increasingly influential both in shaping public policy and in prompting intense debate in France over contentious issues such as national sovereignty, EMU, immigration and the 1996 Intergovernmental Conference. Thus, it was unsurprising that, like the proverbial dog which failed to bark during the night, Europe should be conspicuously absent from the 1995 presidential election debates.

NOTES

1. The author would like to thank both Jeremy Richardson and Ella Ritchie for their comments on earlier drafts of this chapter.

2. Lipset and Rokkan (1967).
3. Kingdon (1984).
4. Tsebelis (1990).
5. Kingdon (1984), p. 20.
6. Ibid., p. 17.
7. Radaelli (1995); Adler and Haas (1992).
8. Haas (1992), p. 3.
9. Kingdon (1984), p. 170.
10. Menon (1996).
11. Sabatier (1988).
12. Radaelli (1995), p. 171.
13. Tiersky (1994).
14. Machin (1993); Tiersky (1994).
15. Guyomarch, Machin and Ritchie (1996).
16. *Libération*, 25 April 1995.
17. *The Economist*, 24 December 1994.
18. *Financial Times*, 1 Februrary 1995.
19. Guyomarch, Machin and Ritchie (1996).
20. Holmes (1987), p. 34.
21. Ross, Hoffman and Malzacher (1987), Mazey and Newman (1987) and Cerny and Schain (1987).
22. Derbyshire (1990).
23. Quoted in Tiersky (1994), p. 217.
24. Hall (1990).
25. Ibid., p. 180.
26. Tiersky (1994), p. 183.
27. Tiersky (1994).
28. See *L'Election présidentielle. 23 avril et 7 mai 1995* (Paris: Le Monde, 1995).
29. Damgaard, Gehrlich and Richardson (1989).
30. Schain (1990).
31. Betz (1994), p. 54.
32. See Richardson (1995), Appleton (1995) and Lawson and Merkl (1988).
33. Hainsworth (1992).
34. Bell (1990).
35. *Libération*, 25 April 1995.
36. Morris (1994), p. 166.
37. Guyomarch, Machin and Ritchie (1996).
38. Menon (1996).
39. Ibid.
40. Ibid.
41. Gaffney (1995).
42. Appleton (1995).

7 Voting Behaviour
Alain Guyomarch

The aim of this chapter is to describe and analyse voting behaviour in the first and second ballots of the 1995 presidential election. For this purpose, two kinds of data are available. The first kind consists of very robust official election statistics[1] (see Appendix 1). These may be disaggregated by place of residence, with detailed statistics for every region, department and commune (see Appendix 3). The second kind consists of rather less robust opinion polls and, in particular, exit polls.[2] If the disadvantage of this second kind of data is that it is limited by the non-availability of disaggregated figures and the absence of a long time-series, its main advantage is that it answers questions directly relevant for reconsidering contemporary theories and models of French voting behaviour.

In the last decade, electoral analysts have attempted to synthesise the main theoretical conclusions of previous research into French voting behaviour.[3] In so doing, a widely accepted general model has emerged. This model is known as the 'demand and supply' model and has been most clearly formulated by Nonna Mayer and Pascal Perrineau.[4] Here, voting behaviour at any particular election is deemed to reflect both the long-term social characteristics of the voters (the 'demand' factors) and the immediate circumstances and conditions of the election (the 'supply' factors). Whether or not a registered voter takes part in either or both ballots, whether he or she casts a valid vote or spoils the paper, whether he or she votes for Chirac, Jospin, Balladur or whoever, the choice depends on decisions taken by the voter at the moment and in the circumstances of the election. In turn, these choices depend on how the voter perceives the options available to him or her and that perception reflects both the election campaign and the voter's socioeconomic background, identity, values and predispositions.

This chapter considers how the French voted in 1995 by examining their behaviour in terms of both 'demand' and

149

'supply'. In the first section, attention is focused on voting behaviour according to objective 'positional' information about the voters (age, sex, socioprofessional category and place of residence). In the second section, attention is focused on subjective 'positional' information about voting (religious and class identities). The third section considers voting behaviour in terms of the political predispositions of the voters, such as left-right affiliations and partisan preferences. The fourth section focuses on how the voters analysed the electoral context and the options that were available to them in 1995. In all these sections, the main concern is to determine the precise composition of the social coalitions which carried Jospin and Chirac into the second ballot and then Chirac to the Elysée Palace. In so doing, comparisons will be made between the 1995 election and previous ones.

Throughout the chapter, an attempt will be made to assess whether findings of recent electoral studies are confirmed by the 1995 results. Is locality still important in the ways which Goguel and Abélès identified?[5] Is religion still the best social indicator of voting, as Converse and Pierce, Michelat and Simon and Lewis-Beck and Skalaban asserted?[6] Do voters still position themselves easily on the left–right axis and is the two-block division of voters still as relevant in 1995 as it was in 1981 or 1988 as Platone argued?[7] Are voters' electoral options institutionally defined as Machin concluded?[8] Is the French voter becoming more rational as Habert and Lancelot believed?[9]

THE SOCIAL BASES OF VOTING

Chirac's victory in 1995 contrasts with his defeat in 1988 by his ability to build a second-ballot social coalition with a majority, or at least plurality, of support. At both the first and second ballots, voting behaviour in terms of voters' objective social characteristics was different in several respects in 1995 when compared with both 1988 and 1981. In terms of both age and sex, the main changes were the growth in support for Chirac among younger and female voters. In terms of socioprofessional origins, a marked change was the decline in workers' votes for the communist candidate and the rise in support for Le Pen and Chirac. In terms of electoral geography, shifts apparent in 1988 were confirmed in 1995 as Le Pen's strength in Alsace and the southeast was maintained. Let us examine each of these trends in more detail.

A breakdown of voting behaviour by age shows some striking changes between 1988 and 1995. At the first ballot in 1995, the most popular candidate for the 18 to 24 age group was Chirac with 25 per cent, whereas he won only 17 per cent in 1988. At that election Mitterrand won 35 per cent of the votes of this age group and Barre 19 per cent. By contrast, in 1995 Jospin won 24 per cent of their votes and Balladur only 12 per cent. Even Le Pen, with 17 per cent, beat Balladur. More important in determining the overall results were changes among the numerically important 25 to 34 age group. A major element in Mitterrand's 1988 victory was his strong appeal to these voters. He took 39 per cent of the total, three times as many as Chirac. In 1995, however, Jospin won only 23 per cent, whereas Chirac won 21 per cent and Le Pen 17 per cent. Chirac also improved on his 1988 score in the 35 to 49 category, going from 17 per cent to 19 per cent.

By contrast, when comparing the 1988 and 1995 presidential elections, Chirac lost first-ballot support in the 50 to 64 and over 65 age groups. In 1988, he won 29 per cent and 31 per cent respectively in these groups, whereas he took only 17 per cent and 18 per cent of their votes in 1995. The most popular candidate among older voters was Balladur who won 25 per cent and 36 per cent of the support in these two groups. However, his popularity here was insufficient to compensate for the low level of support that he gained among the 18 to 24 and 25 to 39 age groups (12 per cent and 16 per cent) where Chirac was at his strongest. So, if Jospin led the first-ballot poll because he won between a fifth and a quarter of the votes in virtually all age groups, Chirac came second because of his strong youth vote. The support of older voters for Balladur meant that Chirac's lead was narrow, but it did give Chirac a second-ballot reservoir of support.

At the second ballot, as in 1988, a majority of older voters chose Chirac. He scored better in the 50 to 64 age group, 57 per cent, than he did in 1988 when he scored 54 per cent. The exit polls provide conflicting evidence about the behaviour of the over 65 group. Ifop recorded a slight loss of votes for Chirac (57 per cent in 1988 to 55 per cent in 1995), while BVA indicated substantial gains (from 57 per cent to 64 per cent). However, these poll results merely reflect conflicting evidence over the extent, rather than the existence, of a substantial pro-Chirac majority among older voters. Differences between the findings of the exit polls are also marked at the other end of the age category. In the 18 to 24 category, Chirac's lead was 51 per cent according to BVA, but 55 per cent according to Ifop. In both cases, however, the results are different to those for 1988, when Chirac only won 44 per cent of the votes in this group. Divergences in poll data do not question Chirac's lead, therefore, merely its extent. By contrast, where exit poll results are strikingly similar is in the two numerically important age groups, 25 to 34 and 35 to 49. In the first, Chirac led with 52 per cent, whereas Mitterrand won the support of 65 per cent of voters in this group in 1988. In 1995, however, many of those who were in the 25 to 34 age in 1988 had now joined the 35 to 49 category and it is here that Jospin scored most highly with 52 per cent.

Differences in voting behaviour between men and women appear to be rather small and similar to those apparent in 1988. At the first ballot in 1995, Le Pen won a higher proportion of the male vote, 17 per cent, than the female vote, 13 per cent, although in 1988 the gap between the two was much bigger, 17 per cent to 10 per cent. Therefore, his overall increase in support mainly reflected increased popularity among women. The breakdown in age groups of female votes (from the BVA poll) shows that the greatest increases in his support were in the 25 to 34 and the 35 to 49 age groups where he won 16 per cent and 13 per cent respectively. At the other end of the political spectrum, Hue won 10 per cent of the male vote and 8 per cent of the female vote. The latter score is an appreciable increase from 1988 when the communist candidate, Lajoinie, won only 5 per cent of the female vote. The biggest gain was in the 25 to 34 age group where 10 per cent of the female vote went

Table 7.1 The changing age/gender composition of the Chirac
electorate (%)

	1995	1988	1981 (Giscard)	Change 1988–95	Change 1981–95
Sex					
Men	52	46	44	+6	+8
Women	53	46	51	+7	+1
Age					
18–24	51	44	37	+7	+14
25–34	52	35	37	+17	+15
35–49	48	43	49	+5	−1
50–64	57	54	53	+3	+4
Over 65	64	57	60	+7	+4

BVA, in *L'élection présidentielle. 23 avril et 7 mai 1995* (Paris: Le Monde, 1995).

to Hue. The first ballot scores of Jospin, 22 per cent of men and 24 per cent of women, were lower than Mitterrand's 1988 scores, 31 per cent and 37 per cent respectively. Balladur, like Barre in 1988, scored slightly better among women, 21 per cent, than among men, 18 per cent, whereas Chirac won 20 per cent of the votes of both men and women. At the second ballot, Chirac won a majority of both men and women. The data in Table 7.1 allows a comparison not only with 1988 but also with 1981. It shows that Chirac's victory in 1995 represented a consolidation of established support for the centre-right candidate, be it Giscard or Chirac, from older voters as well as an increased appeal to younger voters.

Exit poll information also provides data about the changing electoral behaviour of different professional groups (see Table 7.2). The big changes in voting behaviour in 1995 were the marked decline in support for the left among both blue- and white-collar workers, the rise of support for Le Pen among the same groups and the general increase in support for the candidates of the centre-right. The relative successes of Jospin, Hue and Laguiller in 1995 cannot disguise a long-term decline in support for the left in its traditional socioprofessional heartland. Whereas in 1981 Mitterrand, Laguiller and the communist, Marchais, together took two-thirds of the votes of blue-collar workers at the

Table 7.2 Voting behaviour by socioprofessional groups (%)

	Farmer	Shop-keeper	Prof. & exec.	White collar	Blue collar	Other
First ballot						
PCF						
Hue (1995)	5	5	5	10	15	9
Lajoinie (1988)	2	2	1	7	17	7
Marchais (1981)	2	9	7	18	30	12
PS						
Jospin (1995)	13	8	26	23	21	20
Mitterrand (1988)	20	15	24	43	43	33
Mitterrand (1981)	23	14	19	29	33	25
RPR						
Chirac (1995)	29	28	24	17	15	19
Chirac (1988)	36	23	36	18	7	23
Chirac (1981)	36	29	36	18	10	16
Centre-right						
Balladur (1995)	24	27	21	15	10	32
Barre (1988)	16	23	16	15	7	18
Giscard (1981)	33	35	24	17	18	35
FN						
Le Pen (1995)	14	21	6	19	27	12
Le Pen (1988)	18	31	21	11	16	12
Second ballot						
RPR						
Chirac (1995)	77	77	59	49	43	60/42*
Chirac (1988)	71	63	58	42	26	54/38
PS						
Jospin (1995)	23	23	41	51	57	40/58
Mitterrand (1988)	29	37	42	58	74	46/62

* The first figure in the final column refers to the retired and house-wives, the second figure refers to the unemployed.

first ballot, leaving 28 per cent for Giscard and Chirac, in 1995 the three candidates of the left together won only 43 per cent. At the first ballot, the presence of two RPR candidates, Balladur and Chirac, and a former UDF candidate, de Villiers, helps to explain variations in professional support for Chirac. Nonetheless, Le Pen captured 27 per cent of the votes of blue-collar workers, 6 per cent more than

Jospin, 12 per cent more than Hue and 1 per cent more than the combined scores of Balladur and Chirac. Among white-collar workers, the decline of the left was also marked. Jospin and Hue together won a third of these votes, only 1 per cent ahead of the total for Balladur and Chirac. Le Pen was only 4 per cent behind Jospin, with 19 per cent of the support of white-collar workers. This is in stark contrast to 1988 when the gap between Mitterrand and Le Pen in this category was 32 per cent.

At the second ballot, the high level of support for Chirac from among those who had previously voted for Balladur and de Villiers meant that traditional patterns of support for the right reappeared. Support for centre-right candidates among farmers, artisans and small shopkeepers, professionals and business executives, and housewives and the retired has usually been strong. Indeed, in 1988 Chirac's shares of their votes was 71 per cent, 63 per cent, 58 per cent and 54 per cent respectively. However, in 1995 Chirac even increased his support among these groups, winning the support of 77 per cent of farmers, 77 per cent of artisans and small shopkeepers, 59 per cent of professionals and business executives and 60 per cent of the unemployed. By contrast, second-ballot support for the candidate of the left is normally strongest among blue- and white-collar workers. Mitterrand's victory in 1988 reflected the fact that he won the support of 74 per cent of blue-collar workers, 60 per cent of white-collar workers and 62 per cent of the unemployed. In 1995, Jospin also won majority support in these groups, but by greatly reduced margins, 57 per cent among blue-collar workers, 51 per cent among white-collar workers and 58 per cent among the unemployed. Paradoxically, Chirac's gain among the blue and white-collar workers contributed greatly to his victory. Among blue-collar workers, he gained 17 per cent between 1988 and 1995. If the sizes of increased scores among blue-collar workers for Le Pen at the first ballot (11 points) and Chirac at the second ballot (17 points) suggest that the former contributed to the latter, the true picture is probably more complex, since 44 per cent of Le Pen's voters abstained or spoilt their ballots at the second ballot in 1995 and 17 per cent voted for Jospin. At the first ballot, the three centre-right candidates together won 29 per cent of the blue-collar vote, whereas in 1988 Barre and Chirac gained only 14 per cent of their support. In terms of the socioprofessional origins of voters, this 15 point gain in support among blue-collar workers since 1988 appears to be the single most important contribution to Chirac's electoral victory. In 1988, he received the support of only 26 per cent of blue-collar workers, whereas in 1995 43 per cent of that group voted for him at the second ballot.

Other exit poll data appears to confirm this view. In terms of the employment status of voters, Chirac scored highest among those groups which traditionally support the candidates of the centre-right, namely the self-employed and both the retired and housewives, with 78 per cent and 60 per cent respectively at the second ballot. In both categories he improved on the combined scores of the three centre-right candidates at the first ballot, 63 per cent and 54 per cent, and his own 1988 performance, 69 per cent and 54 per cent. By contrast, Jospin's lead was the strongest among the unemployed. His second ballot score of 58 per cent was an improvement on the combined first-ballot scores of all left candidates, 41 per cent, but lower than that of Mitterrand in 1988, 62 per cent.

In terms of electoral geography, loyalty to 'local boys' was especially useful for the centre-right. Chirac's second-ballot victory reflected the first-ballot local strengths of Chirac, Balladur and de Villiers. De Villiers was strongest in his home department, the Vendée, where he led the poll with 22 per cent of the vote. Balladur led the first-ballot poll in seven departments in metropolitan France, including Haute-Savoie, his home department, where he took 24.7 per cent of the poll. However, his best results were in Mayenne and Maine-et-Loire where he won over 25 per cent of the vote and the west and the east of France generally (see Appendix 3). In general, Balladur was weakest where Chirac was strongest and vice versa. The Mayor of Paris had his strongest appeal in that city, winning 32.19 per cent of the vote at the first ballot. He also did well around his home department of the Corrèze (49.30 per cent) and in the neighbouring Cantal, Creuse and Haute-Vienne (40.98 per cent, 34.54 per cent and 28.80 per cent respectively). His lowest results were in the north-east and south. Chirac led the poll in 18 departments, although in the Alpes-Maritimes he led Le Pen by only three votes. Chirac was also runner-up in 37 departments, providing him with a solid base for the second ballot.

Although Jospin led the first ballot with 23.30 per cent of the vote and scored only 2.5 per cent less than Mitterrand in 1981, his second ballot prospects were less than promising. The major problem was that he scored relatively poorly in many of the most highly populated parts of France. Although in Paris Jospin fared only marginally less well than Mitterrand in 1981, in other highly populated departments the drop in votes for the socialist candidate was considerable: 8.2 per cent in the Moselle and Gironde, 7.5 per cent in the Vaucluse and Haut-Rhin, and over 6.5 per cent in the Alpes-Maritimes, Var, Rhône, Bas-Rhin and Seine-et-Marne. Even in traditional left-wing bastions like the Nord, his score fell 4 points when compared with 1981, while in the Haute-Garonne, Jospin's political home, he won 4.5 per cent fewer votes than Mitterrand in 1981.

A second problem for Jospin was that his own areas of relative weakness were not balanced by increases in the scores of other candidates of the left. Although Laguiller and the communist achieved better scores than they had done in 1988, Jospin needed scores comparable to the combined votes of Marchais, Laguiller, Crépeau and Bouchardeau in 1981 in order to have any chance of winning at the second ballot. The decline in the geographical base of communist voting between 1981 and 1995 illustrates the extent of the problem. Their share of the poll fell dramatically in populous urban departments where previously it had been strong. In the Bouches-du-Rhône, the fall was 13 per cent, in the neighbouring Gard 12 per cent, in Seine-Saint-Denis 12 per cent, in the Somme 11 per cent, in the Nord and Pas-de-Calais 9 per cent and in the Val-de-Marne 8 per cent. Whereas in 1981 Marchais's best score of 27.27 per cent was in the urban Seine-Saint-Denis, in 1995 Hue's top score of 15.66 per cent was in the rural Allier. Nor has the decline in votes for a socialist candidate been matched by a rise in support for the Verts. On the contrary, Voynet won 130 000 fewer votes than Waechter in 1988.

By contrast, Le Pen's support has grown slightly since 1988, although his geographical base changed little. In 1995, he

led the poll in seven departments, all of which were in the
east (Bas-Rhin, Haut-Rhin and Moselle) or the south-east
(Loire, Var, Vaucluse and Bouches-du-Rhône). He also won
over 20 per cent in three other departments. Le Pen's support was concentrated in a band of regions to the south,
east and north of the Massif Central from Perpignan to
Evreux, while his support was weakest in the west from Midi-
Pyrénées to Brittany. In some areas where Chirac was strong,
including Paris and the Limousin, Le Pen was particularly
weak and in the Corrèze Le Pen scored 4.58 per cent, his
poorest result in the whole of France.

At the second ballot, the core of Chirac's victory lay in
the 19 departments where he had a second ballot majority
in 1988. In 1995, he took over 55 per cent of the vote in all
these departments, winning over 60 per cent in eight of
them. They lie in the most populous regions of France: the
Ile-de-France, Rhône-Alpes, Provence-Alpes-Côte-d'Azur and
Alsace. Chirac also scored over 60 per cent in one department where Mitterrand had led at the 1988 second ballot,
the Corrèze. Furthermore, he won over 55 per cent of the
vote in seven other departments (Aube, Aveyron, Orne, Haut-
Rhin, Savoie, Seine-et-Marne and Vaucluse). His most important score came in the most populous region in the
country, Ile-de-France. In seven of the eight departments
here, Chirac improved on his 1988 score by over 7.5 points.
In Paris, his increase was only 5.4 points but that took him
to 60.09 per cent. In Seine-Saint-Denis, the traditional communist bastion, he did not lead, but he did improve his
1988 performance by 9.1 per cent. In the second most populous region, Rhône-Alpes, Chirac improved his score by 6
points, leading the poll in seven of the eight departments.
In Provence-Alpes-Côte-d'Azur, France's third most populous region, Chirac's increase was only 5.5 per cent, but he
led Jospin by 17 percentage points. In short, Chirac's victory reflected the fact that his support was concentrated in
the most populous areas.

In contrast, Jospin's second-ballot geographical strength
lay in traditional bastions of the left which are no longer
the most populous regions. Jospin had a majority of votes
in four regions and 26 departments. However, the combined
number of voters in the three most populous regions which

he won, the Nord-Pas-de-Calais, Midi-Pyrénées and Picardie, was less than that of the Paris region. Furthermore, in some traditional left areas, mobilisation for Chirac was considerable. In the Haute-Vienne and Seine-Saint-Denis, former communist strongholds, Jospin's scores were lower than those of Mitterrand in 1988 by 10.1 and 9.1 per cent respectively. In the Indre, Seine-Maritime, Aisne, Oise, Sarthe and Meurthe-et-Moselle, Jospin's 1995 score was down on Mitterrand's 1988 score by more than 7 points. In many parts of the south-west, however, the decline was less marked. In Languedoc-Rousillon and Midi-Pyrénées the fall was below the national average.

If the bases of Mitterrand's 1981 and 1988 social coalition had not disappeared in 1995, it had been so weakened that Jospin had no real chance of success. Jospin scored less well than Mitterrand in all areas and all social groups, but his decline was most marked among urban workers, in line with the decline of left voting strength among workers at all elections of the 1990s.

SOCIAL VALUES, IDENTITIES AND VOTING IN 1995

How does the behaviour of voters in 1995 reflect their values and the subjective perceptions of their social positions? In 1977, Michelat and Simon found that the stronger the Catholic identity of a voter, the more he or she voted for the right, while the stronger the working class identity, the more a voter cast his vote for the left.[10] Similarly, Converse and Pierce examined class status, religious attitudes and political values (summarised as 'attitudes towards de Gaulle') and found that 'religion appears to be a political factor to be reckoned with although not on a par with the Gaullist/anti-Gaullist dimension. Class status runs a poor third.'[11] Since those studies, which were essentially conducted on data from the late 1960s, five factors have changed. Religious practice has declined (only 8 per cent of the population were regular churchgoers in 1990) and the moral force of the Church has weakened appreciably.[12] At the same time, class structures have modified with the rise of the 'new middle classes', whose cultural liberalism contributed to the rise of PS support in the 1970s,[13] and class consciousness has declined mark-

edly. The fifth change is the absence of a dominant cleavage over political values to replace the Gaullism of the late
1960s. The blurring of political values brought about by the
international eclipse of marxism, the rise of the Verts and
the FN, two experiences of *cohabitation*, Mitterrand's Gaullist-
style foreign policy and the socialists' conversion to market
economics mean that opinion pollsters have not found any
'summary of values' to replace 'Gaullism' for time-series
comparisons. As recently as 1992, however, Lewis-Beck and
Skalaban concluded that 'religion and class reliably shape
preferences, with the former more important than the latter. These forces have maintained themselves across the Fifth
Republic.'[14]

Our data from 1995 indicates that some marginal changes
have taken place. The centre-right candidates at the first
ballot and Chirac at the second managed to mobilise more
effectively among practising Catholics than in 1988, but without returning to the pattern of 1981 and earlier elections.
Support among church-going Catholics was one area where
Mitterrand had built up his voting support in the 1980s. In
1988, among regularly practising Catholics, second-ballot
support for Mitterrand increased from 12 per cent in 1981
to 33 per cent. For Jospin, support in this group fell to 26
per cent in 1995. However, this decline does not suggest
that religion was a key element of anti-left mobilisation, since
the drop in poll-share among practising Catholics for the
candidate of the left in 1995 was notably smaller than his
losses among non-practising Catholics and among those with
no religious identity. Jospin gained the votes of only 41 per
cent of non-practising Catholics (who, in 1995, are far more
numerous than practising Catholics), whereas Mitterrand won
a majority in 1988 (56 per cent). Among those with no
declared religion, Jospin's share of the poll, 56 per cent,
was considerably lower than that of Mitterrand in 1988, 74
per cent. Thus, for those with a strong religious identity,
religion is still a good social indicator of voting behaviour.
The problem is that practising Catholics have almost become an endangered species, and among non-practising
Catholics and the non-religious, which is the vast majority
of the voting population, residual religious identity has much
less political salience.[15]

The definitions used for the subjective social class questions of the exit polls allowed voters to position themselves in six groups: privileged, well-off, upper-middle classes, lower-middle classes, popular classes and underprivileged. Interestingly, pollsters no longer refer to 'working' classes. At the first ballot, the most striking result was that 34 per cent of the underprivileged chose Le Pen, whereas only 17 per cent chose Jospin, 15 per cent Chirac and 13 per cent Hue. However, among members of the popular classes, the hegemony of the left, though weakened (53 per cent in total for Jospin, Hue and Voynet combined) is still evident. Nonetheless, Le Pen won 19 per cent of the votes of this group, whereas Balladur and Chirac together took only 24 per cent. The lower-middle classes split almost evenly between the three left candidates (41 per cent) and the three centre-right candidates (40 per cent) with 15 per cent for Le Pen. Not surprisingly, the three centre-right candidates together won majorities among the upper-middle classes, well-off and privileged (53 per cent, 63 per cent and 51 per cent). In these groups, Le Pen scored least well (11 per cent or less).

At the second ballot, however, Chirac's lead in all the upper three categories was substantial, 57 per cent of the privileged, 58 per cent of the upper-middle classes and 71 per cent of the well-off. In contrast, Jospin led in the lower-middle classes (51 per cent), the underprivileged (56 per cent) and the popular classes (62 per cent). Although many of Le Pen's voters abstained or spoiled their papers at the second ballot and two-thirds of his supporters who did vote chose Chirac, it is clear that a substantial number of the underprivileged and popular classes who had voted for Le Pen at the first ballot chose the candidate of the left at the second. Given the general swing to the centre-right across almost all social groups, the voting relevance of these subjective social identities of class and religion appears to have changed little since 1988.

POLITICAL IDENTITIES AND PREDISPOSITIONS

Many studies have shown that, while partisan identification is generally weak in France, the ability of voters to identify their position on a left–right scale remains strong and relevant for voting behaviour.[16] According to voter self-identifications on such a scale, the 1995 results showed one element of change since 1988 and one feature of continuity. Unlike the situation in 1988, when Mitterrand won significant support among those who described themselves as 'on the right', virtually none of those who placed themselves in this category voted for any of the candidates of the left or for Voynet in 1995. By contrast, among those placing themselves 'on the left', a minority voted for candidates of the right. Indeed, among those identifying themselves 'on the extreme left', 5 per cent voted for Le Pen and among those 'on the moderate left', 4 per cent voted for Le Pen and 4 per cent for Chirac. At the political extremes, however, the patterns of 1988 were repeated. The mobilisation of those on the extreme right for Le Pen (77 per cent) was much higher than that of those on the extreme left for Laguiller and Hue combined (63 per cent).

The most striking result, however, was the choice of candidates by those who described themselves as 'neither left nor right'. In this category, 21 per cent chose Chirac, 20 per cent Balladur and 20 per cent Le Pen. However, Jospin received only 14 per cent of their votes, a mere six points ahead of Laguiller. In simplistic terms, the results of the first ballot reflected the fact that virtually all those on the centre-right and extreme right voted for candidates of the centre-right or Le Pen, as did a considerable majority of the 'neither left nor right' group, whereas a minority of left sympathisers also supported those same candidates. The implication was that the outcome of the second ballot was a foregone conclusion.

The second-ballot exit polls indicate that there was a change between ballots, but one which was insufficiently small to alter the anticipated result. Among first-ballot centre-right voters, loyalty to the flag-bearer of the 'family' clearly overcame any bitterness engendered by the personal rivalry between Chirac and Balladur. At the second ballot, 85 per cent of Balladur's voters and 70 per cent of de Villiers' supported Chirac. On the left, voter loyalty within the 'family' was similar, since 83 per cent of Hue's voters and 61 per cent of Laguiller's opted for Jospin. So too did 57 per cent of Voynet's voters, confirming the association of ecologism with the left. By contrast, as in 1988, the FN identity remained distinct from that of the centre-right. At the second ballot, 44 per cent of Le Pen's voters either abstained or spoiled their papers and a further 17 per cent voted for Jospin. In short, this confirms that many FN voters have little sense of solidarity with the parties and candidates of the RPR-UDF coalition. Increasingly, the extreme right's supporters have an electoral identity which is distinct from those on the centre-right.

The impact of voter identification with established political parties in 1995 was demonstrated by exit poll findings about previous voting behaviour, subjective voter identification, consistency of voting behaviour between the two ballots and subjective voter ratings of the importance of partisan identification in determining candidate choice. Previously, voter loyalty to party has been strongest among FN voters, whereas for other voters the notions of coalitions or left and right blocks have been as significant as party labels. This was particularly relevant for the right since both the main candidates came from the RPR, whereas de Villiers had a cross-coalition appeal based on his anti-Maastricht campaign.

BVA indicated that 56 per cent of those who had voted for Mitterrand at the first ballot in 1988 voted for Jospin at the first ballot in 1995. Chirac's appeal to his 1988 voters was slightly lower, at 51 per cent, since 33 per cent voted for Balladur. There was a significant transfer of loyalty from those who voted for Barre in 1988 to Balladur in 1995, 65 per cent. Ifop showed that voter consistency between the 1993 legislative elections and the 1995 presidential election was highest for those who voted RPR-UDF in 1993. In 1995, 84 per cent voted for the centre-right, 38 per cent for both Balladur and Chirac and 8 per cent for de Villiers. Le Pen achieved a similar degree of voter loyalty as 80 per cent of the FN's 1993 voters chose him in 1995. Jospin and Hue achieved slightly lower levels of party loyalty, 69 per cent and 64 per cent respectively. Similar figures emerge from the BVA poll which asked voters to identify which party they 'felt close to'. In this poll, 80 per cent of FN identifiers said that they had voted for Le Pen, whereas 78 per cent of PS identifiers chose Jospin and 72 per cent of PCF identifiers voted for Hue. This poll also confirmed that Balladur was seen as Barre's spiritual descendent. His appeal among UDF sympathisers, 73 per cent, was greater than that of Chirac among RPR voters, 61 per cent.

VOTING AND VOTER PERCEPTIONS OF THE 1995 ELECTION

Voter perceptions of the options available to them in 1995 were influenced not only by the results of previous elections and the campaign but also by the number of previous elections, the types of electoral system used at those elections and the consequent competitive strategies of the parties. An element in voter perceptions of the presidential election was the state of play of political forces before the first ballot. The facts could be read in very different ways. While the presidency had been in the hands of the left since 1981, the RPR-UDF coalition had been in government and had held an overwhelming majority in the National Assembly since 1993. Furthermore, centre-right coalitions ran most regional councils and many local governments. On the one hand, therefore, the election was an opportunity for centre-right voters to end 14 years of socialist rule, to confirm preceding national and local election results and to stop the presidential constraints on governmental action resulting from the period of *cohabitation*. On the other hand, though, they also faced several problems. For example, Balladur could not argue that his government had been toothless because of presidential interventions as this would have made him appear a weak leader. Similarly, there was the threat that fratricidal conflicts, similar to the ones between Barre and Chirac in 1988 and Giscard and Chirac in 1981, would help to create a second-ballot majority for the left (see Chapter 4).

For the socialists, the situation was a chance to re-establish themselves as a credible electoral force after their disastrous performances at the 1993 legislative elections and the 1994 European elections. The depressing score of the official socialist list in 1994, a mere 14.5 per cent, both discredited Rocard as a possible socialist presidential candidate in 1995 and led to widespread anxiety that the PS might be near to collapse. In 1995, the Socialist dream scenario was a massive mobilisation around Jacques Delors to repeat Mitterrand's performance in 1988. The more realistic alternative was to find a candidate who would be able to win through to the second round and lose respectably, thereby reinstating the socialists as the alternative to the centre-right (see Chapter 5).

As Machin has shown, the creation of new sets of elections (European in 1979 and regional in 1986) and the introduction of proportional representation for these and other elections underlined the decreasing salience of majoritarianism in the Fifth Republic.[17] Until 1979, small parties were the main casualties of the coalition-building process as the institutional pressures of the majority runoff electoral system encouraged people not to 'waste' their vote on candidates from small parties (see Chapter 3). Under the new rules, small parties can now survive and even prosper and they can attempt to show their national influence by contesting the first ballots of presidential elections. In 1995, the electoral calendar placed the presidential election after the 1994 European elections and immediately before the June 1995 municipal elections (with its semi-proportional form of representation). This had the perverse effect of encouraging voters to choose 'non-presidential' candidates at the first ballot. Candidates of the main political forces were in competition to win through to the second ballot. However, candidates of the smaller political forces, or individual candidates with no organised backers, sought simply to test their own popularity, or the appeal of their ideas, without a realistic hope of success.

The voters, thus, faced several options at the first ballot (see Chapter 3). One was to express support for a candidate who had no chance of winning through to the second ballot, let alone of being elected. Another was to ensure that their preferred or their least detested candidate won through. A third option (and one which was likely to occur only in a situation like that of 1995 when the opinion polls were unclear as to who would lead the first ballot) was to support a candidate who was not seen as the ideal choice

for president, but who was a good second-ballot opponent for
their preferred candidate to beat. The final option was not to
take part at all so as to express lack of interest in, indifference
to, or dissatisfaction with the final outcome. At the second
ballot, the likelihood that this is the chosen option clearly increases as the choice of candidates is reduced to two.

Indeed, in 1995, this final option was chosen by more
people than at any other presidential election except that
of 1969. Previously, no more than 18.91 per cent of voters
abstained (see Appendix 1). At the first ballot of the 1995
election, though, 21.62 per cent of voters abstained and a
further 2.83 per cent either voted blank or spoiled their
ballot. This compares with figures of 1.31 per cent in 1981
and 1.60 per cent in 1988. At the second ballot of the 1995
election, the non-voting figures were even more significant.
Abstentionism fell slightly to 20.33 per cent (compared to
14.15 per cent in 1981 and 15.93 per cent in 1988), but the
number of spoiled papers rose to an all-time record of 5.97
per cent. In 1995, therefore, only 29.95 million of 39.98
million registered voters cast their ballot for either Chirac
or Jospin. By American standards, this would have been a
triumph of civic duty, but in France such a figure was only
exceeded at the second ballot in 1969, when 31.15 per cent
of voters abstained, reflecting wide indifference to choosing
between the centrist Alain Poher and the Gaullist Georges
Pompidou.

At the first ballot, Ifop asked voters to choose which of
the following explanations best described why they had just
chosen their candidate: 'for him to be elected president',
'for him to be present at the second ballot', 'against the
other candidates', or 'to have my ideas represented'. Not
surprisingly, supporters of Chirac, Balladur and Jospin mainly
chose the first two priorities. Among Chirac's voters, 73 per
cent wanted him to be president, while 8 per cent wished
him to be a candidate at the second ballot. For 65 per cent
of Balladur's supporters, the priority was for him to become
president, while a further 17 per cent wanted him at least
to have a second-ballot chance. Jospin's voters were slightly
less optimistic, since electing him to the presidency was the
priority for 50 per cent, while 30 per cent felt that the main
challenge was to ensure his presence at the second round.

In contrast to these functional approaches were the more symbolic priorities of voters for the other candidates. The representation of ideas was the main motivation for voters choosing de Villiers (65 per cent), Voynet (61 per cent), Hue (53 per cent), Laguiller (42 per cent) and Le Pen (37 per cent), although a strong minority of Le Pen's voters did have illusions about his presidential chances with 27 per cent of them voting for him to be to elected as president and 17 per cent for him to stand at the second ballot. For Laguiller and Voynet, many votes reflected a hostility towards the other candidates (34 per cent and 25 per cent, respectively).

The BVA estimation of how first-ballot voters or abstainers behaved at the second ballot reveals that the number of first-round voters who abstained or wasted their votes at the second round was far greater than the official statistics appear to indicate. At the second round, 34 per cent of first-ballot abstainers voted. By contrast, 31 per cent of Le Pen's voters abstained and a further 13 per cent wasted their votes. Similarly, among 20 per cent of Laguiller's and Voynet's voters abstained and almost 10 per cent spoiled their papers. The second-ballot losses from de Villiers and Hue, however, were much lower, 20 per cent and 14 per cent respectively. The loss from Balladur voters was very small, only 5 per cent. Not surprisingly, among both Chirac's and Jospin's first-round voters, second-ballot losses were insignificant.

The consequence of the low participation at the second ballot was striking. On the one hand, Chirac's margin of victory was a comfortable 1.5 million votes, or 5 percentage points more than Jospin. On the other hand, his total vote was not only less than 50 per cent of registered voters, but also less than 50 per cent of the actual number of voters who went to the polls. Therefore, for the first time since the president was directly elected by universal suffrage in 1965, the winner failed to gain more than 50 per cent of popular support and with it the special legitimacy that such a figure brings. While all his four predecessors had majority support, Chirac has only a plurality.

Does his election nonetheless represent a rational choice by many voters as the Habert-Lancelot thesis might suggest?[18]

At both ballots, Ifop asked voters to select one of four factors which had most influenced their choices: the candidates' personalities, their political origins and backgrounds, their policy platforms or 'the values they represent'. Almost half of those who replied believed that group identities and values were the crucial factors in determining their choices. However, a strong minority of voters saw themselves as voting more 'rationally'. Their choices were based on perceptions of personalities, issues and platforms. Candidates' personalities counted most for 19 per cent of voters at the first ballot and for 16 per cent at the second, while their platforms were the main attraction for 26 per cent of first-ballot voters and 23 per cent of second-ballot voters. In 1995, group identities and party loyalties remained a significant influence on voting behaviour, but these considerations alone did not determine the outcome of the election. If those with strong 'group' loyalties formed the core of voters for the main left and centre-right candidates, a minority of electors saw personalities, issues and platforms as important influences on their choices.

BVA found that perceptions of candidates' personalities at the first ballot varied considerably. For two candidates, Chirac and Balladur, 'presidential stature' was a significant attraction (38 per cent and 32 per cent respectively) and it was Chirac's most important quality. Jospin's presidential stature was rated no more highly than that of Le Pen (6 per cent each), while those of Laguiller, Hue and Voynet barely registered (2 per cent each). In contrast, the strongest appeal of Voynet, Jospin, Laguiller, Hue, Le Pen and de Villiers was the closeness of their views to those of their electors. Almost equally important for Le Pen's voters was that he represented a change (37 per cent), although the other candidates, except Jospin and Balladur, scored over 20 per cent. Balladur most inspired trust among his supporters (41 per cent), followed by Jospin (23 per cent) and de Villiers (22 per cent) with Le Pen scoring most poorly at 5 per cent.

At the second ballot, Ifop found that 'experience' was cited as an important attribute by 53 per cent of Chirac's voters, but by only 14 per cent of Jospin's voters. Similarly, Chirac's 'ability to represent France abroad' was an attraction for 30 per cent of his supporters, while among Jospin supporters only 10 per cent recognised this attribute. Chirac also beat Jospin on 'dynamism' (by 39 per cent to 29 per cent) and 'ability to make decisions' (by 26 per cent to 14 per cent), although on their respective 'abilities to get things done' Chirac and Jospin scored equally well at 26 per cent. In contrast, where Jospin clearly had an advantage was on his 'honesty' (50 per cent to 19 per cent) and 'closeness to French people' (28 per cent to 20 per cent). Jospin's problem was that few of his own voters saw him as a serious presidential contender.

Ifop also provides information about how the electorate saw the main issues and the candidates' platforms. Voters were asked to give two issues on which policy platforms had influenced their choice. The single most cited issue, unemployment, won surprisingly low scores, 29 per cent at the first ballot and 33 per cent at the second. The next four most cited issues at the first ballot were social inequalities (16 per cent), living standards (14 per cent), immigration (13 per cent) and social protection (8 per cent). At the second ballot, the results were similar, except that immigration fell to 11 per cent and education became the fourth most cited issue (9 per cent). A striking aspect of this data was the high number of those who could not or would not identify two issues which had influenced their choices of candidates, 26 per cent at the first ballot and 28 per cent at the second.

These poll findings confirm the complexity of voting behaviour. Most voters were not primarily voting on the basis of issues or personalities at this election. Even those who did often perceived candidates and their platforms in ways which were influenced by their social backgrounds and group loyalties. Many admitted that they voted to express support for a candidate on the basis of group identity, shared values or protest. Some voted in the expectation that their preferred candidate had no chance of getting through to the second ballot, let alone of being elected. If such behaviour may appear 'symbolic' in presidential terms, it is not necessarily irrational and may be 'functional' in the context of the problems associated with wider political competition.

CONCLUSIONS

Reactions to the result of the 1995 presidential election by the candidates themselves give us some indication of the difficulty of assessing the significance of the changes in voting behaviour since 1988. Chirac was obviously delighted with the result and his supporters seem to share his optimism that the social base of the centre-right coalition is still strong, despite the impact of the economic crisis and the attack from the FN. The centre-right coalition, whatever its internal dissentions over leaders and policies, remained the dominant political force in the country and increased its support among young people and in some of the more economically dynamic regions of France. Jospin and the socialists were pleased and somewhat surprised to have lost so well. The expected humiliation did not take place and the results indicated that the social coalition of the left, if battered and reduced, is still a force with potential especially in urban areas. Balladur had the consolation prize of performing creditably himself and seeing his political family win back the presidency. Le Pen succeeded in creating a third force in French politics which is hostile to the two main political blocks. Both Hue and Laguiller saw their scores as successes. Only de Villiers, Voynet and Cheminade bemoaned their failures.

At the second ballot, almost a third of first-ballot abstainers turned out to vote either to support a candidate they wanted or to vote against a candidate they disliked. In contrast, however, large numbers of those who voted for Le Pen, Laguiller and Voynet at the first ballot did not take part in the crucial choice. Hence, although for the majority of French voters the second ballot was primarily about choosing the president, for a significant minority neither candidate was sufficiently attractive or repulsive to merit a trip to the polls. Nonetheless, on the basis of the data currently available, it does not appear that the 'demand and supply' model of voting behaviour needs significant reformulation in the light of the 1995 presidential election.

NOTES

1. See *L'Election présidentielle. 23 avril et 7 mai 1995* (Paris: Le Monde, 1995), *L'Election présidentielle du 24 avril et 8 mai 1988* (Paris: Le Monde, 1988), *L'Election présidentielle du 26 avril et 10 mai 1981* (Paris: Le Monde, 1981) and *L'Election présidentielle de mai 1974* (Paris: Le Monde, 1974).
2. See BVA in *L'Election présidentielle. 23 avril et 7 mai 1995*, op. cit. and Ifop in *Libération*, 28 April and 9 May 1995. For BVA, the sample sizes were 6343 voters in 200 polling stations at the first ballot and 4798 in 159 stations at the second. For Ifop, the sample sizes were 5467 and 5661 voters respectively. All poll references in the text refer to these two sources.
3. Notably, Gaxie (1985) and CEVIPOF (1990).
4. Mayer and Perrineau (1992), pp. 72–111.
5. Goguel (1981 and 1983) and Abélès (1989).
6. Converse and Pierce (1986), Michelat and Simon (1977) and Lewis-Beck and Skalaban (1992).
7. Platone (1990).
8. Machin (1989).
9. Habert and Lancelot (1988).
10. Michelat and Simon (1977).
11. Converse and Pierce (1986), p. 178.
12. Pélassy (1995).
13. Capdevieille, Dupoirier et al. (1981).
14. Lewis-Beck and Skalaban (1992), p. 177.
15. In fact, the 1995 exit polls measure religious practice, whereas Converse and Pierce measured religious identity by asking people to locate themselves on the clerical–anticlerical dimension (1986), p. 178, and Michelat and Simon measured a broader concept of religious culture (1977).
16. Michelat in CEVIPOF (1990), pp. 71–103.
17. Machin (1989).
18. Habert and Lancelot (1988).

8 The French Presidency: The Changing Public Policy Environment
Vincent Wright and Robert Elgie

The 1995 election revealed some valuable lessons about the changing nature of the public policy role of the French presidency. This chapter will begin by exploring the traditional public policy dimensions of the presidency. It will then look at the international and domestic pressures which are reshaping the French public policy environment before turning to the nature of the impact of these pressures on the presidency. It concludes by arguing that a traditionally complex and problem-ridden presidential situation has been rendered even more complex and problematic and that this may have important systemic implications.

THE PUBLIC POLICY ROLE OF THE PRESIDENCY: THREE APPROACHES

In public policy terms there are three ways of exploring the public policy role of the presidency: by looking at the positions occupied by the presidency; by adopting a sectoral approach; and by examining the president's role in the policy cycle. Let us briefly look at each in turn.

The President and public policy – the positional approach

The range and variety of the president's positional powers mean that the institution is inextricably linked with the conduct of public policy-making.

The president as joint holder of core executive authority
The president shares with the prime minister the formal

172

leadership of the executive. On the one hand, the 1958 Constitution appears to give significant powers to the prime minister. Article 20 states that the government decides and directs the policies of the nation and that it has the administration and the armed forces at its disposal. Article 21 then goes on to say that the prime minister is in charge of the government's actions, that he is responsible for national defence and that he issues decrees which have the force of law in all areas in which the legislature is not competent to act. In these ways, the Constitution appears to skew day-to-day decision-making responsibilities clearly in the direction of the prime minister. On the other hand, though, the president is more than a mere constitutional figurehead: Article 8 indicates that the president appoints the prime minister; Article 12 gives the president the power to dissolve the National Assembly; Article 15 states that he is the commander-in-chief of the armed forces; Article 52 authorises him to negotiate and ratify treaties; Article 16 allows him to assume emergency powers during a period of national crisis (as de Gaulle did in 1961); and, finally, Article 5 gives the president an ambiguous and, hence, potentially wide-ranging power, stating that it is his responsibility to make sure that the Constitution is respected, to ensure, by his arbitration, the regular functioning of the organs of government and the continuity of the state and to protect national independence and territorial integrity. In short, the 1958 regime gives the president the constitutional wherewithal to intervene in the policy-making process. The only exception to this rule occurred during the periods of *cohabitation* (1986–88 and 1993–95) when the president was opposed by a majority in the National Assembly. As a result of Article 49, which makes the government responsible to the lower house of the legislature, *cohabitation* provided the opportunity for the prime minister to assume the leadership of the executive and to leave the president with a role in only a small number of policy areas.

The president as part of the governmental machine
The governmental machine formally comprises ministers and junior ministers as well as their private staffs (*cabinets ministériels*) and the various permanent policy coordinating

institutions which ensure the smooth flow of governmental business. Ministers and junior ministers are appointed by the president on the recommendation of the prime minister. The composition of the government is, therefore, their joint responsibility. This is important because ministers (and to a lesser degree junior ministers) have the potential to influence the policy process. They have regulatory powers to make legally binding decisions and they head ministries many of which have an extensive array of field services so ensuring the presence of the centre in the locality. Ministers have both a legal interest in the policy process, as they are personally responsible for all decisions taken in their department, and a political interest, as their careers at least partly depend upon how they perform in office. In realising their legal and political aims, each minister and junior minister is assisted by a *cabinet,* or set of special advisers. *Cabinet* members are hand picked for their loyalty and expertise. They are the minister's faithful servants and expert counsellors. They ensure that the minister's point of view is made known at all stages of the policy process. This is not to say, though, that the president and prime minister are at a comparative disadvantage. They, too, have their personal staffs (known as the *Secrétariat général de la présidence* in the case of the president), which fulfil the same functions as their ministerial equivalents. In addition, the influence of both the president and prime minister is enhanced by their proximity to the government's main policy coordinating institutions. There is a vast array of such institutions, the three most important of which are the *Secrétariat général du gouvernement* which is responsible for laws and decrees and reports to the prime minister, the *Secrétariat général de la Défense nationale* which coordinates defence policy and reports to the president, and the *Secrétariat général du Comité interministériel pour la coopération économique internationale* which is in charge of preparing and administering policy matters with a European Union tinge and often officially reports to the prime minister but, in practice, always falls within the president's orbit.

The president as a key actor in the wider state machine
The wider state machine comprises not only the core ex-

ecutive and the government, but also the administration, army, police, the public industrial and banking sector and a wide range of quasi-state bodies which run a variety of services, such as motorways. The myth of the omnipotent French state (or State) is well ingrained both at home and abroad. Justified theoretically on the basis of a belief in the primacy of the public interest over private concerns and practically in the centre's need to control a potentially rebellious periphery, the desire to create an impartial but controlling central authority has been a preoccupation of French officials for centuries. It has resulted in the formal state control of many aspects of French life and has manifested itself, for example, in the tutelage role of the prefect over local government, the use of the police and security services as instruments of (actual and supposed) counterinsurgency and the nationalisation of major economic interests, such as the Banque de France during the 1937 Popular Front government, Renault immediately following the Second World War, and then a range of multinational subsidiaries, commercial banks, financial companies, arms producers and steel firms during Mitterrand's first *septennat.* It would be wrong to suggest that such a high degree of state control led to straightforward and efficient command and control procedures. Nevertheless, it did implicate central decision-makers (foremost among whom after 1958 was the president) in many of the country's economic, social and political concerns.

The president as a mechanism in the wider decision-making process
Outside the governmental and state policy process, the wider decision-making process is structured around policy networks which include the key public and private actors involved in various sectors such as banking, industry, agriculture and education or its subsectors (university, secondary, primary and nursery education).[1] In this wider process, the role of banks, firms (public and private), professions (doctors, teachers, architects, engineers, lawyers, town planners), and charitable and voluntary associations (the so-called 'third sector') as well as employers' associations and farmers' and industrial workers' unions comes to the fore. Marginalised in the

formal, verticalised governmental and state decision-making process, some groups become critical actors in the horizontally organised and relatively closed sectoral policy networks. For example, French trade unions enjoyed a reputation in Europe for being weak, but few governments dared ignore them when issues relating to secondary education, agriculture or pensions were raised. Hence, as these interests demonstrated their concerns, either privately or often very publicly, so the president and other government and state officials were drawn into policy networks and were instrumental in both the conflict-resolution and more general policy-making process.

The president as an instrument in the governance of the polity
By 'governance' is meant that total range of rules, regulations, institutions (public and private), networks, arrangements, operating codes (written or unwritten) and myths which provide for every democratic polity the four essential and interconnected ingredients of stability, coherence, minimal steering capacity and legitimacy. The presidency, meaning both the occupant of the office and the mode of election, played an essential role in providing those ingredients. Thus, the presidential election contributed, on the one hand, to stability by providing an arena for the articulation of a wide range of grievances and demands at the first ballot and, on the other, to coherence by squeezing querulous partners into two potential government coalitions on the second ballot (see Chapter 3). It contributed to the steering capacity of the polity not only because of its bipolarising pressures, but also because it forced the two major candidates into drawing up reasonably precise programmes which later became the general guidelines of government policy. Above all, the presidential election endowed the system with legitimacy: it connected the electors with the government (no longer, as under the Fourth Republic, were governments patched together in back rooms by party bosses who were oblivious to the will of the electorate); it created a contest of extraordinary political mobilisation with high turnouts; it facilitated the expression of minority opinions; and it solved the problem of succession, which is crucial in all political systems. In short, the presidential election seemingly resolved the

inherent conflict between participation and government: it was a circus with a purpose. The structural yet highly functional ambivalence of the mode of election was reflected in the office, since the president as the *élu du peuple* was, at the same time, the representative of the entire people and, as such, above the political battle, a policy entrepreneur and a party or coalition leader.

The president and public policy – the sectoral approach

The second major approach to studying the public policy dimension of the presidency is to move from position to policy sector. What role did the president play in a particular sector? The weight of evidence suggests that the influence of the president was directly related to the extent to which the president had either constitutional responsibility or a direct personal interest, or whether an issue was politically salient.

Firstly, as indicated above, the Constitution encourages the president to pay special attention to foreign and defence policy-making. As early in the Fifth Republic's political history as 1959, the then President of the National Assembly, Jacques Chaban-Delmas, argued that these areas (as well as Algerian affairs and policy towards the now defunct French-African Community) comprised the president's 'reserved domain'. In them the president was wholly and personally responsible for policy-making. Outside them the government and, especially, the prime minister was responsible for taking policy decisions. Over time, the reserved domain expanded. It came to include economic and monetary politics and constitutional review. Nevertheless, in general the president's constitutional prerogatives meant that he was inescapably preoccupied with 'high' politics such as state craft, diplomacy and the defence of national sovereignty (including the process of European integration), while the prime minister was left to deal with 'low' politics such as how to keep the people off the streets. They also meant that the president continued to have a say in the above areas during periods of *cohabitation.*

Secondly, presidents were quick to intervene in areas in which they had a personal interest. Following the precedent for presidential intervention which was set during the de Gaulle presidency, his successors took it upon themselves to intervene when and where they personally saw fit. So, for example, Pompidou was interested in industrial development, Giscard d'Estaing set great store by social reforms such as the reforms to liberalise the abortion and divorce laws, and Mitterrand immersed himself in penal reform – one of his first acts was the abolition of the death penalty – and broadcasting and cultural matters, personally choosing the architect who designed the glass pyramid in the courtyard of the Louvre. By contrast, in areas where the president had little interest, matters were left to the prime minister, ministers and officials.

Finally, when issues became politically salient, then it was the duty of the president to step in and take charge. So, for example, the prime minister was generally more concerned with policies related to agriculture (except when the farmers were on one of their customary violent rampages), education (except when students were wrecking classrooms or the Latin Quarter) or health (except when doctors were on strike). In times of crisis, therefore, public attention naturally turned towards the president as the symbol of national unity. There was the popular expectation that the president would come to the country's rescue in its moment of greatest need.

The president and public policy – the policy cycle approach

The third major way of analysing the presidential policymaking role is by analysing the activity of the office at the various stages of the policy cycle – agenda-setting, formalisation, implementation, evaluation, legitimisation – or by studying its 'power potential' – for initiating, for facilitating, for inhibiting or for imposing a veto on particular politics.

Policy was initiated by a variety of different actors: state and public officials, private concerns, interest representatives, parliamentarians and, more rarely, political parties. In the initiation process, therefore, it was not unknown for the president to play a reactive rather than a proactive role. This is to discount, though, the role of presidential elections. The election was more than just a mechanism by which to structure party competition, it was an opportunity for candidates to construct and for voters to choose between competing *choix de société*. To this end, the elaboration of an electoral programme was an important part of the presidential equation. It was a mechanism by which to reconcile the conflicting institutional logics of populism and centrism and party and personality (see Chapter 3). The programme was a personal statement, but one which was situated within the broad thrust of party thinking. It was a statement which was designed to maximise popular appeal, but in such a way so as not alienate the waverers and the genuinely undecided. More than that, the programme formed the basis of a contract between the president and the people. However vaguely it might be defined and however many contradictions it might contain, the victorious candidate's programme naturally constituted the new government's charter of action. Prime ministers were appointed on the basis that they would implement the programme and the public was aware that in its implementation their voice had been heard. In this way, presidential elections and candidates' programmes not only played a part in the initiation of policy, but also in its subsequent legitimisation.

In terms of policy formalisation, the president was also a significant political player. There are five main stages to the French policy process.[2] At each of these stages the president's presence could be felt. The first stage is the interdepartmental reunion. This brings together ministerial, prime ministerial and presidential personal staff members as well as the formal participation of one or more members of the *Secrétariat général du gouvernement*. Here, technical and legal decisions are taken, but these are often not without their subsequent political implications. The second stage is the interdepartmental committee. This meeting brings together the same participants as before, but is usually chaired by the prime minister personally and ministers also generally attend. It represents a higher stage in the decision-making process and one in which interministerial conflicts are addressed and, with luck, resolved. The third stage is the interdepartmental council. This meeting is chaired by none other than the president himself in the presence of the prime minister, relevant ministers and the most senior ministerial, prime ministerial and presidential advisers. It is held to arbitrate between conflicting political choices or entrenched interministerial demands and only takes place when reunions and committees have failed to bring about common accord. The fourth stage is the Council of Ministers, which is chaired by the president and does little more than ratify decisions previously taken. The fifth stage is the legislative stage where the prime minister, ministers and their advisers shepherd the government bill through both houses of parliament until it becomes law. To this end, they are aided (and sometimes abetted) by majority spokespersons, parliamentary party group leaders and committee chairs. Presidential intervention in this stage is exceptional but it may occur if an additional impetus needs to be given. In all stages of the policy formalisation process, therefore, there is potential for the president to shape the course of events either directly or through instructions to his advisers.

The president's role in the implementation and evaluation of public policy was less direct. Formally, the role of policy implementation was carried out by ministers, their personal staff and the permanent officials in their department. More generally, the implementation process was overseen by the prime minister, most notably by way of officials in the *Secrétariat général du gouvernement*. To the extent that successful policy implementation was part of the presidential contract, then the president was concerned. The same was true for policy evaluation. For many years, successful policy evaluation procedures in France were comparatively underdeveloped although there were attempts to introduce rationalised budgetary procedures in the 1970s for example.[3] In general, however, in the case of both implementation and evaluation, there was a natural tendency for presidents to be overtaken by political rather than rational considerations in this respect and for these items to be relegated to the lower end of the president's political agenda.

By examining the various stages of the policy cycle it becomes possible to identify the president's 'power potential' – his capacity to initiate or, if necessary, to inhibit policy, to facilitate, or should the need arise, to veto its realisation. It also leads to the twin observations that the president was present at all stages of the policy process, but that the president was merely one political actor among many in this process. So, the president was an initiator of policy, but so too were others with their own separate agendas. The president was present in the formalisation of policy, but not to the exclusion of others who had their own interests to pursue. The president was concerned with the implementation and evaluation of policy, but it was not his main preoccupation. Finally, the president helped to legitimise the policy process, but, as the experience of *cohabitation* showed, legitimacy could be transferred to the prime minister and the government at the drop of an electoral hat.

THE PUBLIC POLICY ROLE OF THE PRESIDENCY: THE TRADITIONAL PICTURE

By combining these three approaches, it is possible to construct a highly complex yet reasonably clear and consistent picture: the president enjoyed veto powers for defence matters, but was powerless in implementing or evaluating highly technical scientific policies; he was generally absent from routinised policy-making, but present when it became politically charged; he enjoyed a potential for initiation in many domains, but his capacity for imposing an effective veto was highly contingent.

In truth, however, plotting presidential power is an intrinsically difficult exercise and not only because it was so patchy across sectors and policy stages. The complication arises from the fact that the president played another vital role as the definer of the parameters of public policy; he traced the sphere of the 'non-sayable' and the 'non-doable'. He was the guardian of that inalienable policy mix which was rooted in political consensus and cultural myth. He was the head of a state which was a self-conscious and active player. To its traditional regalian functions, such as defence of the territorial integrity of the nation, the maintenance of public order and a legal system to enforce contracts and the striking of money, the French state, along with most others in Western Europe, had a wide range of other functions. It was no neutral arbiter. It was an active *tuteur*: it instructed, guided and directed. But it did so in a way which was consistent with a minimum of social and territorial solidarity. It embodied the 'public good', sustained (albeit not very successfully) the *culte du droit* (a profound respect for the law), and defined and conferred citizenship rights which, once acquired, were constitutionally entrenched. Its enlightened aspect was also reflected in its profoundly secular nature and in its role as an economic actor. Through a peculiar and often misunderstood mixture of *dirigisme*, indicative planning, Keynesianism and protectionism, it pursued a policy of economic growth, full employment and social welfare which were seen to be integrally linked.

The state was, therefore, all encompassing. It was charged with a mission of furthering social integration and harmony as well as individual betterment. It was endowed with legitimacy and armed with the instruments of its ambitions. It was apparently omnipresent: the public administration was huge, the state industrial and banking sectors were among the biggest in Europe, especially after 1981, and the state had extensive field services in the provinces, unlike the British state. Secondly, it possessed a whole gamut of policy instruments. Finally, by the practice of *pantouflage* – the movement of public officials into strategic and lucrative posts in the private sector – the state was able to extend its influence since many of its officials had allegedly been socialised into the public ethos and retained close links with the *corps* from which they emanated. France was presented, therefore, as the quintessential state-dominated political system, itself locked into an apparently untouchable and generally enlightened set of shibboleths, the cultural parameters of public policy. When those shibboleths were question, the president, as head of state, was mobilised: 'territorial integrity', 'unity', 'solidarity', 'justice' were the stock phrases of the predictable presidential response.

The public policy role of the presidency was, therefore, generalised and specific, formal and informal, visible and tangible, practical and symbolic. The occupant might be contested, the office only very rarely. It was highly legitimate and, in turn, it conferred legitimacy on the system. Yet the traditional presidential system was both fragile and problematic. It was fragile because part of its legitimacy was instrumental. It was rooted in the interlinking of policy process and policy outcome. When the latter was judged to be satisfactory, the complexities and ambiguities of the former were accepted. When the latter was deemed to be unsatisfactory, the former was called into question. It was problematic for a variety of reasons that sprang from the nature of the French state, the policy-making process and the presidency itself.

The first problem for the presidency lay in the nature of the decision-making process which was both highly complex and much less receptive to state direction than appearances (and academics) suggested. The policy process has always been structured both vertically and horizontally, territorially and sectorally, with overlapping and nebulous jurisdictions in which public, semi-public and private actors interact in constant fashion, blurring the line between public and private interests. Indeed, we have well documented cases of public bodies acting like private agents and private bodies under *de facto* if not *de jure* state control.[4] Keeping some degree of steering capacity or even establishing principles of political accountability in this ill-coordinated and multi-layered decision-making process presented the first problem for the presidency. Even more problematic was the continuing tradition of disgruntled groups taking to the streets in pursuit of their interests: the parameters of some areas of public policy came increasingly to be framed by the unruly who dictated to frightened politicians no-go areas.

Problem number two for the presidency was the nature of the state machine. Far from being an efficient and well-coordinated instrument of public policy, the machine, on closer investigation, proved to be fragmented, compartmentalised, torn by internal tension and rivalries and characterised by the presence of powerful autonomous bodies (the so-called *Etats dans l'Etat*) and groups more committed to their own self-interest than the public good. In many areas of public policy, state *dirigisme*, so beloved by foreign observers, masked the manipulation of the state by private or autonomous public bodies; it was effectively captured by these interests.

The nature of the office presents the third problem for presidential policy-making. There was always a mismatch between the resources available to and the demands placed upon the office. The principal resources were *constitutional* which were ambiguous and regularly contested, *personal charisma* which was often short-lived, *political* which were highly contingent, *patronage* which was limited and often created more enemies than friends, and *legitimacy* which was sometimes ephemeral. The administrative resources of the office were small and offered an inadequate instrument for penetrating the various vertically and horizontally structured policy networks. With this imperfect power base, the office was nonetheless expected to juggle with multiple competing and often conflicting exigencies, which often sprang from the tension between its overarching, integrative and non-partisan function and its direct involvement in politicised policy-making.

PRESSURES ON THE TRADITIONAL MODEL

Four very broad trends which emerged in the 1980s and 1990s were further to destabilise the already constrained, complex and problem-ridden presidential policy role: a general dilution of the country's capacity to define its own policies; a weakening of the position of the state within the French decision-making process; an erosion of the authority within the state machine; and an increase in the intractability of the problems posed to French decision-makers. Several pressures were at work which produced these trends.

The internationalisation and liberalisation of financial and industrial circuits
Internationalisation has many dimensions, one of the most important of which is the increasing interdependence and interlocking of national economies. No country can now ignore the situation and policies of its trading partners, a lesson the French socialists were painfully to learn after 1981. A second dimension of internationalisation relates to the financial services revolution, which was initially unleashed in the United States and then soon gained Britain and quickly spread to France: the 'Little Bang' in the Paris Bourse followed rapidly in the wake of London's 'Big Bang'. Coupled

with this revolution was the rapid internationalisation of industry during the 1980s, the so-called 'frenzied years' characterised by the internationalisation of sales, ownership, investment, acquisitions, mergers, joint ventures and supply agreements. Collapsing regulatory barriers, diminishing telecommunication and transportation costs, more accessible and cheaper international markets and the diversification strategies of the major financial and industrial groups combined to transform the world economy. The ownership of national industry was radically altered; by the beginning of the 1990s a third of quoted French shares were in the hands of foreigners, and French companies indulged in massive raids on foreign stock (between January 1988 and June 1992 France was Europe's most voracious predator, with 775 deals worth £37 billion).[5] The internationalisation and multinationalisation of the French banking industry presented the government with a number of tricky political questions: how to tax such firms most of whose activities are abroad; how to regulate them in such circumstances; how to prevent French firms from exporting their labour needs to cheaper countries; how to attract foreign capital, so badly needed by French companies, or foreign firms, so desirable for employment purposes, without sacrificing a degree of economic sovereignty.

The impact of the European Union
The impact of the EU on French policies was felt in an increasing number of areas: economic, financial, industrial, environmental, social welfare, health, education, immigration and defence. The 'regulatory creep' of Brussels gathered pace throughout the 1980s driven by different coalitions of national and European interests. Quermonne cites the example of the Industry ministry in 1983–84 which had to spend six months writing and rewriting proposals to restructure the clothing and textile sectors in order to comply with Community regulations concerning state aid to ailing industries and competition policy.[6] More generally, French policy was driven by the desire to meet (or at least to be seen to be trying to meet) the criteria for the completion of the Single European Market and now Economic and Monetary Union. Successive governments have followed the so-called *franc fort* exchange rate policy since the mid-1980s,

which has impacted on interest rate policy and narrowed budgetary parameters. In all, together with the internationalisation and liberalisation of both the world and the French economy, Europeanisation has constrained the domestic policy-making process.

An ideological paradigm shift
Throughout the 1980s there was a decided shift in the macroeconomic paradigm from Keynesianism to monetarism, from *dirigisme* to market-oriented solutions, from fiscal expansionism to restraint, from mercantilism to free trade. The shift involved an inevitable questioning of the role of the state and of public provision in all areas of industry and social welfare. It was a shift which was taken on board by almost all of the political elite, although not by a similar proportion of the French people themselves. Both left- and right-wing governments pursued policies between which, to all but the fully initiated, it was distinctly difficult to differentiate. While it may be the case that French governments were never as enthusiastic as the British in espousing the new paradigm, many of their policies still bore a disconcerting resemblance to the Thatcher agenda. Socialist governments invented a discourse of *modernisation* and the 'need to prepare for the open market' in justifying their 'Thatcherism with a human face'. Right-wing governments discovered the apparent inefficiency of the state where they had once championed its wealth-creating role, and promoted free market competition where before they had been wary of its many iniquities. Whereas previously politics was about great debates now the devil was very much in the detail. The effect of the new paradigm on the party system was twofold. On the one hand, it created room for new lines of division to occur between the middle-ground parties and the extremes. On the other, it also created room for fault-lines to appear within the middle-ground parties as modernisers and traditionalists battled it out.

Economic recession and industrial transformation
This is a point which is almost too well known to warrant elaboration. In Chapter 1, David Hanley paints the gloomy picture of a country in which high unemployment has been

taken as axiomatic. The apparently inexorable rise in unemployment to record heights weighs heavily on a state budget which is already being squeezed by the depressed state of the economy and by fiscal resistance displayed by overburdened tax payers. Of course, the impact of the recession remains extremely variable. Most acutely affected were the grant-intensive rust-belt industries of textiles, shipbuilding and steel (coal had severely contracted much earlier). Less severely hit were service industries. Nevertheless, the political implications of the changing economic and industrial base of the country were immediate: disaffection with established leaders, parties and the political class in general and a desire to find self-expression in new forms of political participation or old forms with a new face.

Changing demographic structures and social mores
These changes involved, for example, more elderly people to be looked after by fewer wage earners and more single parents who, being financially dependent on the state, increased the pressure for budgetary expansion.

The technological revolution
The political impact of the technological revolution cannot be underestimated. It has increased the problems of controlling information flows across national boundaries; it has greatly facilitated the liberalisation of the world's financial markets; it has transformed national natural monopolies into sectors susceptible to international or European competition (notably in energy supply and telecommunications); it has deskilled millions of workers and shaken up the labour market generally; it has improved the health of the nation (thus increasing the pressure on public spending); and it has had a significant impact on working practices within the state apparatus.

The changing policy agenda
In part, the issue agenda has been reshaped by worthy causes, most notable among which are feminism and environmentalism, but both of which are also not without their damaging budgetary implications. In the main, though, the changing policy agenda is partly resultant upon the economic recession

which contributed to triggering the miserable litany of rising insecurity, racial tensions, drugs and crime that currently preoccupies policy-makers and provides fertile ground for political elements which many had thought extinct. Today the French are not overly concerned with the merits or otherwise of competing ideologies. Instead, their worries are those which impinge directly on their everyday lives. Immediately after the 1995 election the four priority issues which the French felt that Chirac should address were unemployment (92 per cent), social protection (55 per cent), immigration (38 per cent) and exclusion (37 per cent). For the same four issues, though, the degree of confidence that the French placed in Chirac to tackle them successfully was 55 per cent, 25 per cent, 20 per cent and 20 per cent respectively.[7]

These multiple pressures have fed one another in a dynamic and complex fashion and have clearly reshaped the policy-making environment of France and the role of its president therein. It is now:

More internationalised
Major domestic actors such as banking, industrial and insurance groups are locked into international networks, while domestic decision-making has been penetrated by foreign actors. The blurring of the national identities of multinationals, although exaggerated in the literature, is, nevertheless, a source of real problems for governments everywhere. Equally problematic for domestic decision-makers is the internationalisation of regulatory bodies in an increasing number of spheres ranging from financial services to air transport. The internationalisation of regulatory activity is but an inevitable response to the changing nature of the world economy. The individual state appears powerless to control, for example, the kind of massive abuses that have been committed in financial circles and which have ignored national frontiers.

More Europeanised
Europeanisation has directly and profoundly impacted upon domestic decision-making in a variety of ways. This may be illustrated by taking three major examples. In the first place,

the 'leading constitutional values' of the European Union, which are market protection, price stability, a balanced budget and sound public finances, provide a framework of discipline in which France now has to function. Firmly committed to achieving the convergence criteria enshrined in the Maastricht Treaty and determined to remain within the Exchange Rate Mechanism, France has fixed itself into a currency corset which is regularly adjusted by the German Bundesbank and to which the increasingly independent Banque de France is obliged to respond. Without any doubt, its economic and monetary policy discretion has been singularly restricted. It is also being restricted over its use of protectionist devices and state aids, which now have to be negotiated with Brussels, to cushion its own industry and there have been some famous rows between the French government and the European Commission over subsidies to ailing French companies, notably Air France. Secondly, France, together with all its European partners, has now to live with the principle and the practice of the supremacy of EU law over national law. This principle strikes at the very heart of sovereignty and for some time was rejected by the French Council of State, the country's supreme administrative council. Nevertheless, in 1990 the Council of State acknowledged for the first time in its Nicolo ruling that European law must take precedence over domestic administrative law. Thirdly, France is a signatory to the Schengen Agreement which provides for the abolition of internal frontier controls on goods and people, combined with measures for cooperation among police, immigration, customs and intelligence services as well. Although there have been problems in the implementation of the Schengen Agreement, they would appear to be of a temporary nature.

More privatised, deregulated and marketised
The bureaucratic allocation of resources has been dismantled in a number of ways. The radical privatisation programmes of 1986–88 and post-1993 have resulted not only in the denationalisation of major banks and enterprises, they have also involved the 'privatisation of the logic of the public sector': almost all public-sector managers now enjoy great autonomy and are expected to run their enterprises according

to private-sector criteria. Political interventions in the running of the nationalised sector still occur, but they are becoming the exceptions that prove the rule. Indeed, several prominent nationalised industry chairmen have testified to the freedom they now enjoy. Privatisation has been accompanied by deregulation: France has dismantled some of the rules and regulations for which it was justly infamous thus weakening one of its favourite and much detested weapons. It has also begun to be infected by another British virus: the desire to introduce surrogate or quasi-markets into public service provision by way of competitive tendering and sub-contracting.

More juridicised
Juridicisation refers to the extent to which court decisions themselves, the pedagogical authority of court jurisprudence and the threat of future court censure alters the policy-making process.[8] In all of these respects, the courts have become much more prominent public policy actors. This is true of the European Court of Justice, the Constitutional Council and civil judges. For example, government ministers have been explicitly advised of the attitude that they should adopt towards the European Court. In 1988, prime minister Michel Rocard issued a circular to all ministers in which it was stated: 'You will ensure that your administration's texts and projects conform to the State's obligations towards the Community (treaties, derived Community law and the jurisprudence of the European Court of Justice).' In addition, the Constitutional Council has demonstrated that it is a sporadically assertive body which has been involved in arbitrating some highly sensitive issues and which has provoked the ire of politicians who have denounced the 'government by judges'. In its broadcasting, press, decentralisation, nationalisation, privatisation and other decisions, the Constitutional Council has become a significant actor in the process of which other decision-makers have to take account. Finally, civil judges, like their Italian counterparts, have come to prominence in pursuing the misdemeanours of senior politicians and political parties. The personal finances of Bernard Tapie and the party finances of the PS, PR and CDS have all come under extremely close judicial scrutiny, which has added an

extra dimension to public affairs. It is revealing that the scandal involving Chirac's newly appointed prime minister, Alain Juppé, was finally resolved by a magistrate whose decision might well have brought down the government.[9]

More diffused
With the emergence of new social movements and the proliferation of vociferous single-issue groups, many of which fit uneasily into the normal bargained, bureaucratised and routinised processes of decision-making, the political system has become even more diffused. For example, recent high-profile campaigns have been mounted by and on behalf of the homeless, by intellectuals opposed to the continuing war in Bosnia, by those fearful for the future survival of the Pyrenean bear and by those opposed to Chirac's decision to recommence nuclear tests in the south Pacific. Unlike groups which in the past occasionally erupted into violent demonstrations in order to press their case, these new groups are more likely to be permanent and increasingly institutionalised. Like the older groups, however, they frequently deny the legitimacy of the traditional policy process and refuse to be ensnared by membership of political parties which inevitably involves compromise. They use modern advertising techniques and are highly aware of the importance of professionally organised media campaigns. They are a more difficult target for the state to identify and contain and they increase the level of volatility inherent in the policy process.

More problematic in terms of the policy agenda
Many new politically salient policies are intrinsically difficult to solve: some criminal activity (drugs and money laundering) are international in character; some problems (the breakdown of the family and unfavourable demographic trends) are essentially social in character and not susceptible to political solutions; yet others (a viable independent defence posture, unemployment and the financing of the welfare state) are budgetary in nature and the state, for a variety of reasons, is locked into a budgetary squeeze. In addition, the delays and early teething problems which have emerged in the implementation of the Schengen Agreement

bear testimony to the immense problems confronting French decision-makers as a result of the integration of Europe. Finally, membership of the EU is altering traditional policy networks, reshaping the balance of power within the country, by creating opportunities for some actors while marginalising others (some rich regions, for example, have set up offices in Brussels to exploit the funds available) and triggering institutional innovation for coordinating purposes.

More devolved both territorially and sectorally
Since 1981, France has embarked on an ambitious programme of territorial decentralisation (transfer of power to locally elected politicians) and deconcentration (transfer of power to the state services at the local level). Local officials, both centrally appointed and locally elected and both of which were always more powerful than traditional analyses depicted, have unquestionably strengthened their power bases. However, rather than simply shifting the balance of power from one level of government to another, the move towards decentralisation and deconcentration has also resulted in a multi-tiered policy process in which the various political actors are increasingly interdependent. On the one hand, local politicians have become stronger, but they are still obliged to look to the state's representatives, both at the centre and in the locality, for grants, subsidies, exemptions from regulations and the like. On the other, state officials still need local representatives to deliver services effectively in order to maintain the instrumentality of the policy process. Finally, in common with other European states, the French state has devolved authority in a number of spheres, such as broadcasting and financial services, to semi-autonomous regulatory agencies such as the Conseil Supérieur de l'Audiovisuel or so-called 'third sector' bodies. The result of this policy of territorial and sectoral devolution is a weakening of direct state leverage in decision-making, even in problems such as environmental issues and immigration which have international, social and budgetary ramifications, and an ever more variegated set of actors between whom policy decisions have to be thrashed out.

In short, the traditional public policy-making landscape, already highly problematic for the presidency, has become much more complex and more resistant to political management.

CONCLUSION

The three broad trends which we have identified – a diminished influence for France, a more discrete role for the state as a result of the adjustment of the boundaries between market, state and society, and an increasingly complex, elusive and autonomous policy-making environment – have left the presidency in a distinctly exposed position. Admittedly, there is a danger of exaggerating the extent and impact of the three trends. Thus, France is not an entirely hapless spectator of its own fate and its insertion into international or transnational policy networks may even have increased (however marginally) its influence in some sectors. The state remains the major player or a key actor in many policy areas (health, education, training, pensions) and may even have extended its tentacles into other areas (financial services and the environment notably). Even in the industrial sector, despite the pressures of the GATT and EU, the state retains a role as owner, regulator, trade negotiator, parameter-setter (by its macroeconomic, fiscal, exchange rate, competition and labour market policies) and subsidiser. Finally, the increasing complexity of decision-making does not signify ungovernability (one of the buzz words of pessimistic observers who fail to recognise that vast swathes of public policy are managed in routinised and incremental patterns by discrete policy networks in little need of formal political coordination).

Nevertheless, we should not underestimate the difficulties confronting the political elites and, more especially, the presidency, which continues to play a crucial role at all levels of government and governance. Without doubt, the trends of recent years have rendered more acute the intrinsic dilemmas of the office. Faced with increasingly insoluble problems and squeezed in its resources, it has, nevertheless, to manage continuing high levels of expectation, to be seen as a policy entrepreneur and to endow legitimacy on the system. Political pressure requires visibility, prudence increasingly demands effacement.

The 1995 presidential election was, therefore, a peculiar affair. In itself it was a legitimising agent, yet it fully revealed the high political salience of problems without solutions and the crumbling legitimacy of those institutions, including the presidency, which were being called upon to solve them. Within six months of assuming office, President Chirac was already confronted with the dilemmas of his position and the early evidence suggests that both his willingness and ability to resolve them were somewhat limited.

NOTES

1. A study of one aspect of the French economic policy community is to be found in Hayward (1986).
2. See Elgie (1993), pp. 16–20.
3. Quermonne (1991), p. 271.
4. See Hayward (1986) and Wright (1994).
5. For further details on the issues of internationalisation and liberalisation, see Hayward (1995).
6. Quermonne (1991), p. 310.
7. Figures taken from the poll in *Le Monde*, 11 May 1995.
8. This definition is adapted from Stone (1989), pp. 31–2.
9. As a high-ranking official in the Paris administration he had allocated himself a spacious and elegant apartment in a fashionable part of the capital at a rent which was well below the market value.

Appendix 1
Presidential Election
Results, 1965–95

Note: Figures for candidates correspond to percentage of valid votes cast.

5 and 19 December 1965

	[*First round*]	[*Second round*]
Abstentions	15.25	15.68
Spoilt ballots	0.86	2.31
Charles de Gaulle (Gaullist)	44.65	55.20
François Mitterrand (socialist)	31.79	44.80
Jean Lecanuet (centrist)	15.57	
Jean-Louis Tixier-Vignancour (extreme right)	5.20	
Pierre Marcilhacy (independent)	1.71	
Marcel Barbu (independent)	1.15	

1 and 15 June 1969

	[*First round*]	[*Second round*]
Abstentions	22.41	31.15
Spoilt ballots	1.00	4.42
Georges Pompidou (Gaullist)	44.47	58.21
Alain Poher (centrist)	23.31	41.79
Jacques Duclos (communist)	21.27	
Gaston Defferre (socialist)	5.01	
Michel Rocard (unified socialist)	3.61	
Louis Ducatel (independent)	1.27	
Alain Krivine (extreme left)	1.06	

5 and 19 May 1974

	[*First round*]	[*Second round*]
Abstentions	15.77	12.67
Spoilt ballots	0.77	1.17
Valéry Giscard d'Estaing (centre-right)	32.60	50.81
François Mitterrand (socialist)	43.25	49.19
Jacques Chaban-Delmas (Gaullist)	15.11	
Jean Royer (right)	3.17	

Arlette Laguiller (extreme left)	2.33
René Dumont (ecologist)	1.32
Jean-Marie Le Pen (extreme right)	0.75
Emile Muller (social democrat)	0.69
Alain Krivine (extreme left)	0.37
Bertrand Renouvin (monarchist)	0.17
Jean-Claude Sebag (federalist)	0.16
Guy Héraud (federalist)	0.08

26 April and 10 May 1981

	[*First round*]	[*Second round*]
Abstentions	18.91	14.15
Spoilt ballots	1.31	2.47
François Mitterrand (socialist)	25.85	51.76
Valéry Giscard d'Estaing (centre-right)	28.32	48.24
Jacques Chirac (Gaullist)	18.00	
Georges Marchais (communist)	15.35	
Brice Lalonde (ecologist)	3.88	
Arlette Laguiller (extreme left)	2.30	
Michel Crépeau (left-radical)	2.21	
Michel Debré (Gaullist)	1.66	
Marie-France Garaud (Gaullist)	1.33	
Huguette Bouchardeau (unified socialist)	1.11	

24 April and 8 May 1988

	[*First round*]	[*Second round*]
Abstentions	18.62	15.93
Spoilt ballots	1.60	3.40
François Mitterrand (socialist)	34.10	54.02
Jacques Chirac (Gaullist)	19.94	45.98
Raymond Barre (centrist)	16.54	
Jean-Marie Le Pen (extreme right)	14.40	
André Lajoinie (communist)	6.76	
Antoine Waechter (ecologist)	3.78	
Pierre Juquin (dissident communist)	2.01	
Arlette Laguiller (extreme left)	1.99	
Pierre Boussel (extreme left)	0.38	

23 April and 7 May 1995

	[*First round*]	[*Second round*]
Abstentions	21.62	20.33
Spoilt ballots	2.83	5.97
Jacques Chirac (Gaullist)	20.84	52.64
Lionel Jospin (socialist)	23.30	47.36

Edouard Balladur (Gaullist)	18.58
Jean-Marie Le Pen (extreme right)	15.00
Robert Hue (communist)	8.64
Arlette Laguiller (extreme left)	5.30
Philippe de Villiers (right)	4.74
Dominique Voynet (ecologist)	3.32
Jacques Cheminade (independent)	0.28

Appendix 2
Chronology of Events
Relating to the 1995
Presidential Election

December 1993
19   Senior UDF ministers, François Léotard and Simone Veil, call upon the Prime Minister, Edouard Balladur (RPR), to stand as a candidate at the election.

June 1994
10   Publication of the manifesto-book *Une nouvelle France* by Jacques Chirac (RPR).
19   Following the PS's poor showing at the European elections, Michel Rocard is ousted as party leader and replaced by Henri Emmanuelli.

September 1994
16   Philippe de Villiers resigns from the UDF's Parti Républicain (PR).
18   Jean-Marie Le Pen (FN) announces that he will stand as a candidate.
19–21 Former President Valéry Giscard d'Estaing (UDF) publishes three articles in *Le Figaro* setting out his ideas.
21   Robert Hue (PCF) announces that he will stand as a candidate.
27   Arlette Laguiller (Lutte Ouvrière) announces that she will stand as a candidate.

October 1994
10   The Interior Minister, Charles Pasqua (RPR), writes to RPR/UDF deputies and senators reminding them of their parties' commitment to primary elections.
18   Balladur invites Chirac and Giscard d'Estaing to meet him to discuss the tensions within the right-wing parties.
19   Chirac refuses Balladur's invitation, Giscard accepts.
23   Les Verts select Dominique Voynet as their presidential candidate.
24   Balladur criticises Chirac in an interview with *Le Figaro*.
26   Pasqua announces that he has no intention of standing as a candidate.

November 1994

4   Chirac announces that he is a candidate in an interview with the local newspaper, *La Voix du Nord.*

4–6   The Left-Radical Movement (MRG) officially changes its name to Radical at its Le Bourget party conference.

6   Hue is officially chosen as the PCF's candidate.
In a television interview, Chirac proposes that a referendum be held to ratify the third stage of monetary union.

8   Jacques Delors (PS) publishes a book-interview, *L'unité d'un homme.*

9   The president of the UDF's parliamentary group, Charles Millon, announces that he will stand as a candidate if no other UDF candidate does so.

10   Rocard announces in an interview with *Le Nouvel Observateur* that he will not stand as a candidate.

12   The RPR holds a *réunion exceptionelle* in Paris. Chirac resigns the presidency of the party. Neither Balladur, Pasqua nor Philippe Séguin, the President of the National Assembly, attends.

18–20   The PS holds its congress at Liévin. Emmanuelli declares that it is Delors's 'duty' to stand as the party's candidate.

24   Delors states that he will announce whether or not he is a candidate before Christmas.

20   De Villiers launches his own political organisation, the Mouvement pour la France.

December 1994

1   The RPR/UDF working group on the feasibility of primary elections announces that they would be impossible to organise.

11   Delors announces that he will not stand as a candidate.
Génération Écologie ratifies its leader, Brice Lalonde, as its presidential candidate.

14   The regionalist, Max Siméoni, announces that he will stand as a candidate.
The Tribunal de commerce de Paris declares the Radical businessman, Bernard Tapie, bankrupt, meaning that he cannot hold any elected office for five years and is, in effect, out of the presidential race.

20   Balladur states that he will announce whether or not he will stand at the end of January.

January 1995

4   Lionel Jospin announces that he is ready to stand as the PS's candidate.

8   De Villiers announces that he is a candidate.
The general assembly of the Mouvement écologiste indépendant selects Antoine Waechter as its presidential candidate.

10   Publication of a second manifesto-book *La France pour tous* by Chirac.

11   A PS delegation meets a Radical delegation to discuss electoral tactics.

12	Pasqua writes to Chirac to inform that he will support Balladur. The UDF's Adhérents directs officially vote to support Balladur.
17	Jack Lang announces that he is ready to stand as the PS's candidate.
18	Balladur announces at a press conference held at Matignon that he will stand as a candidate. Emmanuelli announces that he is ready to stand as the PS's candidate.
21	The UDF's Centre des démocrates sociaux (CDS) officially votes to support Balladur. The UDF's Parti social démocrate (PSD) officially votes to support Balladur.
25	Lang announces that he will not seek the PS's nomination.
26	Robert Vigouroux, ex-PS mayor of Marseille, announces that he will support Balladur's campaign.
28	The UDF's PR officially votes to support Balladur.

February 1995

1	The PS's bureau national adopts the party's presidential platform, 'Un nouveau contrat pour la République social'.
2	Hue presents his official programme, 'Propositions pour la France'.
4	The right-wing party, the CNI, votes to support Chirac.
5	At its extraordinary party congress, the PS chooses Jospin as its presidential candidate.
12	The UDF's Parti radical officially votes to support Balladur
13	Balladur presents his presidential programme at a press conference. In an interview with *Le Figaro*, Millon announces that his candidature is no longer 'on the agenda'.
16	Balladur holds his first major electoral meeting.
17	Chirac presents his presidential programme at a public meeting.
20	A BVA opinion poll shows that for the first time Chirac is ahead of Balladur.
21	Jospin presents his campaign team.
24	Jean-François Hory (Radical) announces in an interview with *Le Monde* that he will stand as a candidate.

March 1995

2	Tapie announces that he will not support Hory's campaign and states that he has a *préjugé favorable* for Jospin.
6	Ex-Prime Minister Raymond Barre announces that he will not stand as a candidate.
7	Jospin presents his manifesto *Propositions pour la France* at a press conference. Giscard d'Estaing announces that not he will stand as a candidate.
8	Millon announces that he will support Chirac's campaign. Waechter presents his campaign programme.
9	On TF1, Pasqua states that he has never before seen a campaign 'as disgusting' as this one.
10	Hory presents his campaign programme.

11 The UDF's Clubs Perspectives et Réalités officially vote to support Chirac's campaign.

12 Le Mouvement des citoyens, led by Jean-Pierre Chevènement (ex-PS), votes to support Jospin's campaign.

13 In an interview with *Le Figaro*, François Mitterrand announces that he will vote for Jospin.

15 Noël Mamère and André Buchmann (Convergence Ecologie Solidarité) join Jospin's campaign committee as does Pierre Juquin (ex-PCF).
Lalonde announces that he is withdrawing from the campaign.

16 Voynet presents her campaign programme, 'Pour l'écologie aujourd'hui'.
Jean-Pierre Raffarin (the UDF's spokesperson) announces that he is supporting Chirac as does Bruno Durieux, one of Barre's closest followers.

19 Jean-Pierre Soisson (Mouvement des réformateurs) announces that he is supporting Chirac.
Tapie announces on France 2 that now Jospin is just about assured of being in the second round, he will help Hory's campaign.

24 Former Gaullist Prime Minister Jacques Chaban-Delmas announces that he will support Chirac's campaign.

31 Tapie's bankruptcy is confirmed by the Cour d'appel de Paris.
Hory announces that he is withdrawing from the campaign.

April 1995

4 Le Pen presents his official campaign programme, 'Contrat pour la France'.
Deadline for the candidates' official sponsors to be received by the Constitutional Council. Nine candidates have gained the necessary number of sponsors.

6 The official first-round election campaign begins with, henceforth, equal time on radio and television for all candidates.

16 No more opinion polls may be published in France until after the first ballot. In the last poll, Ifop/Europe 2/*Journal du dimanche*, Chirac is credited with 26.5 per cent, Jospin 20.5 per cent, Balladur 16.5 per cent and Le Pen 13 per cent, but 34 per cent of people say that they may still change their mind.

21 End of the official first-round campaign at midnight.

23 First round of the election. Voting ends at 20.00.
Chirac and Jospin qualify for the second ballot.
At 21.00 Balladur admits defeat and calls on his supporters to vote for Chirac at the second round as does de Villiers.
Laguiller declares that personally she will abstain at the second ballot, but that her supporters should decide for themselves whom to vote for.

24 Barre announces that he is giving his full support to Chirac.
The UDF's different components, the CDS, PR, PSD, Parti radical, Clubs Perspectives et Réalités and Adhérents directs, all officially decide to support Chirac at the second round.

26   The PCF's bureau national declares that it is necessary to defeat Chirac at the second ballot and so its supporters should cast their vote for Jospin.

27   The bureau national of Radical decides to vote for Jospin at the second ballot.

28   The official second-round campaign begins.

    Charles Fiterman (ex-PCF and member of Voynet's *comité de soutien*) states in *Le Monde* that he is now unambiguously supporting Jospin.

29   Chirac holds a campaign rally at La Bagatelle, Paris, attended by Balladur, Giscard d'Estaing, and all the leading RPR and UDF figures (with the exception of Barre), plus de Villiers.

    In the last opinion polls, Chirac leads Jospin by 54–46 per cent for BVA and SOFRES and by 55–45 per cent for CSA and IFOP, but 21 per cent of those polled state that they may yet change their mind.

30   The Conseil national interrégional des Verts officially decides not to support either candidate at the second ballot, but states that Chirac's proposals are opposed to their own.

    No more opinion polls may be published in France until after the second ballot.

May 1995

1   On behalf of the FN, Le Pen announces that the party cannot recommend supporting either candidate at the second ballot and that he will make known how he will vote himself later in the week.

2   In an article in *Le Figaro*, Lalonde announces that he voted for Chirac at the first ballot and will do the same at the second.

    A live television debate between Chirac and Jospin attracts 16.8 million viewers.

3   Giscard d'Estaing announces that he will vote for Chirac.

4   Jospin holds his last major campaign meeting near Toulouse.

5   Chirac holds his last campaign rally at Lyon in the company of Barre.

    End of the official campaign at midnight.

7   Second round of the election. Voting ends at 20.00.

    Chirac wins by 52.6–47.4 per cent.

Appendix 3
1995 Results

FIRST BALLOT BY DEPARTMENT

Department	Jospin %	Chirac %	Balla-dur %	Le Pen %	Hue %	Lagu-iller %	Villiers %	Voy-net %	Chem-inade %
Ain	20.50	19.23	19.80	19.86	6.15	4.89	5.38	3.91	0.28
Aisne	24.38	18.17	15.63	17.69	10.93	5.80	4.70	2.43	0.29
Allier	22.14	21.65	16.78	11.23	15.66	4.78	4.73	2.77	0.27
Alpes-H-Provence	22.70	18.37	16.97	15.79	11.16	5.26	5.23	4.19	0.34
Hautes-Alpes	21.95	20.28	20.47	12.74	8.63	5.13	5.48	4.99	0.34
Alpes-Maritimes	16.36	22.48	20.75	22.48	6.79	3.70	4.51	2.72	0.21
Ardèche	22.98	18.10	20.07	14.18	9.97	5.41	5.04	3.93	0.32
Ardennes	24.29	17.54	17.62	18.04	9.47	5.35	4.69	2.75	0.25
Ariège	33.81	16.68	14.43	10.50	12.46	4.98	3.31	3.51	0.34
Aube	20.13	20.95	19.02	18.29	7.85	4.73	5.97	2.78	0.29
Aude	31.14	18.17	13.75	13.56	11.63	4.89	3.91	2.70	0.25
Aveyron	24.57	26.03	21.05	8.51	6.93	4.73	4.46	3.43	0.30
Bouches-du-Rhône	20.38	16.89	17.80	21.43	11.81	5.00	3.65	2.81	0.23
Calvados	23.81	20.03	20.85	12.40	7.29	6.70	4.98	3.64	0.30
Cantal	21.03	40.98	14.09	7.12	6.84	4.13	3.40	2.07	0.34
Charente	28.08	21.08	16.33	10.21	9.39	5.24	6.22	3.11	0.32

FIRST BALLOT BY DEPARTMENT (continued)

	Jospin %	Chirac %	Balladur %	Le Pen %	Hue %	Laguiller %	Villiers %	Voynet %	Cheminade %
Charente-Maritime	24.68	20.00	19.29	11.31	8.46	4.85	7.80	3.29	0.31
Cher	20.87	20.27	18.00	13.54	13.77	5.43	4.93	2.88	0.32
Corrèze	19.86	49.30	4.61	4.58	13.98	3.42	1.95	2.07	0.22
Corse-du-Sud	18.07	30.41	22.58	11.60	9.11	3.04	2.27	2.65	0.27
Haute-Corse	22.55	31.40	18.09	9.83	10.16	3.06	2.22	2.44	0.27
Côte-d'Or	23.67	20.96	18.77	15.84	6.22	5.14	5.19	3.98	0.25
Côtes d'Armor	27.58	19.13	20.12	8.84	11.20	5.49	3.68	3.72	0.25
Creuse	24.80	34.54	10.99	7.03	11.86	4.26	3.47	2.77	0.29
Dordogne	25.05	25.42	13.88	8.76	14.15	4.38	5.09	2.97	0.30
Doubs	24.79	20.72	18.40	15.40	5.37	5.40	4.70	4.96	0.26
Drôme	23.40	16.96	18.72	17.36	8.16	5.26	5.49	4.34	0.31
Eure	20.69	19.48	18.68	18.37	8.53	5.68	5.23	3.03	0.31
Eure-et-Loir	21.37	18.82	20.36	18.22	6.79	5.07	6.18	2.94	0.24
Finistère	26.14	21.78	21.06	9.20	7.46	6.08	3.85	4.20	0.24
Gard	21.54	16.16	16.34	20.28	12.82	5.16	4.48	2.99	0.24
Haute-Garonne	31.87	18.29	16.02	12.63	7.76	6.05	3.46	3.66	0.27
Gers	29.50	21.24	17.61	9.33	8.33	4.82	5.61	3.18	0.37
Gironde	27.70	19.50	17.72	12.77	8.48	5.95	4.61	3.01	0.27
Hérault	24.16	17.70	16.13	18.96	10.24	5.22	4.12	3.25	0.22
Ille-et-Vilaine	25.64	21.04	22.47	8.98	6.30	6.52	4.48	4.33	0.25
Indre	23.87	21.21	16.99	13.01	10.68	5.16	5.85	2.91	0.33
Indre-et-Loire	24.62	18.08	21.21	12.97	7.61	5.32	6.27	3.63	0.29
Isère	25.19	15.78	17.95	17.48	8.63	5.99	4.33	4.39	0.26
Jura	21.88	17.33	20.24	15.46	8.24	5.31	5.41	5.87	0.27
Landes	31.96	21.18	17.51	8.90	9.53	4.24	4.20	2.22	0.27
Loir-et-Cher	22.68	17.66	20.09	15.36	8.54	4.93	7.38	3.08	0.28
Loire	20.39	17.66	18.85	21.08	8.46	5.05	4.90	3.36	0.25
Haute-Loire	20.29	22.92	19.78	15.80	6.67	5.46	5.42	3.33	0.33
Loire-Atlantique	26.15	18.50	20.90	9.61	7.19	6.20	6.97	4.21	0.28
Loiret	20.97	20.47	20.11	15.83	8.08	5.03	5.85	3.35	0.30

Lot	29.00	25.29	13.73	7.71	10.94	5.02	4.35	3.66	0.30
Lot-et-Garonne	23.42	20.19	16.43	14.74	10.63	4.98	6.28	3.01	0.30
Lozère	20.56	26.84	24.35	9.62	7.03	4.13	3.94	3.24	0.30
Maine-et-Loire	20.92	20.03	25.08	10.09	5.47	5.35	8.98	3.78	0.30
Manche	20.20	24.04	24.19	11.06	5.81	5.66	5.32	3.40	0.33
Marne	20.57	20.84	18.85	17.62	7.46	5.82	5.25	3.30	0.29
Haute-Marne	21.04	19.64	17.89	20.35	6.91	5.30	4.99	3.53	0.35
Mayenne	19.74	23.66	26.76	9.47	4.71	5.15	6.43	3.76	0.32
Meurthe-et-Moselle	23.61	17.72	18.07	18.12	8.34	6.47	3.94	3.46	0.27
Meuse	21.24	17.40	21.34	19.75	5.96	5.31	5.06	3.62	0.32
Morbihan	22.63	19.97	23.37	13.79	7.14	5.34	4.06	3.48	0.23
Moselle	19.40	17.18	20.47	23.82	5.73	6.43	3.57	3.10	0.29
Nièvre	30.03	18.04	15.81	11.86	12.66	4.49	4.22	2.62	0.27
Nord	23.23	16.85	17.53	18.18	11.93	5.63	4.04	2.38	0.24
Oise	20.81	19.70	16.00	20.48	9.15	6.00	4.60	2.97	0.29
Orne	19.81	23.18	21.58	14.81	5.64	5.30	5.92	3.45	0.31
Pas-de-Calais	25.17	16.90	15.97	15.21	13.90	6.17	4.26	2.16	0.26
Puy-de-Dôme	25.38	22.48	16.79	11.00	9.55	6.92	4.12	3.46	0.30
Pyrénées-Atlantiques	25.59	23.04	21.16	9.61	7.10	5.58	3.99	3.65	0.28
Hautes-Pyrénées	28.34	20.02	17.60	9.38	12.11	5.30	3.78	3.18	0.30
Pyrénées-Orientales	23.03	19.01	15.70	19.45	10.64	4.88	4.36	2.71	0.22
Bas-Rhin	16.72	16.63	24.73	25.83	2.86	4.79	4.30	3.82	0.32
Haut-Rhin	17.09	16.72	24.24	24.80	3.56	5.06	4.37	3.84	0.32
Rhône	21.71	18.51	20.65	19.14	6.57	5.10	4.29	3.79	0.25
Haute-Saône	24.95	19.66	18.10	16.71	6.55	5.03	4.95	3.77	0.28
Saône-et-Loire	24.88	20.31	19.10	13.24	9.12	4.84	5.25	2.99	0.27
Sarthe	23.48	18.77	21.63	11.43	8.67	5.94	6.12	3.65	0.32
Savoie	21.33	18.65	20.30	16.82	7.94	5.30	5.10	4.29	0.27
Haute-Savoie	18.50	20.04	24.71	16.43	5.02	4.91	5.39	4.67	0.33
Paris	26.02	32.19	16.60	9.25	4.68	4.83	2.60	3.63	0.19

FIRST BALLOT BY DEPARTMENT (*continued*)

	Jospin %	Chirac %	Balladur %	Le Pen %	Hue %	Laguiller %	Villiers %	Voynet %	Cheminade %
Seine-Maritime	23.65	16.95	18.32	15.79	11.63	6.47	3.85	3.08	0.26
Seine-et-Marne	21.25	22.76	15.57	18.40	8.24	5.53	4.63	3.37	0.25
Yvelines	21.36	25.95	19.57	13.78	6.36	4.90	4.44	3.41	0.23
Deux-Sèvres	25.53	21.81	20.61	7.38	5.71	5.71	9.06	3.86	0.33
Somme	22.79	18.85	16.99	15.24	12.43	5.86	5.13	2.43	0.28
Tarn	28.17	19.65	17.64	12.95	8.04	5.00	4.92	3.34	0.30
Tarn-et-Garonne	26.11	19.94	15.98	15.77	7.74	4.82	6.21	3.09	0.33
Var	17.30	19.06	21.09	22.35	8.24	4.18	4.98	2.57	0.22
Vaucluse	20.27	16.67	17.79	23.12	8.55	4.67	5.36	3.30	0.27
Vendée	19.47	18.20	20.18	7.31	4.75	4.52	22.02	3.26	0.28
Vienne	25.41	21.82	18.27	10.49	8.26	5.39	6.15	3.89	0.32
Haute-Vienne	27.41	28.80	10.72	7.57	13.76	4.97	3.36	3.15	0.26
Vosges	22.01	19.78	17.99	19.99	5.69	5.54	5.14	3.53	0.34
Yonne	20.79	20.23	19.08	17.04	8.17	4.95	5.99	3.43	0.31
Territoire de Belfort	25.80	18.15	15.44	18.75	7.36	6.09	3.66	4.53	0.22
Essonne	24.14	22.78	15.54	14.35	9.10	6.00	3.94	3.92	0.23
Hauts-de-Seine	23.07	26.56	19.25	11.65	7.90	4.72	3.36	3.26	0.22
Seine-Saint-Denis	23.39	19.90	11.79	18.78	14.09	5.79	2.87	3.15	0.23
Val-de-Marne	23.64	23.40	14.94	13.33	12.59	5.25	3.20	3.44	0.21
Val-d'Oise	22.24	22.05	14.90	17.50	10.66	5.36	3.79	3.28	0.23
Overseas departments and territories									
Guadeloupe	35.13	38.23	14.48	3.06	3.57	2.25	0.91	1.41	0.95
Guyane	24.15	39.84	16.88	8.08	1.90	3.76	1.87	2.63	0.90
Martinique	36.40	29.14	23.58	1.65	3.54	2.67	0.90	1.27	0.85
Mayotte	5.22	39.23	47.16	1.32	1.61	1.04	1.20	1.72	1.52
Nouvelle-Calédonie	15.87	42.97	26.57	8.17	0.70	1.51	1.85	1.72	0.65
Polynésie française	12.51	51.63	24.93	3.12	1.23	1.63	2.68	1.54	0.72
La Réunion	30.36	35.18	13.53	2.89	10.54	2.42	2.23	1.91	0.94
St-Pierre-&-Miquelon	17.31	33.97	23.48	7.51	4.78	6.41	2.78	3.35	0.41
Wallis-et-Futuna	29.88	43.53	21.80	1.22	0.60	0.87	0.55	0.70	0.87

SECOND BALLOT BY DEPARTMENT

Department	Jospin %	Chirac % .
Ain	42.57	57.42
Aisne	54.54	45.45
Allier	50.25	49.74
Alpes-de-Haute-Provence	47.94	52.05
Hautes-Alpes	45.03	54.96
Alpes-Maritimes	34.52	65.47
Ardèche	48.37	51.62
Ardennes	53.28	46.71
Ariège	59.83	40.16
Aube	44.68	55.31
Aude	55.62	44.37
Aveyron	44.12	55.87
Bouches-du-Rhône	45.51	54.48
Calvados	48.88	51.11
Cantal	37.05	62.94
Charente	53.07	46.92
Charente-Maritime	48.31	51.68
Cher	49.34	50.65
Corrèze	38.63	61.36
Corse-du-Sud	37.87	62.12
Haute-Corse	42.72	57.27
Côte-d'Or	45.80	54.19
Côtes d'Armor	54.05	45.94
Creuse	46.35	53.64
Dordogne	49.98	50.01
Doubs	52.40	47.59
Drôme	47.17	52.82
Eure	47.03	52.96
Eure-et-Loir	45.72	54.27
Finistère	48.83	51.16
Gard	48.92	51.07
Haute-Garonne	54.47	45.52
Gers	50.77	49.22
Gironde	51.21	48.78
Hérault	48.92	51.07
Ille-et-Vilaine	48.81	51.18
Indre	50.29	49.70
Indre-et-Loire	49.42	50.57
Isère	50.16	49.83
Jura	47.71	52.28
Landes	52.70	47.29
Loir-et-Cher	48.20	51.79

Department	Jospin %	Chirac %
Loire	44.54	55.45
Haute-Loire	42.24	57.75
Loire-Atlantique	49.66	50.33
Loiret	43.90	56.09
Lot	51.88	48.11
Lot-et-Garonne	47.94	52.05
Lozère	38.55	61.44
Maine-et-Loire	43.01	56.98
Manche	41.14	58.85
Marne	45.47	54.52
Haute-Marne	47.82	52.17
Mayenne	40.50	59.49
Meurthe-et-Moselle	51.99	48.00
Meuse	47.70	52.29
Morbihan	46.61	53.38
Moselle	48.67	51.32
Nièvre	57.05	42.94
Nord	53.69	46.30
Oise	48.89	51.10
Orne	42.38	57.61
Pas-de-Calais	57.28	42.71
Puy-de-Dôme	48.88	51.11
Pyrénées-Atlantiques	46.10	53.89
Hautes-Pyrénées	53.41	46.58
Pyrénées-Orientales	48.23	51.76
Bas-Rhin	41.10	58.89
Haut-Rhin	43.55	56.44
Rhône	42.07	57.92
Haute-Saône	49.61	50.38
Saône-et-Loire	48.62	51.37
Sarthe	50.79	49.20
Savoie	43.92	56.07
Haute-Savoie	38.05	61.94
Paris	39.90	60.09
Seine-Maritime	53.22	46.77
Seine-et-Marne	44.50	55.49
Yvelines	39.35	60.64
Deux-Sèvres	47.51	52.48
Somme	53.12	46.87
Tarn	50.56	49.43
Tarn-et-Garonne	49.07	50.92
Var	38.40	61.59
Vaucluse	44.14	55.85
Vendée	39.62	60.37
Vienne	49.72	50.27

Department	Jospin %	Chirac %
Haute-Vienne	51.87	48.12
Vosges	48.57	51.42
Yonne	45.17	54.82
Territoire de Belfort	51.40	48.59
Essonne	46.69	53.30
Hauts-de-Seine	40.97	59.02
Seine-Saint-Denis	51.84	48.15
Val-de-Marne	47.01	52.98
Val-d'Oise	46.22	53.77

Source: *Le Monde*, 9 May 1995.

Overseas departments and territories	Jospin %	Chirac %
Guadeloupe	55.10	44.90
Guyane	42.57	57.43
Martinique	58.89	41.11
Mayotte	31.65	68.35
Nouvelle-Calédonie	25.90	74.10
Polynésie française	39.02	60.98
La Réunion	56.07	43.93
St-Pierre-&-Miquelon	39.13	60.87
Wallis-et-Futuna	44.70	55.30

Source: *Le Figaro*, 9 May 1995.

FIRST BALLOT BY REGION

Region	Jospin %	Chirac %	Balladur %	Le Pen %	Hue %	Laguiller %	Villiers %	Voynet %	Cheminade %
Alsace	16.87	16.66	24.52	25.40	3.14	4.90	4.32	3.82	0.31
Aquitaine	26.90	21.42	17.68	11.24	9.42	5.31	4.68	3.04	0.27
Auvergne	23.08	24.76	16.93	11.35	10.36	5.73	4.40	3.06	0.30
Bourgogne	24.48	20.13	18.49	14.57	8.62	4.89	5.22	3.31	0.27
Bretagne	25.50	20.63	21.77	10.09	7.82	5.91	4.03	3.97	0.24
Centre	22.36	19.34	19.77	14.91	8.87	5.15	6.08	3.19	0.28
Champagne-Ardenne	21.35	19.95	18.46	18.29	7.89	5.39	5.24	3.10	0.29
Corse	20.50	30.94	20.13	10.63	9.67	3.04	2.23	2.53	0.26
Franche-Comté	24.26	19.40	18.42	16.08	6.52	5.37	4.80	4.85	0.26
Ile-de-France	23.31	25.14	16.25	14.09	8.73	5.23	3.54	3.44	0.22
Languedoc-Roussillon	24.16	17.92	16.07	18.23	11.08	5.05	4.21	3.00	0.23
Limousin	24.30	36.98	8.64	6.43	13.49	4.30	2.88	2.70	0.24
Lorraine	21.28	17.82	19.39	21.07	6.51	6.18	4.09	3.33	0.29
Midi-Pyrénées	29.39	20.31	16.85	11.42	8.64	5.34	4.26	3.44	0.29
Nord-Pas-de-Calais	23.96	16.87	16.93	17.04	12.67	5.83	4.12	2.29	0.24
Basse-Normandie	21.68	22.10	22.17	12.44	6.41	6.03	5.30	3.51	0.31
Haute-Normandie	22.74	17.71	18.42	16.57	10.68	6.22	4.27	3.06	0.27
Pays de la Loire	22.74	19.31	22.36	9.58	6.38	5.56	9.95	3.80	0.29
Picardie	22.48	18.97	16.20	18.00	10.70	5.89	4.79	2.64	0.28
Poitou-Charentes	25.76	21.06	18.70	10.01	8.00	5.25	7.35	3.52	0.32
PACA	18.94	18.76	19.20	21.57	9.41	4.50	4.43	2.91	0.23
Rhône-Alpes	21.92	17.96	20.03	18.24	7.44	5.26	4.79	4.04	0.27

Source: *Le Monde*, 25 April 1995.

SECOND BALLOT BY REGION

Region	Jospin %	Chirac %
Alsace	42.11	57.88
Aquitaine	49.76	50.23
Auvergne	46.54	53.45
Bourgogne	48.42	51.57
Bretagne	49.40	50.59
Centre	47.43	52.56
Champagne-Ardenne	47.38	52.61
Corse	40.54	59.45
Franche-Comté	50.57	49.42
Ile-de-France	43.90	56.09
Languedoc-Roussillon	49.40	50.59
Limousin	46.22	53.77
Lorraine	49.55	50.44
Midi-Pyrénées	48.03	51.96
Nord-Pas-de-Calais	55.07	44.93
Basse-Normandie	44.77	55.22
Haute-Normandie	51.33	48.66
Pays de la Loire	45.70	54.29
Picardie	51.93	48.06
Poitou-Charentes	49.48	50.51
Provence-Alpes-Côte-d'Azur	41.42	58.57
Rhône-Alpes	44.50	55.49

Source: *Le Monde*, 9 May 1995.

Bibliography

Abélès, M. (1989) *Journées tranquilles en '89*, Paris: Odile Jacob.

Adler, E. and Haas, P.M. (1992) 'Conclusion: epistemic communities, world order and the creation of a reflective research programme', *International Organization*, Vol. 46, No. 1, pp. 367–90.

Appleton, A. (1995) 'Parties under pressure: challenges to "established" French parties', *West European Politics*, Vol. 18, No. 1, pp. 52–77.

Bacqué, R. and Saverot, D. (1995) *Chirac Président, les coulisses d'une victoire*, Paris: Editions du Rocher.

Balladur, E. (1990) *Douze lettres aux Français trop tranquilles*, Paris: Fayard.

Bell, D. (1990) 'A hunger for power: Jacques Chirac', in Gaffney, J. (ed.), *The French Presidential Elections of 1988*, London: Gower.

Betz, H.-G. (1994) *Radical Right-Wing Populism in Western Europe*, London: Macmillan.

Blondel, J. (1975) 'The rise of a new-style President', in Penniman, H. (ed.), *France at the Polls. The Presidential Election of 1974*, Washington DC: American Enterprise Institute, pp. 41–69.

Boy, D. and Mayer, N. (eds) (1990) *L'élécteur français en questions*, Paris: Presses de la FNSP.

Bresson, G. and Thénard, J.-M. (1989) *Les 21 jours qui ébranlèrent la droite*, Paris: Grasset.

Buffotot, P. (1993) 'Le référendum sur l'Union européenne', *Modern and Contemporary France*, Vol. 1, No. 3, pp. 277–86.

Buffotot, P. and Hanley, D. (1995) 'Les élections européennes de juin 1994: élection européenne ou élection nationale?', *Modern and Contemporary France*, Vol. 3, No. 1, pp. 1–18.

Capdevieille, J., Dupoirier, E., Grunberg, G., Schweisguth, E. and Ysmal, C. (eds) (1981) *France de gauche, vote à droite*, Paris: Presses de la FNSP.

Cayrol, R. (1985) 'Le rôle des campagnes électorales', in Gaxie, D. (ed.), *Explication du vote*, Paris: Presses de la FNSP, pp. 385–417.

Cerny, P. and Schain, M. (eds) (1987) *Socialism, the State and Public Policy in France*, London: Frances Pinter.

CEVIPOF (1990) *L'électeur français en questions*, Paris: Presses de la FNSP.

Charlot, J. (1995) *Pourquoi Jacques Chirac*, Paris: Editions de Fallois.

Chirac, J. (1994) *Une nouvelle France*, Paris: Nil.

Colliard, J.-C. (1995) 'Le processus de nomination des candidats et l'organisation des campagnes électorales', Wahl, N. and Quermonne, J.-L. (eds), *La France présidentielle. L'influence du suffrage universel sur la vie politique*, Paris: Presses de la FNSP, pp. 67–93.

Converse, P.E. and Pierce, R. (1986) *Political Representation in France*, Cambridge, Mass.: Harvard University Press.

Cotta, M. (1995) *Les secrets d'une victoire*, Paris: Flammarion.

Damgaard, E., Gehrlich, P. and Richardson, R. (eds) (1989) *The Politics of Economic Crisis: Lessons from Western Europe*, Aldershot: Avebury.

Derbyshire, I. (1990) *Politics in France from Giscard to Mitterrand*, Edinburgh: Chambers.

Dreyfus, F.-G., Morizet, J. and Peyrard, M. (eds) (1993) *France and EC Membership Evaluated*, London: Pinter.

Duhamel, A. (1987) *La Ve Président*, Paris: Gallimard.

Duhamel, A. (1989) *Les habits neufs de la politique*, Paris: Flammarion.

Duhamel, O. (1985) 'Les logiques cachées de la Constitution de la Cinquième République', in Duhamel, O. and Parodi, J.-L. (eds), *La Constitution de la Cinquième République*, Paris: Presses de la FNSP, pp. 11–23.

Duhamel, O. (1986a) 'Questions constitutionnelles pour l'après-mars 1986', *Projet*, No. 198, March–April, pp. 12–18.

Duhamel, O. (1986b) 'L'hypothèse de la contradiction des majorités en France', in Duverger, M. (ed.), *Les régimes semi-présidentiels*, Paris: PUF, pp. 257–72.

Duhamel, O. (1987) 'Remarques sur la notion de régime semi-présidentiel', in *Droits, institutions et systèmes politiques. Mélanges en hommage à Maurice Duverger*, Paris: PUF, pp. 581–90.

Duhamel, O. (1993a) *La gauche et la Ve République*, Paris: Quadrige.

Duhamel, O. (1993b) *Les démocraties, régimes, histoire, exigences*, Paris: Editions du Seuil.

Duhamel, O. (1995) 'La valse des héros', in Duhamel, O. and Jaffré, J. (eds), *L'Etat de l'opinion 1995*, Paris: Editions du Seuil, pp. 37–57.

Duhamel, O. and Jaffré, J. (1987) *Le nouveau président*, Paris: Editions du Seuil.

Duhamel, O. and Jaffré, J. (eds) (1992) *SOFRES: l'état de l'opinion 1992*, Paris: Editions du Seuil.

Duverger, M. (1967) *Les partis politiques*, Paris: Armand Colin.

Duverger, M. (1986) 'Duverger's Law: Forty Years Later', in Grofman, B. and Lijphart, A. (eds) *Electoral Laws and their Political Consequences*, New York: Agathon Press, pp. 69–84.

Elgie, R. (1993) *The Role of the Prime Minister in France, 1981–91*, London: Macmillan.

Estier, C. (1995) *De Mitterrand à Jospin. Trente ans de campagnes présidentielles*, Paris: Stock.

Fishburn, P.C. (1986) 'Social choice and pluralitylike electoral systems', in Grofman, B. and Lijphart, A. (eds), *Electoral Laws and their Political Consequences*, New York: Agathon Press, pp. 193–202.

Furet, F., Julliard, J. and Rosanvallon, P. (1988) *La République du centre: la fin de l'exception francaise*, Paris: Calmann-Lévy.

Fysh, P. (1995) 'Gaullism and the new world order', in Jenkins, B. and Chafer, A. (eds), *France: From Cold War to the New World Order*, London: Macmillan, pp. 181–92.

Gaffney, J. (1995) 'France', in Lodge, J. (ed.), *The 1994 Elections to the European Parliament*, London: Pinter, pp. 84–106.

Gaxie, D. (ed.) (1985) *Explication du vote*, Paris: Presses de la FNSP.

Giscard d'Estaing, V. (1991) *Le Pouvoir et la Vie*, Vol. 2: *L'Affrontement*, Paris: Compagnie 12.

Goguel, F. (1981 and 1983) *Chroniques électorales*, Vols 1–3, Paris: Presses de la FNSP.

Grofman, B. and Lijphart, A. (eds) (1986) *Electoral Laws and their Political Consequences*, New York, Agathon Press.

Grunberg, G. (1993) 'Le comportement électoral en France', in Chagnollaud, D. (ed.), *La vie politique en France*, Paris: Editions du Seuil, pp. 385–401.

Guettier, C. (1990) 'Les candidats à l'élection présidentielle sous la V^c République', *Revue du droit public et de la science politique en France et à l'étranger*, No. 1, pp. 49–131.

Guyomarch, A., Machin, H. and Ritchie, E. (1996) *France in the European Union*, London: Macmillan.

Haas, P.M. (1992) 'Introduction: epistemic communities and international policy coordination', *International Organization*, Vol. 46, No. 1, pp. 1–36.

Habert, P. and Lancelot, A. (1988) 'L'émergence d'un nouvel électeur?', in Habert, P. and Ysmal, C. (eds), *Les élections législatives de 1988*, Paris: Le Figaro/Etudes Politiques, pp. 16–23.

Habert, P., Perrineau, P. and Ysmal, C. (eds) (1993) *Le vote sanction*, Paris: Département d'Etudes Politiques du Figaro and Presses de la FNSP.

Hainsworth, P. (1992) 'The extreme right in post-war France: the emergence and success of the Front National', in Hainsworth, P. (ed.), *The Extreme Right in Europe and the USA*, London: Pinter, pp. 29–60.

Hall, P.A. (1986) *Governing the Economy. The Politics of State Intervention in Britain and France*, Cambridge: Polity Press.

Hall, P.A. (1990) 'The state and the market', in Hall, P.A., Hayward, J. and Machin, H. (eds), *Developments in French Politics*, London: Macmillan, pp. 171–87.

Hall, P.A., Hayward, J. and Machin, H. (eds) (1994) *Developments in French Politics*, London: Macmillan.

Hayward, J. (1986) *The State and the Market Economy. Industrial Patriotism and Economic Intervention in France*, Brighton: Harvester Books.

Hayward, J. (ed.) (1993) *De Gaulle to Mitterrand: Presidential Power in France*, London, Hurst.

Hayward, J. (ed.) (1995) *Industrial Enterprise and European Integration*, Oxford: Oxford University Press.

Holmes, P. (1987) 'Broken dreams: economic policy in Mitterrand's France', in Mazey, S. and Newman, M. (eds), *Mitterrand's France*, London: Croom Helm, pp. 33–55.

Imbert, C. and Julliard, J. (1995) *La droite et la gauche: qu'est-ce qui les distingue encore?*, Paris: Laffont/Grasset.

Kingdon, J. (1984) *Agendas, Alternatives and Public Policies*, New York: Harper Collins.

Lawson, K. (1981) 'The impact of party reform on party systems', *Comparative Politics*, Vol. 13, No. 4, pp. 401–19.

Lawson, K. and Merkl, P. (eds) (1988) *When Parties Fail: Emerging Alternative Organisations*, Princeton NJ: Princeton University Press.

Lewis-Beck, M.S. and Skalaban, A. (1992) 'France', in Franklin, M., Mackie, T. and Valen, H. (eds), *Electoral Change: Responses to Evolving Social and Attitudinal Structures in Fifteen Countries*, Cambridge: Cambridge University Press, pp. 167–78.

Lijphart, A. (1994) *Electoral Systems and Party Systems. A Study of Twenty-Seven Democracies*, Oxford: Oxford University Press.

Lipset, S.M. and Rokkan, S. (1967) *Party Systems and Voter Alignments: Cross-National Perspectives*, New York: Free Press.

McCarthy, P. ed. (1994) *France–Germany, 1983–1993*, London: Macmillan.

Machin, H. (1989) 'Stages and dynamics in the evolution of the French party system', in Mair, P. and Smith, G. (eds), *Understanding Party System Change in Western Europe*, London: Frank Cass.

Machin, H. (1990) 'Changing patterns of party competition', in Hall, P.A., Hayward, J. and Machin, H. (eds), *Developments in French Politics*, London: Macmillan, pp. 33–54.

Machin, H. (1993) 'The President, the parties and parliament', in Hayward, J. (ed.), *De Gaulle to Mitterrand: Presidential Power in France*, London, Hurst, pp. 120–49.

Machin, H. and Wright, V. (1982) 'Why Mitterrand won: the French presidential elections of April–May 1981', *West European Politics*, Vol. 5, No. 1, pp. 5–35.

Machin, H. and Wright, V. (eds) (1985) *Economic Policy and Policy Making under the Mitterrand Presidency*, London: Pinter.

March, J.G. and Olsen, J.P. (1984) 'The new institutionalism: organizational factors in political life', *American Political Science Review*, Vol. 78, No. 3, pp. 734–49.

Mayer, N. and Perrineau, P. (1992) *Les comportements politiques*, Paris: Armand Colin.

Mazey, S. and Newman, M. (eds) (1987) *Mitterrand's France*, London: Croom Helm.

Menon, A. (1996) 'France and the IGC of 1996', *Journal of European Public Policy*, Vol. 3, No. 2.

Michelat, G. and Simon, M. (1977) *Classe, réligion et comportements politiques*, Paris: Presses de la FNSP.

Morabito, M. (1995) *Le chef de l'Etat en France*, Paris: Monchrestien.

Morris, P. (1994) *French Politics Today*, Manchester: Manchester University Press.

Mossuz-Lavau, J. (1994) *Les Français et la politique*, Paris: Odile Jacob.

Nay, C. (1994) *Le Dauphin et le Régent*, Paris: Grasset et Fasquelle.

Parodi, J.-L. (1973) *La Ve République et le système majoritaire*, Paris: Institut d'études politiques.

Parodi, J.-L. (1978) 'Les règles du scrutin majoritaire', *Projet*, No. 122, pp. 191–200.

Parodi, J.-L. (1980) 'Effets et non-effets de l'élection présidentielle au suffrage universel direct', *Pouvoirs*, No. 14, pp. 5–14.

Parodi, J.-L. (1981) 'Lo scrutinio uninominale maggioritario a doppio turno in Francia', *Il Mulino*, No. 273, January–February, pp. 24–38.

Parodi, J.-L. (1983a) 'La Cinquième République à l'épreuve de la proportionnelle. Essai de prospective institutionnelle', *Revue française de science politique*, Vol. 33, No. 6, pp. 987–1008.

Parodi, J.-L. (1983b) 'L'élection présidentielle de 1969 ou l'enracinement par l'exception', in *La Présidence de la République de Georges Pompidou*, paper presented to the FNSP conference, 24–25 November, Paris.

Parodi, J.-L. (1985) 'Imprévisible ou inéluctable, l'évolution de la Cinquième République?', in Duhamel, O. and Parodi, J.-L. (eds), *La Constitution de la Cinquième République*, Paris: Presses de la FNSP, pp. 24–43.

Parodi, J.-L. (1989) 'Le nouvel espace politique français', in Mény, Y. (ed.), *Idéologies, partis politiques et groupes sociaux*, Paris: Presses de la FNSP, pp. 147–57.

Passeron, A. (1984) 'Le parti d'un homme', *Pouvoirs*, No. 28, pp. 27–34.

Pélassy, D. (1995) *Sans foi, ni loi!*, Paris: Fayard.

Perrineau, P. (ed.) (1994) *L'engagement politique: déclin ou mutation?*, Paris: Presses de la FNSP.

Perrineau, P. and Ysmal, C. (eds) (1995) *Le vote des douze. Les élections européennes de 1994*, Paris: Département d'Etudes Politiques du Figaro and Presses de la FNSP.

Platone, F. (1990) 'Public opinion and electoral change', in Hall, P.A., Hayward, J. and Machin, H. (eds), *Developments in French Politics*, London: Macmillan.

Quermonne, J.-L. (1991) *L'appareil administratif de l'Etat*, Paris: Editions du Seuil.

Radaelli, C. (1995) 'The role of knowledge in the policy process', *Journal of European Public Policy*, Vol. 2, No. 2, pp. 159–84.

Richardson, J. (1995) 'The market for political activism: interest groups as a challenge to political parties', *West European Politics*, Vol. 18, No. 1, pp. 116–39.

Riker, W.H. (1986) 'Duverger's law revisited', in Grofman, B. and Lijphart, A. (eds), *Electoral Laws and their Political Consequences*, New York: Agathon Press, pp. 19–42.

Ross, G. (1987) 'Adieu vieilles idées: the middle strata and the decline of Resistance-Liberation Left discourse in France', in Ross, G. and Howorth, J. (eds), *Contemporary France*, Vol. 1, pp. 57–83.

Ross, G., Hoffman, S. and Malzacher, S. (eds) (1987) *The Mitterrand Experiment*, Cambridge: Polity Press.

Sabatier, P. (1988) 'An advocacy coalition framework of policy change and the role of policy-oriented learning therein', *Policy Sciences*, Vol. 21, pp. 129–69.

Schain, M. (1990) 'Immigration and Politics', in Hall, P.A., Hayward, J. and Machin, H. (eds), *Developments in French Politics*, London: Macmillan, pp. 253–68.

Scrutator (1995) *Marathon pour l'Elysée*, Paris: Plon.

Séguin, P. (1994) *Ce que j'ai dit*, Paris: Grasset.

Shonfeld, W.R. (1981) 'The RPR, from a *Rassemblement* to the Gaullist movement', in Andrews, W.G. and Hoffman, S. (eds), *The Fifth Republic at Twenty*, Albany, NY: State University of New York Press, pp. 91–111.

Shugart, M.S. and Taagepera, R. (1994) 'Plurality versus majority election of presidents. A proposal for a "double complement rule"', *Comparative Political Studies*, Vol. 27, No. 3, pp. 323–48.

Steinmo, S., Thelen, K. and Longstreth, F. (eds) (1992) *Structuring Politics*, Cambridge: Cambridge University Press.

Stone, A. (1989) 'Legal constraints to policy-making: the Constitutional

Council and the Council of State', in Godt, P. (ed.), *Policy-Making in France. From de Gaulle to Mitterrand*, London: Pinter, pp. 28–41.

Tiersky, R. (1994) *France in the New Europe*, Belmont: Wadsworth Publishing.

Todd, E. (1988) *La nouvelle France*, Paris: Editions du Seuil.

Todd, E. (1994) *Aux origines du malaise politique français*, Paris: Fondation Saint-Simon.

Tsebelis, G. (1990) *Nested Games. Rational Choice in Comparative Politics*, Berkeley: University of California Press.

Wright, S.G. and Riker, W.H. (1989) 'Plurality and runoff systems and numbers of candidates', *Public Choice*, Vol. 60, pp. 155–75.

Wright, V. (1989) *The Government and Politics of France*, 3rd edn, London: Unwin Hyman.

Wright, V. (ed.) (1994) *Privatization in Western Europe, Pressures, Problems and Paradoxes*, London: Pinter.

Ysmal, C. (1989) *Les partis politiques sous la V^c République*, Paris: Monchrestien.

Ysmal, C. (1992) 'La diversité des forces "anti-système"', in Habert, P., Perrineau, P. and Ysmal, C. (eds), *Le Vote Eclaté, les élections régionales et cantonales des 22 et 29 mars 1992*, Paris: Presses de la FNSP, pp. 187–208.

Index